£25

Candidate Selection in Comparative Perspective

Candidate Selection in Comparative Perspective

The Secret Garden of Politics

edited by
Michael Gallagher and Michael Marsh

SAGE Modern Politics Series Volume 18
Sponsored by the European Consortium for
Political Research/ECPR

SAGE Publications
London • Newbury Park • Beverly Hills • New Delhi

Editorial material © Michael Gallagher and Michael Marsh 1988
Chapter 1 © Michael Gallagher 1988
Chapter 2 © Lieven De Winter 1988
Chapter 3 © David Denver 1988
Chapter 4 © Jean-Louis Thiébault 1988
Chapter 5 © Geoffrey Roberts 1988
Chapter 6 © Michael Gallagher 1988
Chapter 7 © Douglas A. Wertman 1988
Chapter. 8 © Rei Shiratori 1988
Chapter 9 © Ruud Koole and Monique Leijenaar 1988
Chapter 10 © Henry Valen 1988
Conclusion © Michael Gallagher 1988

First published 1988

SAGE Publications Ltd
28 Banner Street
London EC1Y 8QE

SAGE Publications Inc
2111 West Hillcrest Street
Newbury Park, California 91320

SAGE Publications India Pvt Ltd
C-236 Defence Colony
New Delhi 110 024

SAGE Publications Inc
275 South Beverly Drive
Beverly Hills, California 90212

British Library Cataloguing in Publication Data
Candidate selection in comparative
    perspective: the secret garden of
    politics. — (Sage modern politics series; 18)
    1. Nominations for office
    I. Gallagher, Michael, 1951–   II. Marsh,
    Michael
    324.5   JF2081
    ISBN 0–8039–8124–4

Library of Congress catalog card number 87–062227

Printed in Great Britain by J. W. Arrowsmith Ltd, Bristol

Contents

List of tables

Preface

A commentator on politics in the United Kingdom once described candidate selection as 'the secret garden of British politics'. The remark has wider application. The selection of candidates has regularly been referred to by political scientists as a 'key' or 'crucial' part of the political process, but in most countries it usually takes place well away from the glare of public scrutiny. Nor has it really received much academic attention, especially on a comparative basis.

In consequence, we organized a workshop on 'Candidate selection in comparative perspective' as part of the European Consortium for Political Research joint sessions in Barcelona in March 1985. This book developed from that meeting, at which preliminary versions of seven of its chapters were presented. Besides the introduction and conclusion, the two new chapters are Chapters 5 and 7. Richard Katz, a participant in the workshop, was unable because of the pressure of other tasks to write the Italian chapter as originally scheduled, and his place was taken by Douglas Wertman. In addition, we felt it desirable to include a chapter on Western Europe's most populous country, West Germany, which Geoffrey Roberts agreed to write. We are particularly grateful to these two authors for contributing chapters on schedule at short notice. The Dutch chapter draws on two papers presented separately in Barcelona by Ruud Koole and Monique Leijenaar respectively.

Five other papers were presented at the Barcelona workshop, each of which was of excellent quality but had to be omitted for reasons of space and/or thematic unity, since the book is organized on a country-by-country basis. John Bochel, in 'The selection of candidates: an analytical framework', argued for the utility of a comparative framework which would emphasize the functions of candidate selection for various elements of the party organization. Richard Katz, in 'Nomination strategies in systems with intraparty preference voting', discussed the role of voters in choosing their deputies when the electoral system permits this. Michael Marsh presented 'Nominating unattractive candidates: small businessmen in Irish political recruitment', which sought explanations for the parties' persistent selection of large numbers of small businessmen, despite their apparent lack of popularity with the voters.

Donald R. Matthews, in 'Political recruitment and institutional change: the case of the US Congress', outlined recent changes in the American political system and their impact on the behaviour of congressmen. Diane Sainsbury presented 'Women's routes to national legislatures: a three-country comparison', a subject which merits a book in its own right. She argued that the nature of candidate selection in Sweden was conducive to the selection of a relatively high proportion of women, whereas selection procedures in Britain and the USA made it harder for women to win nomination.

Our thanks must go first of all to the contributors to the book, most of whom managed to keep reasonably close to the agreed schedule, and all of whom displayed considerable patience and co-operation in dealing with what may have seemed an interminable series of questions, suggestions and comments. In addition, Sage's editorial director, David Hill, and the series editor, Michael Laver, made some helpful suggestions on the text, and responded speedily to all our questions. We are also grateful to Ken Newton, Michael Laver's predecessor, who helped to get the project under way. Last, but certainly not least, we should like to thank Miriam Nestor, who typed more than one version of five of the chapters in this book, and has played a large part in creating the finished product.

1

Introduction

Michael Gallagher

This book is about ways in which political parties select their candidates for elections to national parliaments. The significance of candidate selection is easy to underestimate. It may seem at first sight to be one of the more obscure functions performed by political parties, a mere administrative procedure carried out in a back room, of concern only to those directly involved. In fact it has far wider implications. The quality of candidates selected determines the quality of the deputies elected, of the resultant parliament, often of the members of the government and, to some extent, of a country's politics. A change in parties' selection procedures in any given country might thus have direct consequences for the way politics operate there. Moreover, the way in which political parties select their candidates may be used as an acid test of how democratically they conduct their internal affairs.

In this introductory chapter we shall outline the main lines of inquiry the book will follow, and review the existing literature on the subject. First, the chapter will elaborate on the reasons why candidate selection is widely seen as important. Second, it will identify the main questions to be asked when trying to build up a descriptive picture of the way candidates are picked. Third, it will discuss the theories advanced as to the factors which influence the selection of candidates. Finally, it will discuss the ways in which different selection processes might have distinct consequences. The validity of the hypotheses discussed in this chapter will be considered, in the light of the available evidence, in the concluding chapter.

The importance of candidate selection

Candidate selection has often been identified as a crucial part of the political process, but it has received comparatively little attention. For only a few countries do detailed studies of selection practices exist; for most countries the subject is dealt with in rather cursory fashion by textbooks giving a general introduction to the government and politics of the country. Attempts to study the subject cross-nationally have faced the formidable obstacle of a paucity of reliable and contemporary information from all but a few polities, principally Britain and the USA. Marvick (1976: 40) comments that 'few recruitment studies have drawn systematically on a quantitative data base', and suggests that 'recruitment theories and models have thus far tended to be formulated with specific data configurations in mind'. There is a tendency for single-country studies to frame a rather sweeping 'general theory' which fits the specific data set, with the writer then calling for 'further research' from other people to test its wider applicability. Even so, a few pioneering ventures have sought to examine candidate selection comparatively, enabling certain tentative conclusions to be framed about the extent of variation between and within countries, the main independent factors determining what form candidate selection takes within any country, and whether different selection practices have distinct consequences (see Czudnowski, 1975: 219–29; Duverger, 1964: 353–64; Epstein, 1980: 201–32; Ranney, 1981).

Candidate selection has been identified as important for two reasons: it is a key stage in the political recruitment process, and it is an important arena of intraparty conflict. With regard to the first of these, access to any political elite is controlled by a series of 'gatekeepers', and the narrowest gate of all is that guarded by the candidate selectors. As Pesonen (1968: 348) points out, 'the nomination stage eliminates 99.96 percent of all the eligible people. The voters choose from only 0.04 percent.' For this reason most writers on elites or recruitment stress the vital role of candidate selection. Czudnowski (1975: 219) describes it as 'perhaps the most crucial stage in the recruitment process'. Crotty (1968b: 260) observes that

> The party in recruiting candidates determines the personnel and, more symbolically, the groups to be represented among the decision-making elite. Through recruitment, the party indirectly influences the types of policy decisions to be enacted and the interests most likely to be heard. Candidate recruitment then represents one of the key linkages between the electorate and the policy-making process.

It is clear that the values of the selectorate, often a small number of activists, frequently have more impact than those of the voters. This applies especially under electoral systems which do not permit voters any degree of choice between candidates of the same party; picking candidates then often amounts to picking deputies. Moreover, since deputies wish to be in good standing with their selectorate, their behaviour is likely to be affected by their knowledge of what the selectors want (Putnam, 1976: 56).

The importance of candidate selection as a key process within the party and a key arena of internal power struggles has been argued most quotably by Schattschneider (1942: 64 and 100), whose best-known observation on the subject is perhaps over-cited but under-examined. He states that

> The nominating process . . . has become the crucial process of the party. The nature of the nominating procedure determines the nature of the party; he who can make the nominations is the owner of the party. This is therefore one of the best points at which to observe the distribution of power within the party.

Endorsing this statement, Ranney (1981: 103) adds that

> the most vital and hotly contested factional disputes in any party are the struggles that take place over the choice of its candidates; for what is at stake in such a struggle, as the opposing sides well know, is nothing less than control of the core of what the party stands for and does.

Michels (1915: 183–4), too, stressed candidate selection as central in the struggle for power within parties, illustrating the point with a quote from Karl Kautsky. Hennessy (1968: 2), echoing Bryce's earlier statement, says, 'The chief thing *is* the selection of candidates.' Riggs suggests that the most useful basis for constructing a typology of parties is not one of the commonly employed functional criteria, but the structural criterion of how a party selects its candidates, and he outlines a scheme (1968: 62–6) for classifying parties according to their 'nominator structures'.

Apart from the internal conflict it may generate, selecting candidates is an important part of any study of political parties because it is one of their main activities. Kirchheimer (1966: 198) commented that 'the nomination of candidates for popular legitimation as office-holders . . . emerges as the most important function of the present-day catch-all party'. Jupp (1968: 58) has gone further, arguing that picking candidates is not just the most important thing parties do, it is virtually the only thing they do: 'the European mass party is becoming limited to electioneering and the selection of candidates'.

Undoubtedly, ordinary members cannot realistically expect to play a role in laying down party policy or formulating election manifestos, and even when the membership does succeed in altering party policy via a resolution passed at conference, it is notoriously difficult for the party at large to compel the parliamentary leadership to implement it in government. Consequently, the contest over candidate selection is generally even more intense than the struggle for control over the party manifesto. Moreover, it is far easier to analyse the outcome, and so the subject is more amenable to systematic cross-national study.

This book has four main aims. First, it will provide descriptions of candidate selection in nine countries, employing a common framework to enable comparisons to be drawn. Second, it will seek to identify the most important influences on the nature of the candidate selection process. Third, it will attempt to establish the consequences of candidate selection, by asking whether different processes are different in their outcomes. Finally, it will constitute a test of the importance of candidate selection as a topic for research, making possible an assessment of statements like those quoted above.

The process of candidate selection

In describing the process of candidate selection within each country, chapters will focus on three main questions. How centralized is the process? How extensive is participation in it? And what qualities do aspirants need in order to be selected?[1]

Across the world, selection practices vary greatly, and the locus of effective control of the process ranges accordingly. At one extreme (excluding cases where there is no screening at all), candidates might be picked in a vote by all party supporters; at the other, they can be chosen by the party leader alone. Between these possibilities the spectrum includes, in decreasing order of openness, selection by all party members in the constituency; by a subset of constituency party members; by the regional organization; by the national executive; or by the national faction leaders. Interest groups affiliated to the party may also play a role in selecting candidates; where they do, the decisive actors might be local or national. Even when the crucial decision is taken at the same level in several parties, the involvement of party members can still vary widely, and the proportion of party voters who participate in the process will also differ from party to party, depending on how many voters are registered members of the party.

The existing literature suggests that the locus of control usually lies somewhere between the two extremes, without always being precise as to exactly where. Ranney (1981: 82–3) concludes that 'the most common pattern is selection by constituency party agencies under some form of supervision by national or regional agencies, and the next most common is selection by national agencies after consideration of suggestions made by constituency and regional agencies'. Even knowing that selection is made by constituency agencies, of course, still leaves open the question of how widely party members and voters are involved. Epstein (1980: 225) sums up the pattern by observing that 'oligarchical control over candidate selection is usual, but it is not always managed in the same way'. Czudnowski (1975: 220) arrives at much the same conclusion: except in the USA, 'the selection of candidates follows the pattern of all institutions; i.e. important decisions are made informally by groups of influentials, and ratification is more often a procedural formality'. For Obler (1974: 163) the general practice is that 'extra-parliamentary party leaders usually pick the nominees in closed private meetings and then submit their choice to rank and file party members and/or delegates who nearly always grant their approval'.

Devising a research strategy to pin down the exact point in the party where the decision is made is not straightforward. One complication which arises when trying to explain the degree of centralization is that the dependent variable itself may vary not only between parties but perhaps even within them. It is possible that the central organization possesses more influence or control over some candidacies than over others. Under the British electoral system, for example, the centre might have more influence over the nomination in constituencies where the party is very strong (so that even an unpopular, imposed candidate will win the seat) or where it is weak (where there is no significant local organization to resent the centre's action) than in a marginal constituency. Similarly, under list systems, the centre might have more leverage over filling some positions on the list than others. It is also quite probable that the selectors, whoever they are, will apply rather different criteria in these different cases, and will, for example, take less heed of the voters' wishes when selecting candidates for safe and for hopeless seats (or list positions) than for marginal ones.

Clearly, any study of candidate selection must go far beyond, while not ignoring, examination of what party constitutions say about it. One of the earliest students of the subject, Ostrogorski (1970, I: 448), commented that 'the procedure laid down by the rules for the selection of the candidate . . . is simply a formality which just puts the finishing touch on the work of the wire-pullers'. Another difficulty is that it is not always clear, *pace* Schattschneider, that any one really does 'control' nomination. Instead, the outcomes of the selection process often reflect the results of a complex set of interactions between many actors within the party (and perhaps some outside it), in which different actors have different degrees of influence but none has complete control.

The task of studying candidate selection is complicated further by the knowledge that the most effective influence may be wielded in private. An obvious example concerns the amount of power exercised by national agencies. In many countries, candidates are selected locally, with a central agency such as the national executive having a right, under party constitutions, to veto the choice. The extent to which this right is exercised can vary greatly, even between two parties whose constitutions are similar. At first sight, it might seem reasonable to try to measure the extent of central involvement by counting the number of times national agencies alter the composition of a locally selected panel. The difficulty is that the absence of such overt central intervention may signify not powerlessness but satisfaction with the panel selected locally, or even successful central intervention behind the scenes at an earlier stage. The more the process involves such backstage negotiations, possibly encompassing trade-offs in other areas of party activity, the less easy it is for the researcher to reconstruct the process in its totality. As Duverger (1964: 354) has remarked, 'parties do not like the odours of the electoral kitchen to spread to the outside world'.

The ideal research method would probably be to conduct in-depth interviews with all those involved in the selection process: central party officers, deputies, selected candidates, unsuccessful aspirants, local party elites, ordinary branch members and so on. Given limited resources, this type of strategy is rarely realistic. Instead it is more feasible to try to tackle questions which can be answered without the need for such a comprehensive approach. Do central agencies monitor closely the affairs of their party around the country? Does it help or hinder an aspirant's prospects of being selected to be regarded as a favourite of central office? When conflict between local and national party organizations does emerge, what is the outcome? Even though these questions too constitute only indirect indicators of the power of the centre, answers to them should be informative.

The third question to be addressed when outlining the process of candidate selection is that of the qualities aspirants need in order to boost their chances; what are the selectors looking for, and why? Party constitutions may state basic requirements of eligibility, such as a minimum period of membership, but rarely go further. Seligman (1971: 12) usefully suggests that the criteria can be dichotomized as either ascriptive or achievement-related, or, to put it another way, objective and subjective personal characteristics. The former would include age, family, social status, race, religion, gender, group affiliation and locality, while examples of the latter are expertise in organizing, communication or bargaining, a record of service in the party organization, and ideological orthodoxy. Under electoral systems using multi-member constituencies, the selectors may employ both criteria, aiming for a ticket which 'balances' certain ascribed characteristics and then using achieve-ment criteria to pick the individuals. When groups are organized around these ascribed characteristics, a pattern described by Duverger (1964: 54–5) as 'social decentralization', Czudnowski (1970: 231–2) raises the question of how much control the party retains over the selection of individuals once it has been decided that a balance is to be sought; in some circumstances, the party may 'contract out' the task of selection, by allowing the groups them-selves to pick the individuals.

When a balanced ticket is sought, we want to know what qualities the selectors decide to balance, and why. When they use achievement-related criteria, do they seem to be looking primarily for candidates who will keep in close touch with the constituency or for candidates who seem likely to make good parliamentarians and/or ministers? As for why the selectors use the criteria they do, the most obvious consideration is the reaction of the voters: the selectors may employ whatever criteria are relevant to producing a ticket with the greatest electoral appeal. But it is not always this simple. The choice likely to be most popular with the voters may not be of greatest appeal to the members; it may even be unacceptable to them, and Seligman (1971: 15) believes that 'party unity is often a higher priority than immediate electoral victory'.

Once again, there are methodological problems to confront when trying to answer the question. One common approach is to compare the backgrounds of selected candidates, or even deputies, with those of party voters, and to assume that differences between the two reveal what the selectors were looking for. This assumption seems to be made by Ranney (1981: 97–102), but is not very sound (see the discussion in Holland, 1986: 6–8). For example, it is well known that the great majority of almost all parties' candidates are men, but it does not follow that the selectors have a conscious preference for men. It could be that they are looking for some other quality, such as a high socio-economic status, which men are more likely than women to possess. The same is true of the other qualities which deputies and candidates tend to possess: if selectors consis-tently pick highly educated candidates, this may be not because they want educated candidates per se but because they want articulate candidates, who, it so happens, are likely to be relatively well educated. Alternatively, it may be that the obstacles placed in the way of women or those with little education wishing to participate actively in politics are such that few even put themselves forward for selection.

A refinement is to compare those selected with unsuccessful aspirants, and to draw inferences about the selectors' preferences from the differences. This approach may throw light on the selectors' values (as is demonstrated by Holland, 1986), and any information it yields is of inherent interest, but it is not entirely satisfactory as a way of answering the question of what the selectors are looking for. Using unsuccessful aspirants as a control group ignores that majority of party members who do not seek nomination, for one reason or another, possibly simply because they believe that they do not possess the qualities the selectors are looking for. It is quite probable, indeed, that successful and unsuccessful aspirants will have more in common with each other than either has with ordinary party members, let alone voters.

Some of the background characteristics of deputies, no doubt, really are sought by selectors, but others are not. In the general absence of data drawn from interviews with selectors, there is a need for care when attempting to decide exactly what the selectors are looking for and why.

Influences shaping the candidate selection process

Parties differ, even within the same country, with regard to their rules governing candidate selection, the locus of control (or greatest influence) over the process, the involvement of party members and the qualities which stand aspirants in good stead. Explaining these variations, one of the aims of this book, involves examining the impact on the selection process of each of a set of factors, the most important of which are legal provisions (where they exist), governmental organization, the electoral system, political culture and the nature of the party. This list, of course, does not imply that each factor is significant in every country, or that no other factor is significant in any specific country.

The first of these, legal provisions, play an important role in countries where they exist, but such countries are in a small minority. The second, the political structure of the country, is likely to affect the structure of the parties within it. Harmel (1981: 86), using data collected by Janda which refers to the period 1957–62, concludes that general party decentralization (of which control over candidate selection is one indicator) is quite strongly related to decentralization of power within the polities where the parties operate. Although Duverger (1964: 393–403) suggests that it is party structure which 'exercises a fundamental influence on the degree of separation or concentration of powers' (p. 398), most writers see the causal relationship running in the other direction. Epstein (1980: 31–4; cf. Lawson, 1976: 79, 228) comments that party organization 'tends to parallel government organization', for obvious reasons, and gives examples of federal systems where the parties are strongest at the regional level, with national parties being little more than loose federations of regional organizations. Thus we could expect to find that parties operating in centralized unitary states will, other things being equal, have relatively centralized procedures for selecting candidates, that in federal countries power will lie with the state organizations and that, in countries where local government is strong, candidate selection will be controlled by the local party organization.

The third factor, the electoral system, is often held to exert great influence on many features of a country's politics, including candidate selection. Czudnowski (1975: 221) posits a strong link between the two:

> Party selection seems to be closely related to the electoral system. When a candidate has to be *elected* by a local or regional constituency, he will tend to be *selected* by the local or regional party organization. In large multi-member constituencies, with proportional assignment of seats from party lists, including national party lists, central party organizations have a far greater influence, if not a monopoly, on candidate selection.

Hermens (1972: 51–8), in whose splenetic vision practically every conceivable political evil invariably ensues once a PR system is introduced, predictably sees PR as having grim consequences for internal party democracy. Under list systems, he says, the deputy depends on the party, not the voter; the national leader of the party is likely to gain control of the local or provincial selection committees and hence of the entire selection process; and, in consequence, 'the national party leader can bring dozens of parliamentary careers to an end by a mere stroke of a pen' (p. 55). In contrast, 'the relationship between individual deputies and the national leader' under a plurality electoral system is, naturally, 'truly democratic' (p. 54).

More soberly, Epstein (1980: 225–6) argues that 'to a considerable extent, greater centralization is associated with a nation's electoral system', suggesting that central control is more likely under PR systems because of the larger constituencies they involve. Butler (1981: 20) maintains that one reason for Anglo-Saxon countries' unwillingness to adopt electoral systems involving lists is 'a reluctance to accept the central-party dominance over candidate selection that goes with list systems of proportional representation'. In contrast, Duverger (1964: 59–60) suggests that the impact of the electoral system on the degree of general centralization of parties is highly uncertain. Elsewhere (1964: 356–9) he argues that large constituencies and list systems increase the influence of 'the party' relative to the candidate, but does not go on to offer suggestions as to which specific agencies of the party acquire this additional influence. Clearly, it is plausible that in large constituencies, where voters are unlikely to have personal knowledge of the candidates and are more likely to rely on party label or sub-group membership as a voting cue, the centre has more scope to intervene actively.

A rather similar, though distinct, hypothesis relating centralization to the electoral system would employ the degree of voter choice rather than the area covered by a constituency as the independent variable: the smaller the role of the voter in deciding which candidates are elected, the greater the power of the parties' national agencies. Thus an electoral system involving constituencies which either return just one member, with only one round of voting, or return several members under a rigid (non-preferential) list system, could be expected to increase the role of central agencies in candidate selection. In contrast, when the electoral system provides for preferential voting, allowing electors to choose the individuals they wish to represent them, local agencies can argue that the party ticket must be assembled carefully, with sensitivity to the voters' wishes, and that only the local organization is in a position to know just what ticket will be of most appeal to voters in the constituency.

Political culture too could help explain the form selection takes. Political culture, denoting generally people's attitudes towards political phenomena, is naturally influenced strongly by historical experience. Consequently, party members in one country may accept a minimal degree of involvement in internal decision-making, one which would provoke party members elsewhere to protest, simply because they have never known a different state of affairs. But even though members in one country may be largely ignorant of practices in other countries, they are likely to know what pertains in other parties in their own country, which suggests that changes in selection procedures in one party, especially ones which increase ordinary members' power, may trigger demand for similar changes in other parties. Specific features of political culture may have an impact: centralization may be low in countries with a localistic political culture, and members may demand a high degree of involvement in countries whose political culture stresses the merits of participation.

Turning to the fifth factor, the nature of the party, theorists of political parties have long argued that different types of party are distinctive in their organization and decision-making processes. Wright incorporates the various models of parties and how they behave into a dichotomy between two ideal types, the Rational-

Efficient party and the Party Democracy type. He outlines their characteristics thus (1971b: 7):

> Briefly summarized, the Rational-Efficient party has exclusively electoral functions and is programmatically occupied with winning elec-tions rather than with defining policy. The Party Democracy type is more policy-orientated, ideological, and concerned with defining policy in an internally democratic manner involving rank-and-file member participation. Electoral success is viewed not as an end in itself but rather as a means to the implementation of policy ends.

The two naturally differ considerably when it comes to candidate selection (Wright, 1971c: 44–5). In an archetypal case of the former, candidates 'are often recruited from outside the party organization — the prime consideration being the voter appeal of the candidate'. But in the Party Democracy model, candidates

> tend to be recruited and promoted from within the organization. Norms of loyalty and service to the organization are important. Leaders must gain and retain the loyalty of the members, as well as appeal to voters as representatives of the party. These patterns are made possible by the more highly organized structure and party control over the nomination of candidates for public office in the Party Democracy model.

This largely reiterates Duverger's distinction (1964: 359), though of course Duverger was claiming to be describing empirically observable categories rather than ideal types:

> Cadre parties, which have no strong financial backing and live in perpetual money difficulties, are always soft-hearted towards candidates willing to cover the costs of the campaign, and in practice investiture is obtained without any great difficulty. Mass parties, which are generally parties of the Left, have less taste for this capitalist form of individual candidature. Moreover their constitutions often contain clauses intended to prevent an independent personality from receiving party support at the last moment: only those who have been party members for a certain amount of time can stand for election with party support.

Seligman (1967: 312) makes much the same point: 'Parties that centralize candidate recruitment are those with explicit ideologies and bureaucratized organizations.' He argues further (1967: 303) that the qualities the selectors are looking for will vary according to party type. Permanent minority parties (which in a non-American context must be narrowed to parties which are permanently excluded from government), he says,

> tend toward purism and sectarianism; their candidates are more concerned with expressing ideological integrity than with winning the broadest spectrum of popular support. In contrast, a party with expecta-

tions of governing will select candidates with the skills, abilities and resources to win and govern.

It is, clearly, plausible that more ideological parties will be more rigorous in the demands they make of candidates, and that their selectors will seek evidence of commitment and programmatic purity, while pragmatic parties' selectors, being entirely election-orientated, will be highly tolerant of any candidate who seems likely to be electorally popular. But it is also possible that the once standard differentiation between ideological mass parties and pragmatic cadre parties has been rendered largely obsolete by time (some would argue that it was never valid in any case), and that differences in candidate selection processes are not related systematically to parties' positions on the left–right spectrum, or to how clearly defined their political programme is.

The nature of the party, of course, goes beyond this particular dichotomy: centralization could also be related to the heterogeneity of a party's support. When a party draws votes from different social groups in different constituencies, it might make sense to allow the local organization discretion to tailor its ticket and its campaign to the local situation. With, no doubt, such parties in mind, Eldersveld (1964: 9) argues that the 'widely varying local milieus of opinion, tradition, and social structure' faced by parties 'encourages the recognition and acceptance of local leadership, local strategy, local power'. In contrast, parties drawing support from just one category of voters would have less incentive to decentralize the candidate selection process.

Consequences of the candidate selection process

At the start of this chapter we outlined the views of several writers on the key role of candidate selection in political recruitment and intraparty conflict. If candidate selection really is important, and it matters who the selectors are, what qualities they seek and whom they select, then it should presumably be possible to identify distinctive consequences of different methods of selection. The most obvious way of exploring the impact on recruitment is by analysing two aspects of deputies, their backgrounds and their behaviour. Candidate selection may also have consequences in a third area, namely the cohesion and power structure of the party itself.

The first question, the impact on the composition of legislatures, has received surprisingly little attention, even in studies of candidate selection. Some, indeed, have doubted whether there is a relationship between the two. Goodman, Swanson and Cornwell (1970), having derived mixed findings from examination of the backgrounds of delegates to constitutional conventions in four states in the USA, conclude (p. 102) that perhaps, 'given provisions for popular election of some sort, outcomes are similar, regardless of *structural* differences'. Czudnowski (1975: 228) endorses this view, and suggests rather sweepingly that a selection process should be seen only as a consequence of political decisions: 'considering selection systems as independent variables leads to descriptive analyses of little theoretical relevance'.

In contrast, Loewenberg and Patterson, having outlined selection practices in several countries, conclude (1979: 97) that 'these differences in the recruiting mechanisms have a profound effect on the composition of parliaments'. Ostrogorski commented scathingly on the outcomes of selection processes on both sides of the Atlantic. He suggested (1970, I: 507–8) that the influence wielded by the ubiquitous 'wire-pullers' of the central organization in the British Liberal Party at the turn of the century produced mainly MPs who were 'mediocrities whose sole qualifications are their wealth and their willingness to yield a blind obedience to the party and its leader'. He was no more impressed by the choices made by locally autonomous 'lower grade conventions' in the USA, which he said generally selected 'candidates who are decidedly bad from the standpoint of morality and intelligence' (II: 237). More sanguinely, Keynes, Tobin and Danziger (1979), from a study of state legislators in Connecticut, Pennsylvania and Washington, find that the less open the nominating system, the more likely are legislators to have served in party and public offices. This finding, though, probably has little applicability outside the USA, since virtually all other countries' nomination systems are 'closed' in American terms, in that they are controlled by the party organization and exclude ordinary voters.

A priori, it is plausible to anticipate a clear relationship between the degree of centralization in the candidate selection process and the composition of the resulting parliamentary group, with regard to familiar background variables like education, age, local roots, relationship to former deputies, and gender. Party leaders are likely to place a high priority on having an effective parliamentary group, especially in countries where cabinets are drawn from parliament, so if leaders control the process one could expect deputies to be relatively well educated and also young, since they will not have had to spend years establishing a base in the party organization or in local politics. They may have past experience of working in the party's central research organization or with the leadership in some capacity. In contrast, when selection is firmly under the control of local members, more interested in whether aspirants have 'paid their dues' with a solid track record at local level than in their likely parliamentary capacities, the resulting parliamentarians might be older and less well educated, more likely to have local roots and to be long-standing members of the local party organization. For this reason, Duverger (1964: 162–8) suggests that centralized parties will have younger and better-educated parliamentary groups, and produces some data from the French National Assembly of 1946 to support his argument.

It is possible that a locally controlled process will result in a higher proportion of deputies who are related to previous deputies, as locally prominent political families manage to pass a seat on from one generation to another. It is not apparent that any relationship is to be expected in advance between the proportion of women candidates selected and the degree of centralization, although Castles (1981: 25) seems to regard centralized candidate selection as an important intervening variable in the relationship between electoral systems and the number of women in parliament. He argues (without providing any evidence) that list systems of PR tend to produce centralization of candidate selection, and implies that a national selectorate may be more inclined to select women than local selectors.

Turning to the second question, the impact of candidate selection on deputies' behaviour and hence on the nature of the legislature, there is every reason to anticipate a clear relationship. One of the assumptions on which liberal democracy rests is that politicians' behaviour will be affected by the knowledge that they depend on the electorate for re-election, so presumably it will also be affected by the wishes of the selectorate, especially where the latter are placed in a particularly powerful position by the electoral system. Butler (1981: 22) writes that 'the different degrees of headquarters control over national and regional lists explain many of the differences in the behaviour patterns of individual politicians', without specifying what sort of patterns follow from what degree of centralization. The selectors' views are likely to have an impact on legislators' behaviour not only because of their power to deselect an incumbent. In Mezey's words (1979: 151) 'the expectations of those with whom a role occupant such as a legislator must interact will have a particularly strong effect on the incumbent's role perceptions'. The selectors' influence may be especially strong when they play an important role in the deputy's pre-legislative socialization, as well as having close contact with him or her after the deputy enters parliament.

The selection process might have an impact both on the cohesion of parliamentary parties and on the roles on which deputies concentrate. Where nominations are controlled centrally, we might expect to find that deputies follow the party line faithfully in parliament, as disloyalty will mean deselection. If local members or a local elite control the process, deputies might flout the whip occasionally if they are pulled in a different direction by local factors or the ideological views of local activists. If they do not depend on any organ of the party for reselection, one might expect to find low levels of party discipline in parliament.

The roles adopted by deputies are also likely to be influenced by whoever controls the selection process. Assuming that parties' central bodies attach most value to deputies' activities at the national level, and that ordinary members are more concerned with the local visibility of their parliamentary representatives (assumptions which may not be universally valid), we should expect to find that when the selection process is centrally controlled, deputies concentrate most of their energies on parliamentary duties, and when it is locally controlled, they spend more time on constituency work and other activities which keep them in contact with the local membership.

As for the third question, the impact on parties, control of candidate selection may well reinforce as well as reflect existing power structures within the organization. The extent of members' involvement in the process may largely colour their general view of the legitimacy of party institutions. If it is extensive, the result may be a greater degree of party cohesion and more willingness to allow key decisions in other areas, such as party policy, to remain in the hands of a small group of national leaders. But the reverse is also possible; party cohesion may be threatened unless control of selection procedures is maintained by an oligarchy mindful of the need to preserve a delicate balance between different interests within the party. The same considerations apply, *a fortiori*, to the involvement of ordinary voters.

If it is established that different candidate selection processes do have distinct consequences, the question still remains as to whether the selection process is really an important causal agent. If a Party Democracy type of party selects candidates high in ideological commitment, and has a highly disciplined parliamentary party whose members concentrate on promoting the party's policies rather than on constituency work, then we should probably attribute the nature of the parliamentary party to the nature of the party as a whole rather than to its candidate selection process specifically. It is possible, then, that in some or many cases candidate selection may be an intervening variable rather than an independent one. Even in these cases, of course, candidate selection would still be important, as the mechanism through which the membership stamps its mark on the parliamentary group. The material contained in this book should enable us to draw conclusions as to whether candidate selection is more cause or consequence; it is a vital process with an independent effect of its own, does it merely reflect other factors in the social and political environment, or might it play both roles on different occasions?

The country studies

Chapters 2 to 10 of the book will explore these ideas in each of nine countries. The countries covered are sufficiently similar to permit meaningful comparisons to be drawn, and the fact that governments in each need the support of a majority in the legislature justifies the concentration on selection at parliamentary elections. But, at the same time, they encompass a wide range of characteristics. Their electoral systems fall into four broad categories. Britain has single-member constituencies (as has France except in 1986); Belgium, the Netherlands, Norway and France (in 1986) have list systems which provide little or no opportunity for voters to overturn the party's ranking of candidates; Ireland, Italy and Japan have preferential systems in which the voters' wishes are very important. West Germany is a particularly interesting case, since its electoral system combines two forms (single-member and non-preferential list), enabling comparisons to be drawn between the process and outcome of candidate selection under the two forms.

In other ways too the countries provide useful contrasts. Powerful factions are a feature of parties in Italy and Japan. Interest groups play important roles in parties in Britain, Belgium and Italy. France, Ireland and Japan are often regarded as countries where localism is exceptionally strong, and Britain as a country where it is exceptionally weak. In Norway and West Germany candidate selection is affected by legal provisions. In Belgium, Britain, Ireland and the Netherlands there have been changes in candidate selection in recent years. Overall, the range of countries covered ensures that the conclusions reached should be soundly grounded, and avoids the danger noted by Marvick (cited earlier in the chapter) of extrapolating from a very limited data set.

The fact that all nine countries belong to the developed world and have competitive party systems makes it easier to use a common framework for each chapter. We have not covered the United States of America partly because the legislature must contend with the president for authority, but mainly because parties do not play the central role in candidate selection which they enjoy in Europe and Japan. We are interested not primarily in the factors which motivate individuals to seek candidacies but in the process by which parties allocate the rewards of nomination. We are asking not *whether* parties select candidates but *how* they select them.

The fact that none of our chapters is about an uncompetitive system or a less developed country does not imply that we do not regard the topic as a worthwhile area of research in such contexts. On the contrary, when elections do not enable voters to exercise a choice between parties or even between candidates, the candidate selection stage may be the only place where genuine competition takes place. As Hermet (1978: 12) has put it:

> Analysing the candidate-selection machinery offers a much wider and more useful base for understanding rivalries, compromises and man-oeuvres for seduction or intimidation, which frequently constitute the real purpose of non-competitive elections. The composition of the list of candidates offered to the voter reflects an infinite number of ideological nuances, even within nominally single-party systems.

Of course, a difficulty in studying candidate selection in such systems is that the process is usually carried out far from the public eye, especially when genuine rivalry is involved. For less developed countries, the problem, as so often, is a simple lack of basic information. Even so, there have been valuable studies of candidate selection both in the uncompetitive systems of Eastern Europe and in some less developed countries, especially in Africa and Asia. Their findings, along with those from studies of candidate selection in competitive party systems not covered in this book, will be drawn on in the concluding chapter, which will examine the propositions put forward above in the light of the available evidence.

Notes

I should like to thank Michael Laver and Michael Marsh for comments on an earlier draft.

1. Throughout this book we use 'aspirant' to denote a person seeking a candidacy, and 'deselection' to denote the refusal of the selectors to reselect an outgoing deputy as a candidate.

References

Butler, David (1981) 'Electoral Systems', pp. 7–25 in Butler, Penniman and Ranney (1981).

Butler, David, Howard R. Penniman and Austin Ranney (eds)(1981) *Democracy at the Polls*. Washington, DC: American Enterprise Institute.

Castles, Francis G. (1981) 'Female Legislative Representation and the Electoral System', *Politics*, 1 (2): 21–7.

Crotty, William J. (ed.) (1968a) *Approaches to the Study of Party Organization*. Boston, MA: Allyn & Bacon.

Crotty, William J. (1968b) 'The Party Organization and its Activities', pp. 247–306 in Crotty (1968a).

Czudnowski, Moshe M. (1970) 'Legislative Recruitment under Proportional Representation in Israel: A Model and a Case Study', *Midwest Journal of Political Science*, 14 (2): 216–48.

Czudnowski, Moshe M. (1975) 'Political Recruitment', pp. 155–242 in Fred I. Greenstein and Nelson W. Polsby (eds), *Handbook of Political Science:. Volume 2, Micropolitical Theory*. Reading, MA: Addison-Wesley.

Duverger, Maurice (1964) *Political Parties*, 3rd ed. London: Methuen.

Eldersveld, Samuel J. (1964) *Political Parties: A Behavioral Analysis*. Chicago, IL: Rand McNally.

Epstein, Leon D. (1980) *Political Parties in Western Democracies*, revised ed. New Brunswick, NJ: Transaction Books.

Goodman, Jay S., Wayne R. Swanson and Elmer E. Cornwell (1970) 'Political Recruitment in Four Selection Systems', *Western Political Quarterly*, 23 (1): 92–103.

Harmel, Robert (1981) 'Environment and Party Decentralization: A Cross-National Analysis', *Comparative Political Studies*, 14 (1): 75–99.

Hennessy, Bernard (1968) 'On the Study of Party Organization', pp. 1–44 in Crotty (1968a).

Hermens, Ferdinand A. (1972) *Democracy or Anarchy?* New York: Johnson Reprint (first published 1941).

Hermet, Guy (1978) 'State-Controlled Elections: A Framework', pp. 1–18 in Guy Hermet, Richard Rose and Alain Rouquié (eds), *Elections without Choice*. London: Macmillan.

Holland, Martin (1986) *Candidates for Europe: The British Experience*. Aldershot: Gower.

Jupp, James (1968) *Political Parties*. London: Routledge & Kegan Paul.

Keynes, Edward, Richard J. Tobin and Robert Danziger (1979) 'Institutional Effects on Elite Recruitment: The Case of State Nominating Systems', *American Politics Quarterly*, 7 (3): 283–302.

Kirchheimer, Otto (1966) 'The Transformation of the Western European Party Systems', pp. 177–200 in Joseph LaPalombara and Myron Weiner (eds), *Political Parties and Political Development*. Princeton, NJ: Princeton University Press.

Lawson, Kay (1976) *The Comparative Study of Political Parties*. New York: St. Martin's Press.

Loewenberg, Gerhard and Samuel C. Patterson (1979) *Comparing Legislatures*. Boston, MA: Little, Brown.

Marvick, Dwaine (1976) 'Continuities in Recruitment Theory and Research: Toward a New Model', pp. 29–44 in Heinz Eulau and Moshe M. Czudnowski (eds), *Elite Recruitment in Democratic Politics*. Beverly Hills, CA and London: Sage.

Mezey, Michael L. (1979) *Comparative Legislatures*. Durham, NC: Duke University Press.

Michels, Robert (1915) *Political Parties*. London: Jarrold & Sons.

Obler, Jeffrey (1974) 'Intraparty Democracy and the Selection of Parliamentary Candidates: The Belgian Case', *British Journal of Political Science*, 4 (2): 163–85.

Ostrogorski, M. (1970) *Democracy and the Organization of Political Parties*, 2 vols. New York: Haskell House (first published 1902).

Pesonen, Pertti (1968) *An Election in Finland*. New Haven and London: Yale University Press.

Putnam, Robert D. (1976) *The Comparative Study of Political Elites*, Englewood Cliffs, NJ: Prentice-Hall.

Ranney, Austin (1981) 'Candidate Selection', pp. 75–106 in Butler, Penniman and Ranney (1981).

Riggs, Fred W. (1968) 'Comparative Politics and the Study of Political Parties: a Structural Approach', pp. 45–104 in Crotty (1968a).

Schattschneider, E.E. (1942) *Party Government*. New York: Holt, Rinehart & Winston.

Seligman, Lester G. (1967) 'Political Parties and the Recruitment of Political Leadership', pp. 294–315 in Lewis J. Edinger (ed.), *Political Leadership in Industrialized Societies*. New York: John Wiley.

Seligman, Lester G. (1971) *Recruiting Political Elites*. New York: General Learning Press.

Wright, William E. (ed.) (1971a) *A Comparative Study of Party Organization*. Columbus, OH: Charles E. Merrill.

Wright, William E. (1971b) 'Theory', pp. 3–16 in Wright (1971a).

Wright, William E. (1971c) 'Comparative Party Models: Rational-Efficient and Party Democracy', pp. 17–54 in Wright (1971a).

2

Belgium: democracy or oligarchy?

Lieven De Winter

The Belgian 'poll system', a type of intraparty primary in which dues-paying members could vote and select their parliamentary candidates, has for a long time been considered a rare exception to Michels' Iron Law of Oligarchy (Obler, 1974: 164). Most scholars of Belgian politics have focused on selection methods used in the 1960s (Ranney, 1981; Epstein, 1980; Irving, 1979; Dewachter, 1967; Debuyst, 1967). However, since then, dramatic changes in the actual selection processes have taken place in most parties, making the Belgian case more complex, and less of an example of intraparty democracy (De Winter, 1980).

The first part of this chapter describes the main features of the Belgian electoral and party system. Next, the major parties' selection rules and actual selection procedures are examined. The third part deals with selectors' preferences and their role expectations. Finally, the impact of candidate selection on the nature of the parliamentary party and the behaviour of parliamentarians is illustrated.

The impact of the electoral and party system

The electoral system
Intraparty selection procedures in Belgium are adapted to procedures governing general elections. The 212 members of the Chamber of Representatives are elected through a proportional representation system from thirty multi-member constituencies. Parties in each constituency normally draw up lists which include a number of candidates equal to the number of representatives to be elected. They vary from two representatives in the Ieper constituency to thirty-three in Brussels-Hal-Vilvord.

The ordering of candidates on the electoral lists is of particular importance because in practice voters decide only on the number of seats a party will receive, not on who will fill them. There are two ways of casting a vote: a list vote and a preference vote.[1] Every candidate whose number of preference votes reaches the eligibility figure (calculated by dividing the party's total vote by the number of seats it won, plus one) is seated. Usually, only the head of a list manages to reach such a high number. If the head of the list has received fewer preference votes than this figure, list votes are added to his or her preference votes until the required figure is reached. This procedure is repeated for the candidate situated in the second place on the list and so on until all the party's seats have been allocated. However, if the list votes are used up before all the seats have been assigned, the remaining seats are accorded to the candidates with the most preference votes.

With large numbers of voters casting list rather than preference votes this seat-allocating procedure makes the ordering of candidates by the parties crucial in the election process. Belgian voters have rarely managed to alter the ordered list. Following the establishment of universal male suffrage in 1919 and until the last election of 1985, only twenty-six of the 4295 seats in the Chamber (0.61 percent) were accorded to candidates who had been elected 'out of order,' i.e. elected while a candidate placed higher on the list was not. The proportion of preference votes in the total vote has increased steadily (from 16.4 percent in 1919 to 51.9 percent in 1978, and has since stabilized itself slightly below that level). Although this has increased the likelihood that candidates will be elected in a different order from that of their appearance on the list, the number of candidates elected 'out of order' has not increased at all.

So the Belgian voters decide only on the number of seats a party gets; the parties themselves decide who will receive them. Hence party officials have come to think in terms of safe, combative and hopeless list positions. In choosing candidates they are naturally most concerned about who occupies the safe and combative positions, and they often fill the hopeless spots with well-known personalities who may attract voters but who have no serious intention of pursuing a parliamentary career.

The level of competition and the relevance of the intraparty selection process is determined by the number of safe party seats in each constituency. In constituency parties which have no hope of electing even one representative the designation of candidates engenders little interest. Often local party leaders must search for party members willing to be nominated. Only when a constituency party expects to elect at least several representatives if there is sufficient competition among aspirants and concern among the rank-and-file to warrant the expense, time and energy required to involve the different levels of the party organization in the selection process. The focus of this chapter is on the procedures through which the successful candidates are selected.

In addition, only the selection of candidates for the House of Representatives is examined. The Belgian Senate has exactly the same powers and functions as the Chamber of Representatives, and approximately the same distribution of seats among parties. Most of its members are directly elected but data on their selection is scarce.[2]

The party system

For seventy years, from the end of the 1890s until at least 1965, the Belgian party system constituted a clear-cut example of Sartori's (1976) three-party type, in which the three 'traditional' parties, Christian Democrats, Socialists and Liberals shared governmental offices in different coalition combinations. Although the relative strength of these parties changed considerably throughout that period, they usually attracted over 90 percent of the total vote.

In the 1960s three regionalist parties (the Rassemblement Wallon (RW) in the French-speaking Walloon constituencies, the Front Démocratique des Francophones (FDF) in Brussels, and the Volksunie (VU) in Flemish constituencies) emerged and were electorally so successful (22.3 percent of the vote in 1971) that they could not be neglected in the governmental coalitions in the 1970s.[3] The growing salience of the linguistic and regional cleavages, on which their success was based, internally divided the Christian Democrats, Liberals and Socialists, and each traditional party split into two organizationally and programmatically independent Flemish and French-speaking branches (respectively in 1968, 1972 and 1978). These linguistically homogeneous branches, being finally liberated from the electorally unprofitable politics of compromise within their former national party, gradually took up most issues raised by the regional parties. During the first half of the 1980s they managed to crush the electoral appeal of the FDF and the RW. The Volksunie is also in decline, but it still represents an important part of the Flemish electorate. Finally, in the 1985 general election the ecology parties (ECOLO and AGALEV) made a breakthrough and for the first time since 1925 the Parti Communiste Belge (PCB) was not represented in Parliament.

Since the party system seems to be reverting to its three-party format (but in a 'Belgian' three by two version), only the selection of parliamentary candidates by the traditional parties is discussed in detail.[4]

The selection of parliamentary candidates: intraparty rules and practice

The procedures by which Belgian political parties select their parliamentary candidates are not governed by public law, but by rules made, amended, interpreted and enforced entirely by party agencies. These are contained in the constituency charters, and often in the national charter, of each party. Most of these charters call for the poll system. Although procedures regulating this system vary considerably according to constituency and party, all polls are organized along the following lines:

1. All parties set eligibility requirements for candidacy. In some parties they are extremely demanding, in others very easy to meet. Personal exceptions under certain circumstances are allowed, but have to be approved by constituency and/or national party agencies.

2. All persons who are members of the party for more than a specified period prior to the poll are enfranchised. Some parties require membership only at the moment of the candidate selection itself, while other parties demand a more long-term commitment.

3. The poll is a contested election. In practice the number of aspirants usually exceeds the number of safe and combative places to be filled.

4. Most voting members mark their preferences for one or more of the aspirants. The voting procedures differ widely among constituency parties. The candidate who attracts the most votes is placed at the head of the list, and so on according to the number of votes received.

The Liberals were the first to organize polls, in the late 1840s. They hoped, by stressing the distinctiveness of Liberal candidates and by involving voters in the choice of candidates, to mobilize support for the party in general elections. Recognizing the electoral benefits the Liberals derived from this organizational technique, the Catholics started to adopt this procedure in the 1860s. The Socialists were not going to deny their members the right to participate in candidate selection, having led the fight to extend the suffrage. By the end of the 1940s polls had become an accepted tradition in party life (Obler, 1974: 167).

However, although the above procedures are still explicitly contained in the charters of most traditional parties, in many parties the actual use of the poll has been declining drastically since the 1960s. We shall now look at practices within each party.

The Christian Democratic parties

Intraparty rules. The national charter of the Flemish Christelijke Volkspartij (CVP, Christian Popular Party) calls for the use of the poll system but leaves the constituency parties to make the practical arrangements.

The charters of most CVP constituency parties stipulate the use of a particular type of poll system – one based on a 'model list'. The constituency committee establishes an alphabetical list of all aspirants and its preferred list of candidates. The latter is the so-called model list. Each voter may cast his or her ballot for either the entire model list or for particular candidates on the alphabetical list. In the latter case the voter must order the candidates according to preference. If a majority of votes is cast for the model list, it becomes the final electoral list. If it is rejected, the votes cast for aspirants on the alphabetical list are considered in order to rank the candidates. The total vote for each aspirant is calculated by adding the votes received on the alphabetical list to the total number of votes cast for the model list (if the candidate appears on the latter). The aspirant with the highest number of votes is placed at the head of the list, the one with the second highest number in the second place, and so on, until all places have been allocated. As a result of these tabulating procedures, voters in the CVP polls have rarely managed to alter the model lists.[5] However, some constituency parties apply the 'pure' poll system, in which no model list is used. In this system the number of preference poll votes alone determines the selection and order of the candidates for the final list.

In 1965 it became obligatory that final lists drawn up by each constituency party be approved by the National Party Bureau. The Bureau has the power to alter the order of the list, and to add or remove candidates.[6]

The national charter of the French-speaking Parti Social Chrétien (PSC) stipulates that a poll must be organized for every general election, except in the case of premature elections, into which category most of the elections in Belgium fall.[7] The PSC constituency parties apply the same model list system as the CVP, but with a different counting method when the model list is rejected. If as a result of premature elections there is not sufficient time to organize a poll, the constituency committee establishes the final list, which must be approved by a four-fifths majority. If the list receives between a half and four fifths of the vote, a constituency congress consisting of delegates of the local branches is organized. Should the congress reject this list, the national party leadership (comité directeur) formulates it.

The eligibility requirements within the Christian Democratic parties are not very stringent. There is an age limit of 65, and a prohibition against holding a seat in Parliament while serving as the mayor or alderman of a city of more than 30,000 inhabitants. Candidates in the PSC must have belonged to the party for at least two years.

Candidate selection in practice. Parties tend to deviate from these internal rules, particularly when elections are held unexpectedly. In addition, in the Christian Democratic parties the internal party selection process is preceded by a selection process within the major intraparty pressure groups.

In Table 2.1, which describes the evolution of the use of the poll system in the traditional parties in the 1958–85 period, representatives of each party are distinguished according to their language, and presented as a separate parliamentary party.[8]

Table 2.1 *Representatives selected by polls, 1958–85*[a]

	CVP		PSC		SP		PS		PVV		PRL		Total	
		%		%		%		%		%		%		%
	n	poll	n	poll	n	poll	n	poll	n	poll	n	poll	n	poll
1958	68	95.6	36	87.1	34	75.9	50	100.0	10	60.0	11	100.0	190	94.7
1961	65	74.5	31	92.9	35	60.0	49	90.0	8	0.0	12	100.0	200	75.8
1965	54	69.1	23	57.9	29	52.6	35	94.7	20	14.3	28	52.4	189	60.4
1968	51	3.9	18	0.0	29	45.0	30	93.1	19	10.5	28	61.1	175	32.9
1971	46	4.3	21	14.3	29	21.4	32	75.0	21	0.0	15	20.0	164	23.5
1974	50	0.0	22	13.3	26	15.4	33	87.9	21	0.0	12	0.0	164	23.4
1977	56	0.0	24	0.0	27	22.2	35	62.9	17	0.0	16	6.3	175	17.3
1978	57	0.0	25	32.0	26	0.0	32	28.1	22	15.0	15	23.1	177	11.6
1981	43	0.0	18	25.0	26	25.0	34	82.4	28	18.2	24	41.2	173	31.4
1985	49	81.6	19	0.0	32	21.9	35	78.8	22	17.6	25	50.0	182	50.6

[a] Percentages are based on the number of representatives for whom data on selection procedures was available.
Source: See note 16 and De Winter, 1980. In the period under consideration, all elections were premature except for those in 1958 and 1965.

CVP representatives are classified as either MPs selected through a poll (usually the model list system) or as those selected through any other procedure (usually a congress of delegates of local branches or a decision by the constituency party leaders).[9] Table 2.1 shows that in the 1958–81 period the use of the poll system dropped dramatically. In 1958, 95.6 percent of all CVP representatives were placed on the electoral lists through some kind of poll system. From 1965 until 1981 the poll system nearly vanished. Surprisingly, it was widely practised again in 1985, probably due to the fact that for once the elections did not come as a surprise. Thus party leaders could not use the unexpectedness of the elections as an excuse for not organizing polls.

Most representatives who were selected through the poll system gained their place through an approved model list. This calls into question the significance of the high number of representatives selected under the poll system in the 1958, 1961, 1965 and 1985 elections in regard to the apparent democratic nature of the selection procedure. Model lists are very difficult for party members to modify. Hence in most cases the preferences of constituency party officials who draw them up, and not the members' preferences, decide which candidate will get which place on the final list. Even the growing tendency to reject the model lists in the 1958–65 period never resulted in a large modification of the proposed order of candidates.

Although information on the participation of party members is scarce, the data for the 1958, 1961, 1965 and 1985 elections suggest a declining participation rate. In 1958, 51 percent of the members of constituencies using the poll system actually voted. In 1961, 1965 and 1985 the figures were 40, 38 and 25 percent respectively. This decline may indicate dissatisfaction among party members with the oligarchic model list procedure. In constituencies which applied the poll system in the sixties, poll participants constituted approximately 5 percent of those who voted for the constituency party. In 1985 this proportion dropped to 2.5 percent. In Table 2.2 the overall participation rates of members of each traditional party for 1985 are compared. The constituency parties that did not provide for a poll or other forms of direct member participation are also included in the figures.

Table 2.2   *Members' direct participation in candidate selection in the 1985 general election*

Parties	% of national party membership	% of national party electorate
CVP	21.4	1.9
PSC	0.0	0.0
SP	9 5	1,3
PS	38.0	7.6
PVV	0.3	0.0
PRL	2.3	0.2
Total weighted average	12.1	2.1

All figures are estimates, sometimes based on information from only a small number of constituencies. For participation rates in only the constituencies where a poll was organized see sections on individual parties.

The evolution of the use of the poll procedure in the PSC is analogous to the one of the CVP (Table 2.1), except in two respects. First, following the 1968 election some PSC constituency parties continued to use polls. Second, the PSC did not revive the use of the poll in 1985, probably due to the attempt to offer some safe places to members of the Alliance Démocratique (i.e. former RW politicians).

The role of the 'standen' in the selection process. The CVP is a Flemish Catholic catch-all party which appeals to workers, the middle class and farmers.[10] These three socio-economic categories are highly organized. The Algemeen Christelijk Werkersverbond (ACW) represents the workers, the Nationaal Christelijk Midden-standverbond (NCMW) the middle classes, and the Boerenbond (BB) the farmers. All consider the CVP to be the sole political representative of their interests. All three have active sections at the constituency level and are represented as *standen* (estates) in the constituency parties. Each tries to maximize its power within the party through controlling the selection of political personnel at all levels.

As religion became politically less salient in the sixties, the socio-economic cleavage gained in importance and increasingly divided the three interest groups. On the eve of elections all groups try to secure as many safe places on the electoral lists as possible. The designation of candidates must therefore be understood as a focal point of factional conflict.

Party leaders strive to compose lists that will not alienate these interest groups and their followers. This explains the wide use of the model list system instead of the pure poll. Party members voting in a pure poll are not likely to produce such balanced lists. For one thing they are not usually representative of those who vote for the party in the general election. Political participation is unequally spread amongst different social categories, and so is party membership. Second, even in the absence of bias, the pure poll method could fail to result in a balanced list if one faction, supported by a majority of the poll voters, managed to win all or most of the safe places. Members' growing tendency to reject model lists in the sixties – the result of the growing uneasiness between the factions – disturbed the already difficult compromise between the leaders of these factions. In addition, factional fights involving the rank-and-file endanger the unity of the party with potentially damaging electoral consequences. Hence constituency party leaders gradually started to abolish direct member participation.

The control of candidate selection by leaders of interest groups secures them an important tool for the enforcement of conformist political behaviour on the part of their representatives, both inside and outside Parliament. This control is highly institutionalized (Smits, 1982). Delegates of the three interest groups in the constituency party committee come to an agreement regarding safe places which they can reserve for their own candidates. In most constituencies an enduring agreement has been reached. Of the CVP representatives elected in 1978, 60.7 percent were elected on fixed places which had been reserved for a particular group over a period of time, while 30.4 percent were elected in constituencies where the interest group leaders negotiated an agreement valid for only one election on the eve of the composition of the lists.

So nearly all CVP representatives obtained their seat because one of the standen offered them a safe place on an electoral list. In 1985, 46.9 percent of the CVP representatives belonged to the ACW group, 12.3 percent to the BB, 26.5 percent to the NCMV and 8.2 percent were backed both by the BB and the NCMV. Only a few were not backed by any of the groups. These 'sans familles' CVP parliamentarians are usually national party leaders or Cabinet members, with a strong electoral appeal. They cannot be neglected in the bargaining process between the groups.

Not much is known about the procedures through which the intraparty pressure groups select their candidates. In some constituencies a poll among all pressure group members is organized, in others a congress of delegates of the local branches decides. Finally, in some cases the constituency committees hold a secret vote. What is evident is that the existence of intraparty interest groups and their increasingly uneasy alliance explains many features of the candidate selection system within the CVP: the predominance of the model list system over the pure poll, the growing tendency in the sixties to reject the model lists, and the near total abolition of any form of poll system in the seventies.

In the PSC constituency parties, socio-economic interest groups are less well organized. In addition, many changes occurred in the institutionalized representation of the three social categories within the party framework. French-speaking Catholic workers are organized in the Mouvement Ouvrier Chrétien (MOC). The MOC factions seeking political representation by the PSC are organized in the Démocratie Chrétienne (DC). Committees at the constituency level have their representatives in the constituency 'comité directeur'. They recognize parliamentary candidates as their political representatives in the PSC and promote their candidates' selection by the comité directeur and also sponsor their election.

The representation of the Catholic middle classes in the PSC has undergone many organizational changes. Until 1983 they were represented by the Centre Politique des Indépendants et Cadres Chrétiens (CEPIC). CEPIC was abolished in 1983 because intra-party left–right conflicts were about to threaten the very existence of the party. Yet, the disappearance of CEPIC has not decreased the impact of middle-class and right-wing tendencies on the PSC in a significant way. The French-speaking Catholic farmers' organization, the Alliance Agricole Belge, is not officially recognized by the party, but does have individual representatives defending agricultural interests. Finally, there also exists an unstructured group of 'sans familles' PSC politicians unrelated either to the DC or CEPIC.

Stable institutionalized agreements between the representatives of the socio-economic interest groups within PSC constituency parties are less common than in the CVP. In many constituencies there is no tradition of bargaining or seat-sharing. Consequently conflicts between the DC and CEPIC on the eve of elections have been more frequent, and usually more bitter. Since the PSC is also smaller than the CVP, it can count only on one safe seat in many constituencies, so often there is no package of seats to share between the tendencies. This usually results in the selection of a neutral, 'sans familles' candidate, acceptable to all factions. Of the twenty-five PSC representatives in 1978, ten were 'sans familles', ten belonged to the DC and five to CEPIC.

Socialist parties

Intraparty rules. The national party charter of the French-speaking Parti Socialiste (PS) contains no stipulations regarding candidate selection. Therefore constituency parties may choose the methods they wish to apply. Most constituency charters call for use of the pure poll system (as described above for some CVP constituency parties). In some constituencies the party committee can decide to place a specific candidate 'hors poll'. This means that it reserves to this candidate a safe place, usually at the top of the final candidate list. In this case the poll only determines the selection of candidates for the lower places. This procedure is usually applied to protect candidates who are of great value to the national party leadership such as the party president, former ministers or valuable legislators who lack sufficient popularity among constituency party members to ensure their placement at the top of the list. However, the national party agencies have no right to interfere with constituency party arrangements concerning candidate selection.

The national party charter of the Flemish Socialistische Partij

(SP) also contains no rules concerning the composition of candidate lists. As in the PS, most constituency party charters prescribe the use of the pure poll system and the national party leadership has no right to interfere with constituency party arrangements concerning candidate selection.

In the Socialist parties eligibility requirements are generally stringent though they differ widely among constituencies (Ceuleers, 1978). Most charters require a minimum party membership of five years, and a minimum membership in the Socialist trade union and Socialist health insurance fund of five years. In addition some constituencies' charters require membership in the Socialist co-operative and annual minimum purchases, subscription to the party newspaper, the holding of some party office, the enrolment of children in state rather than private (i.e. Catholic) schools, a high level of party activity, that private insurance be held through the Socialist insurance company, membership of spouse in the party, the trade union and the medical insurance fund, and membership of children in party youth organizations. Under the national charter candidates may not be over 65, be seated on the board of directors of private enterprises or hold more than one public office.

These stringent eligibility conditions are not always strictly enforced. Today some are completely unenforcable due, for instance, to the disappearance of party newspapers and of many co-operatives. Also, in order to attract new voters, the national party leadership of the SP have recently promoted the opening of some constituency lists to famous left-wing personalities with few organizational ties to party structures. Similarly the national party leadership of the PS has encouraged the inclusion of candidates from the French-speaking regionalist parties. However, many constituency parties have successfully resisted these enlargements of their candidate lists by strictly applying their charters' eligibility requirements.

Practice. In Table 2.1 Socialist representatives are classified into two categories: those who were selected through a pure poll procedure and those who were not. The non-poll procedures include selection through an 'hors poll' placement or through a congress of delegates of local party branches who approve a list proposal compiled by the constituency committee. Table 2.1 reflects a dramatic decline in the use of the poll system in the SP, and only a slight decrease in the PS.[11] In constituencies where a poll was organized about 60 percent of PS members and 45 percent of SP members participated. This participation rate has remained fairly stable over the entire period under consideration (Ceuleers and De Winter, 1986). In the eighties the members of the PS and SP constitute 21 percent and 16 percent respectively of those parties' electorates (Vanpol, 1983, 1984).

In most cases where no poll method is used, the constituency committee draws up a list which is then presented for approval at a constituency congress of delegates of the local party branches. Sometimes these delegates are bound by their local members to support certain candidates; in other cases they have freedom of choice. The voting mechanisms at these congresses also vary widely. Approval of the proposed list is usually not problematic because leaders of local branches are also members of the committee which draws up the list.

The causes of decline of the poll system in the SP are not as clear as in the case of the CVP–PSC. The socio-economic composition of the Socialist electorate is more homogeneous than the Christian Democratic one. Candidate selection is thus not a focal point of factional conflict between socio-economic categories.

Nevertheless, several causes of decline can be identified. First, a general member poll does not generate the most attractive electoral list. It favours candidates who are backed by one or more organizations of the Socialist movement. Socialist trade unions and health insurance organizations often support particular candidates during the selection process. Leaders of the trade union and health care organizations can mobilize their rank-and-file members, and even their personnel (for which party membership is often required), to vote for them in the poll elections. The support of trade union and health care organizations also offers financial advantages. Since these are the financial backbone of the Socialist movement, they pay for most of the general electoral party propaganda. Sometimes they also contribute substantially to the personal campaign funds of the candidates they support. Under the poll system candidates were usually eager to gain the support of the aged, who were traditionally overrepresented among party members. Thus many candidates were active in, or at least paid attention to, Socialist organizations for older citizens. Young candidates only had a chance when they could rely on the backing of the party youth movement. Nearly all female Socialist parliamentarians held leadership positions in Socialist women's organizations before their election to Parliament. Membership in a strong local party branch was also important because local party members tended to support candidates from their own community. Holders of local public office, such as mayors, were favoured too, due to the local visibility and service nature of their positions. Finally, incumbents who concentrated on constituency service could appeal to the many party members in their clientele. As can be seen, the poll system favours candidates with a high popularity among party members and strong roots in Socialist organizations. Yet such candidates are not always capable of attracting votes from new electors who are either not part of the Socialist movement or who are less integrated into it, such as Catholic workers and the more radicalized 'May 68' generation.

Second, the poll system prevented the 'recuperation' of New Left activists and intellectuals – a natural Socialist recruitment reservoir at the beginning of the seventies – since these categories were not inclined to invest years of participation in the local social life of Socialist organizations before being heard in national politics.

Third, the poll system generated parliamentarians who were not always seriously concerned with their genuine parliamentary work. Under this system, candidates generally raise the necessary support for their selection through devotion to their constituency. Political performance on the national level is a much less effective means of assuring selection in the poll process. Only those politicians with a highly visible position in national politics, such as party leaders and ministers, do not have to rely solely on their local popularity. The use of the 'hors poll' system proves that in many cases even these national positions are not sufficient to secure party leaders first place on the final electoral list under normal poll procedures. Hence under the poll system parliamentary technocrats or specialists could hardly survive.

Finally, it is obvious that the poll system gives rise to strong rivalries between Socialist candidates for the conquest of new or the maintainance of old followers; between the party apparatus, the trade unions and the health organizations, and between local branches, each supporting their own candidates. Candidates had to tackle their fellow comrades first in the weeks preceding the poll, and had less time and energy left for campaigning against the other parties and their candidates.

So the Flemish Socialist constituency parties gradually started dropping the poll system.[12] Abolition was favoured by several factors. First, in many small constituencies with only one Socialist representative polls were never held. Hence the tradition of the poll was not strongly embedded in the political culture.

Second, in 1976 Karel Van Miert, a new and young candidate, was elected national co-president. His organizational ties to the Socialist world were limited and his political career had been rather technocratic. His main goal was to infuse new blood into the party by recruiting young candidates and left-wingers from outside traditional Socialist structures. So from the end of the seventies on, attempts were made to gain votes among Catholic workers by presenting well-known left-wing Catholic personalities (including priests). Given the strong anti-clerical sentiments of rank-and-file members, the recruitment of these new types of candidates would have been impossible under the poll system.

The break-up of the Belgian Socialist Party in 1978 also favoured the rise of the new party leadership. Since most of the Socialist party machinery at the national level (the political secretariat, parliamentary staff, etc.) was formerly dominated by French speakers, the Flemish Socialists had to create their own national structures. The group of 'Young Turks' around the new president had little difficulty placing their people into these new positions. Their aim was to increase the power of the national party leadership over the constituency leadership. One way of doing this was to further the recruitment of political personnel who supported the party's rejuvenation. According to the national party charter, the national leadership still does not have formal powers to interfere with selection procedures in the constituency parties; but it can and does exert considerable informal pressure when it comes to the promotion of new candidates.

The Young Turks have been most successful in smaller constituencies where Socialist organizations are usually less well organized and the party apparatus is smaller, less bureaucratized and thus easier to take over. In large constituencies with an older Socialist tradition there is more resistance.[13] In the traditionalist strongholds, such as Antwerp and Ghent, Socialist organizations and local branches are better organized, party leadership is more bureaucratized, and membership is proportionally larger. They continue to use the poll system (or a constituency congress of mandated delegates) and send the more traditional types of representatives to Parliament.

The absence of some of the factors that contributed to the gradual decline in the use of the poll system in the SP explain why this system has remained fairly common in PS constituency parties. First, the PS is the strongest party in Wallonia, and in every Walloon constituency can count on winning at least one – and usually more than one – seat. Thus candidate selection is, and has always been, a real, and not only a symbolic function, of every single constituency party. Consequently, each constituency party developed the necessary rules and procedures. The PS opted for the pure poll system. Thus this system became one of the most important aspects of members' participation in intraparty decision-making. The high level of participation of PS members in the poll (usually more than half) shows that participation in the poll represents an important and widespread aspect of the political culture and practice of PS party members.

Second, use of the poll has not only been more widespread in PS constituencies than in the SP, it also has a longer tradition. The former Belgian Workers Party scored its first electoral successes in the Walloon industrialized constituencies, and advanced – except for some industrial cities – only slowly in Flemish constituencies. Hence PS organizations at constituency and local level usually have a much longer institutional history and experience than those of the SP, and tend to conduct intraparty business in a more bureaucratic way. The high level of institionalization of PS constituency party life makes procedural changes in the performance of any of its functions – including candidate selection – rather difficult.

On the other hand, the PS is aware of and tries to cope with some of the deficiencies of the poll system. For example, the danger of inbreeding due to the stringent eligibility conditions has been tackled by weakening these requirements considerably. The tendency now is to retain only those requirements concerning 'pure party' participation, for instance a minimum period of membership. However, these changes are insufficient to allow the selection of candidates who are complete newcomers to the Socialist world, such as former FDF–RW parliamentarians. Some of them have been given a chance on Socialist lists through 'hors poll' placement, but only after strong pressure from the national party leadership on the constituency party.

Hence candidate selection within the PS has undergone some modifications. However, contrary to those in the SP, these changes have usually occurred within the poll system, thus modifying only some of its specific operational features.

The Liberal parties

Intraparty rules. The national charter of the Flemish Partij voor Vrijheid and Vooruitgang (PVV, Party for Liberty and Progress) recommends the use of a general member poll, but allows other procedures. Constituency parties must establish their own rules and act accordingly. The national Party Bureau and the Party Council can give recommendations concerning candidates and their order of appearance on the list of a given constituency. These must be communicated to all participants in the poll, or whatever other selection procedure is used. The recommendations are not binding. If no internal agreement on candidate selection is reached within a constituency party the national Party Bureau can intervene arbitrarily.

Traditionally, eligibility requirements are not demanding in the PVV. Today only an age limit of 65 exists and the national Party Bureau can allow exceptions even to this rule.

The present national charter of the French-speaking Parti Réformateur Libéral (PRL, the former Parti de la Liberté et du Progrès) gives constituency party organizations full freedom to establish their candidate selection procedures, but the national Commission de Conciliation et d'Arbritrage can intervene in the selection process in case of conflict within constituency selection committees. PRL candidates cannot be older than 65. This age limit can be overruled through the results of a poll, or by a two-thirds majority vote in the constituency selection committee, but these exceptions must be approved by the national Party Bureau.

Practice. In Table 2.1 PVV representatives are divided into two categories: those who were selected through a pure poll procedure and those who were not. The non-poll procedures include selection through an 'hors poll' placement, through a decision taken by the constituency committee or through a congress of delegates of local party sections who approve a list proposal compiled by the constituency committee.

A decline in the use of the poll system is already noticeable by the beginning of the 1960s. Of PVV representatives elected in the 1958–85 period less than 10 percent were selected through a poll. In most non-poll selection procedures, constituency party committees compiled the candidate lists. In some constituencies a relatively small group of people (a 'comité des sages', or the head of the list at the previous elections) drew up the list. In most cases these proposed lists were approved by a constituency congress of local branch delegates.[14] Data on the participation rate of members (of the PVV as well as of the PRL) are too scarce to draw significant conclusions about its evolution. In 1958–65 usually about half of the members of constituency parties who held polls participated, representing approximately 6 percent of the electorate voting Liberal in those constituencies (De Winter, 1980). In the 1980s members of the PVV and PRL represent respectively 8.6 and 12.0 percent of the parties' electorate (Vanpol, 1983, 1984).

An important cause of the decline in use of the poll system in the Liberal parties during the sixties was the electoral strategy of Omer van Audenhove, the new national president. To attract middle-class and conservative Catholic voters to the hitherto anti-clerical Liberal movement, he wanted to place prominent Catholic political personalities on the liberal lists. His efforts met practically no resistance in the smaller constituencies, where primaries according to the poll system had not been held in the past. But in the larger and politically more significant constituencies, such as Brussels and Liège, the poll system was still in use. It was unlikely that traditional party members, who harboured strong anti-clerical sentiments, would support Catholic aspirants. After unsuccessfully trying to abolish the Brussels poll the president managed to reserve two safe places (the third and the sixth) on the Chamber list for Catholic candidates in the 1965 elections. Both candidates were elected. In 1968 safe places were not reserved for anyone, and both candidates had to compete for places with other aspirants. They ended up in combative positions and only one of the candidates was re-elected. But given the electoral success of the party most constituency parties continued to include Catholic candidates on their lists and strengthened the party's electoral support among Catholics. Ideologically, the party took a neutral position on religious issues such as abortion and education.

As in the case of the Flemish Socialist Party, the leaders of the national Liberal Party viewed the poll as an obstacle blocking the expansion of the party's electoral base. 'In their eyes, the major purpose of the party is to acquire as much political power as possible by attracting as many votes as possible. To achieve this goal, they argue, members must be excluded from the selection procedure' (Obler, 1974: 184). In a few constituencies Liberal organizations played a prominent role in the selection process. For example, a safe place was reserved in some constituencies for candidates representing the Liberal health insurance organization.

The French-speaking Liberals turned away from the poll system after 1965, but contrary to their Flemish counterparts they have gradually re-adopted it since 1978.[15] In the 1958–85 period 42.8 percent of French-speaking Liberal representatives were selected through a poll. In the constituencies which did not organize polls in 1985 the constituency party committee usually drew up a list which was approved by an enlarged constituency committee or a congress of local delegates.

The decline in the use of the poll system is not only due to the desire to incorporate conservative Catholic candidates in the PRL lists. In 1976 the Walloon nationalist RW lost nearly its entire conservative wing, including many parliamentarians, to the Liberals. In order to make this defection successful, these incumbents had to be secured safe places on Liberal lists, against the will of the hitherto more 'Belgicist' party members. In most cases this inclusion was facilitated through restricting the direct participation of party members in candidate selection processes.

Minor parties
The constituency committees of the Volksunie draw up candidate lists which must be approved by a constituency congress composed

of delegates of local branches. These lists must then be approved by the national Party Council, which is composed of delegates from each constituency. The Council can alter candidate lists by a simple majority vote. Incumbents are automatically assigned the same place they held on the previous electoral list, unless two-thirds of the constituency congress vote otherwise.

The Commission Electorale of the FDF selects all candidates for the lists in the three constituencies of Brabant province. In the Rassemblement Wallon, the ally of the FDF which participates in all other French-speaking constituencies, the comité directeur of each constituency draws up a model list which must usually be approved by an enlarged comité directeur. In some constituencies the lists have to be approved also by a general assembly of party members.

In the Communist Party the Central Committee draws up the list for all constituencies after consulting the constituency parties.

Selectors' preferences

Given the very decentralized nature of the selection procedures used and the wide diversity of selecting agencies (ranging from party members to a small number of constituency party leaders) the preferences of the selectors of a given party are hard to establish. No direct survey on selectors' preferences has ever been carried out in Belgium, but some indirect indicators, based on MPs' perceptions of selectors' preferences, do give a preliminary idea about the major differences in preferences of the selectorates of the various parties.[16]

In Table 2.3 representatives' perceptions of their selectors' preferences are grouped according to Bochel and Denver's (1983: 53) three groups of categories (objective personal characteristics, subjective personal characteristics, and political characteristics). Within each group, some concerns are mentioned quite frequently. Territorial balance and electoral value are particularly important in most parties. It is logical that selectors try to attract voters by composing a balanced ticket which presents candidates from most regions within their constituency. The same considerations apply for the representation of women, and of age and professional categories. However, since most constituency parties have only one candidate elected a balance is often impossible. This suggests that considerations concerning a balanced ticket refer more to the composition of the entire candidate list than to the selection of individual candidates. Subjective personal characteristics are

Table 2.3   *Candidates' characteristics preferred by parties' selectorates as perceived by representatives (in percent)*

	CVP	PSC	SP	PS	PVV	PRL	Total %	n
Number of respondents	47	14	18	20	17	10		126
Objective personal characteristics	46.8	78.6	61.1	50.0	70.6	100.0	62.7	79
amongst which are: territorial and linguistic balance	40.4	78.6	50.0	50.0	64.7	100.0	55.6	70
gender, age, professional balance	12.8	7.1	11.1	15.0	35.3	30.0	16.7	21
Subjective personal characteristics	21.3	0.0	33.3	20.0	29.4	20.0	21.4	27
amongst which are: popularity	10.6	0.0	22.2	15.0	11.8	10.0	13.5	17
Political characteristics	100.0	100.0	94.4	80.0	82.4	80.0	92.1	116
amongst which are: electoral value	61.7	71.4	50.0	15.0	52.9	70.0	53.3	67
support from pressure group	95.7	92.9	5.6	0.0	5.9	0.0	47.6	60
party record and intraparty support	57.4	57.1	72.2	80.0	47.1	20.0	58.7	74
local office and constituency record	14.9	21.4	27.8	0.0	29.4	30.0	18.3	23
national political and parliamentary record	10.6	0.0	27.8	5.0	0.0	0.0	8.7	11

mentioned only by 21.4 percent of the respondents and consist of rather vague attributes such as 'popularity', 'ability to get on with people', 'hard working' and 'integrity'.

Table 2.3 reveals interesting differences between parties as far as the political characteristics are concerned, differences which seem to be related to the different nature of their selection procedures and of their selectorates. Not surprisingly pressure group support seems only of concern to Christian Democrat selectors, while party record and support by intraparty organizations (such as strong local branches, youth and women's organizations) seem to be dominant criteria for Socialist selectors. Other political characteristics include local office record, constituency record and the candidates' views on important issues.[17]

Representatives also have the impression that their selectors hold strong expectations about the behaviour of their candidates once elected. As shown in Table 2.4, these expectations refer to a wide range of activities and most of them concern activities outside Parliament.

Representatives' activities most expected by selectors are constituency case work and 'local presence', i.e. Fenno's (1978) 'home style' activities which include participating in the cultural and socio-economic life of the constituency. Many MPs spend their evenings and weekends going to balls, to inaugurations of exhibitions, shops, fairs and markets, to funerals and weddings, celebrations of cultural and sporting organizations, etc. Party work on different levels is also widely expected. Some MPs must be the 'motor' of their constituency and local parties. In addition, selectors strongly expect proper moral behaviour, especially concerning family morals and drinking. But expectations regarding genuine parliamentary work are also widely held.

Table 2.4 *Selectors' role behaviour expectations as perceived by representatives (in percent)*

Behavioural expectations with regard to:	%	n
Parliamentary work	50.8	64
Party work	82.5	104
Pressure group work	31.0	39
Constituency work and local public office	88.9	112
Personal subjective characteristics	31.7	40
Total number of respondents		126

The nature of the parliamentary party

Are selectors' preferences reflected in the nature of the parliamentary party with regard to its background and behaviour? It was argued above that age, sex, occupation, education and local residence were primarily of concern for balancing the entire ticket, but not for selecting candidates in safe and marginal places. Parties do differ on some of these background variables, but it is unclear whether this is caused by differences in selectors' preferences.

Women representatives are rare, except in the CVP. Since the seventies this party has increased the proportion of women in local, constituency and national party leadership positions by using statutory quotas. However, quotas do not exist for the selection of parliamentary candidates.[18] As for educational background, the Socialist parties show the highest proportion of MPs without a regular university degree, a fact reflecting the working-class nature of the parties' recruitment pool. They also show the most marked overrepresentation of teachers. Liberal professions (doctors, lawyers, pharmacists, etc.) are most likely to be found in the Liberal parties. MPs holding leadership positions within the socio-economic pressure groups and party-linked cultural and service organizations are overrepresented in the CVP and the SP.

Residence in the electoral constituency is not a legal requirement for eligibility. However, carpetbagging and 'parachuting' is very rare, and most MPs have strong local ties. On the average, Belgian representatives have lived outside their constituency for less than four years.

The average duration of a parliamentary career in 1978 was 7.7 years. There are some differences between parties, but these can easily be caused by varying electoral fortunes. Certainly, different rates of deselection are not responsible since open deselection is infrequent. In the CVP the order of the list is sometimes altered due to changes in the relative power of the standen in the constituency party, or the necessity of giving the first place to a representative who established a national career (as minister or party president) since the previous elections. Socialists' polls often change the order of candidates, but seldom so drastically that incumbents are downgraded to marginal or hopeless places. In any case, deselection seldom comes unexpectedly, and candidates who fear deselection usually retreat with honour and do not seek renomination.

MPs who combine their mandate with a local office are mostly found in the Socialist parties and the PRL. But this fact is also related to the local power of each party and its rules governing the incompatibility between local and national public offices.

During their term MPs also fulfil leadership functions in a wide variety of non-parliamentary organizations. Socialist representatives are mostly active in their party, in socio-cultural party organizations, and in the social health sector (primarily in the *mutualités*, the parties' mutual medical aid funds). CVP representatives are more engaged in socio-economic pressure groups (i.e. the *standen*). Liberal MPs are most active in their party organizations, in private finance, commerce and industry. PVV representatives are also very active in their *mutualité*, the 'front line' of Liberal constituency case work.

The nature of the parties and of their selection procedures seems to have only a minor impact on the political cohesiveness of the parliamentary groups. In spite of the difference in interest of the standen in the CVP and the PSC, and their control over the selection of parliamentary candidates, voting discipline in Parliament is quite strong. CVP–PSC representatives are expected to defend their stand's interests within the parliamentary committee and within the national and constituency party committee. But the standen have their own representatives within the national party bureau and the Cabinet, and compromises between the standen are usually elaborated at that level. The party and the standen try to maintain a public image of unity. Thus voting discipline has to be strong. In addition, in Belgium party discipline is and has always been strong within every parliamentary group. Christian Democratic representatives are only slightly less disciplined than their Socialist and Liberal colleagues (Langerwerf, 1980; Holvoet, 1980). In general, intraparty factionalism, ideological disputes or conflicts concerning territorial interests very rarely manifest themselves in voting rebellions within a parliamentary group.

Parliamentarians' behaviour

Do selectors' preferences affect the behaviour of representatives, in and outside Parliament? Do parliamentarians engage and specialize in certain forms of behaviour, such as parliamentary work, constituency work and party work, because their selectors want them to? In order to answer these questions, data aggregated on the level of the parliamentary party are less useful, given the heterogeneity of a party's selectorate and of its preferences. With the data at our disposal, the behaviour of individual legislators can be related to their perception of the preferences of those who selected them.[19] In Table 2.5 for each specific behavioural role expectations held by selectors, representatives are divided into those who think that their selectors hold that expectation, and those who do not. If selectors' preferences do affect legislators' behaviour, there should be a significant difference between the groups with regard to the time spent on each activity under consideration.

Table 2.5   *Impact of selectors' preferences on legislators' behaviour*[a]

Hours spent weekly on	Expectation held by selectorate	Expectation not held by selectorate	Total
Parliamentary work	30.3 hrs ($n=70$)	26.2 hrs ($n=61$)	28.4 hrs
Local and constituency party work	4.6 hrs ($n=116$)	2.9 hrs ($n=21$)	4.2 hrs
Pressure group work	3.4 hrs ($n=29$)	2.3 hrs ($n=109$)	2.5 hrs
Constituency case work			
hours per week	8.3 hrs ($n=98$)	6.0 hrs ($n=37$)	7.7 hrs
cases per year	2315 cases ($n=100$)	1397 cases ($n=39$)	2058 cases
Local presence	4.8 hrs ($n=92$)	4.3 hrs ($n=43$)	4.7 hrs

[a] Selectors' preferences as perceived by representatives.

Table 2.5 shows this is so.[20] The impact of selectors' role expectations is most obvious with respect to individual constituency work, followed by pressure group work and local and constituency party work. Genuine parliamentary work and local presence are only slightly affected by selectors' role expectations. These data prove that selectors' preferences – or, better, legislators' perceptions of selectors' role expectations – do have an impact on legislators' behaviour, but that other factors exert an influence as well. Indeed, many representatives spend a considerable amount of time on activities which their selectors do not expect at all.

The method of selection also appears to affect behaviour. A distinction is made in Table 2.6 between representatives selected through a poll (pure poll or model list) and those selected in a different way. The two groups do differ significantly on several behavioural dimensions. As expected, representatives selected through a poll are more constituency-oriented, although both groups spend a similar amount of time on genuine parliamentary work and pressure group work.

Table 2.6   *Impact of selection procedures on representatives' behaviour*

Hours spent weekly on	Selected through poll procedure (n=25)	Selected through non-poll procedure (n=99)	Total (n=124)
Parliamentary work	30.2 hrs	30.0 hrs	30.0 hrs
Local and constituency party work	4.5 hrs	4.2 hrs	4.2 hrs
Pressure group work	2.5 hrs	2.7 hrs	2.7 hrs
Constituency case work			
hours per week	10.6 hrs	7.4 hrs	8.1 hrs
cases per year	2797 cases	1789 cases	1994 cases
Local presence	7.4 hrs	4.3 hrs	4.9 hrs

Conclusion

The nature of the Belgian electoral system makes the selection of parliamentary candidates the most crucial phase in the recruitment process of political elites. Voters decide only on the number of seats a party will receive, and the constituency parties decide who will fill these seats. And a parliamentary seat is usually a necessary step to higher political offices, such as party presidency and the Cabinet.

Until the sixties the three major Belgian parties offered their rank-and-file members substantial opportunities to participate in and even determine the outcome of this recruitment process. The poll selection method often allowed members, rather than constituency party leaders, to choose nominees.

In the eyes of national and constituency party leaders this democratic mass participation had many deficiencies. It tended to overemphasize tensions between different intraparty factions (divided along social, religious and linguistic lines). It also rendered difficult the recruitment of potentially valuable new candidates who lacked popularity among local party members, thereby preventing the composition of the optimally attractive electoral lists.

At the end of the sixties, in most parties (except the PS), the leaderships began to replace general member polls with more oligarchic selection procedures (such as decisions taken by the constituency party committee or a congress of delegates of local party sections). In these cases rank-and-file members exercise only an indirect influence, if any at all, on the selection of their representatives in Parliament.

The evidence on whether candidate selection methods have an impact on legislators' electoral attractiveness, background and behaviour is mixed. There is no doubt that the introduction of a new type of Liberal candidate – through the adoption of new selection procedures – accompanied by a major shift in party ideology, raised Liberal party support considerably in the sixties. In other parties the electoral effect of abrupt changes in selection procedures is less clear. Candidates placed on the CVP's model lists were more or less the same as those of the previous election, but in 1985 their selection was democratically legitimized by the polls which, given the low participation rates, did not raise much enthusiasm. As for the SP, the renewal of its political personnel and its stronger ideological profile, both starting at the end of the seventies, only began to pay off in electoral terms in 1985. Hence it is obvious that factors other than changes in selection procedures and in types of candidates selected influence the rise and fall in party support.

As far as time spent on constituency work, pressure group work, local and constituency party work, and constituency presence are concerned, candidate selection procedures and the expectations selectors hold concerning the behaviour of their representatives (or at least legislators' perceptions of these expectations) do affect representatives' behaviour. On the other hand, genuine parliamentary work and legislators' background characteristics do not seem to be affected by candidate selection procedures.

At the 1985 election some parties unexpectedly reintroduced the poll in several constituencies. Whether this was the death throes of the poll system, or the inauguration of a new era for it, has yet to be seen.

44   Lieven De Winter

Notes

I wish to thank Huri Tursan from the EVI for her many constructive suggestions about the content and language of this chapter.

1. For details see G. van den Berghe on Belgium in Hand et al. (1979).
2. In general the selection of senatorial candidates is more oligarchic than that of representatives. For the election of the directly elected senators some constituencies are merged. As agreements have to be made between the party committees of different constituencies in order to secure a regionally balanced candidate list, the poll system is often abandoned. The decision as to which candidates shall be co-opted as provincial senators is made by the provincial and national party leadership. The national co-opted senators are selected by the national party leadership alone. Many of the provincially and nationally co-opted senators were unsuccessful candidates for the House or for the Senate. Further information on the composition of the Senate lists can be found in the *Cahiers Hebdomadaire du CRISP* published after each general election.
3. The RW joined a governmental coalition in the 1974–7 period, the VU from 1977 to 1978 and the FDF from 1977 to 1980.
4. After the break-up of the traditional parties, none of the linguistic branches has ever joined governmental coalitions without the inclusion of their linguistic counterparts.
5. For a more detailed description of this system in operation in the sixties, see Obler (1973: 171–8), Debuyst (1967: 165–292) and Dewachter (1967: 110–66).
6. As in other parties where the national leadership has the right to overrule the outcome of constituency selection procedures, this intervention hardly ever amounts to a blunt rejection of the constituency party's decision. In the rare cases when the national leadership does intervene, this usually consists only of trying to persuade the quarrelling camps to agree to a compromise.
7. Of the fourteen post-war elections only three (1954, 1958 and 1965) were held at the end of the prescribed four-year period.
8. The Christian Democrats split in 1968, the Liberals in 1972 and the Socialists in 1978. Until their break-up they presented unilingual lists in the sixteen Flemish constituencies and the thirteen Walloon constituencies. In Brussels they usually presented a list with both Flemish and French-speaking candidates. On these bilingual lists, Flemish candidates were usually underrepresented in regard to the parties' proportion of Flemish voters, a situation which led to the presentation of two unilingual lists several years before the national parties split up. Thus for election years in which a party was still linguistically united on the national level (and had a united parliamentary party), the Flemish parliamentary party in Table 2.1 consists of those MPs elected in the sixteen Flemish-speaking constituencies and the Flemish-speaking MPs elected on the bilingual Brussels list (or on the unilingual Flemish Brussels list). The French-speaking parliamentary party consists of the MPs elected in the thirteen French-speaking constituencies and the French-speaking candidates on the bilingual Brussels list (or on the unilingual francophone Brussels list).
9. *Parachutages*, the imposition of a non-local candidate by the national party leadership, and other interventions on behalf of specific candidates by the national party leadership are rare.
10. In the EEC Parliament the CVP belongs to the European Peoples' Party group.
11. The low number for 1978 is due to a rule, applied in most constituencies,

which stipulated that in case an election is held less than eighteen months after the previous election, the previous list is used again.

12. It must be noted that one of the other selection procedures has more or less the same deficiencies as the poll. In some constituencies the members of the local branches hold a secret vote on all aspirants, and then send their delegates with an imperative mandate to the constituency selection congress where a vote is taken on each candidate. Under this procedure, just as under the poll, only the popularity of a candidate among constituency party members decides his or her selection.

13. For instance, in 1985 Karel Van Miert promised the PAKS movement (Progressief Akkoord van Kristenen en Socialisten, Progressive Agreement between Christians and Socialists, a group of left-wing activists within the Catholic trade union) two safe places on Socialist lists. The national leadership asked the Ghent constituency to put the major PAKS spokesman second on its candidate list for the Senate, but the constituency selection congress brought him down to the fourth – hopeless – place. In order to keep his promise, Van Miert had to offer this candidate a seat as a nationally co-opted senator.

14. In half of the constituencies which did not apply the poll procedure in 1985 the decision was taken by the constituency committee, in the other half by a congress of delegates of the local sections. In some cases they were approved by a general assembly of members. Occasionally the 'hors poll' method was used.

15. The polls held by the Liberal parties in the early sixties and in the eighties were not organized on the same principles. Whereas the former resembled the 'pure poll' as commonly used in the PS, the more recent ones are 'general assemblies of members' which vote on a model list proposed by the constituency party leadership. Only if a majority rejects the model list can members attending the assembly vote on the candidates individually. Although every party member is allowed to vote in these assemblies, usually only a few (between 50 and 500) show up. This explains the low scores of the PRL in Table 2.2, despite the fact that, in 1985, members had the opportunity to participate directly in the selection of half of the PRL's representatives.

16. The data presented are based on the responses of 155 representatives who served in the 1978–81 legislative term to the following open-ended question: 'What are the required characteristics of a candidate in order to get selected for an eligible place on the candidate list of your constituency party?' The data on candidate selection are part of larger survey representing the empirical basis of the author's doctoral project on the determinants of legislative role behaviour. All representatives were interviewed by the author himself, most of them during the first half of 1983. The project was funded by the Fonds National de la Recherche Scientifique.

17. Although unequally spread among parties as well, other characteristics were mentioned too infrequently to draw useful conclusions.

18. Of all the representatives elected in 1981 and 1985, 5.6 percent and 8.0 percent respectively were women. As in 1978, most women representatives belonged to the CVP (50 percent and 35.3 percent).

19. Data on the selectors' expectations are based on legislators' perceptions of their selectorates' expectations. These perceptions can be accurate, biased, incomplete or even absolutely wrong. But the accuracy of legislators' perceptions does not really matter as far as the question whether selectors' expectations affect parliamentarians' behaviour is concerned. MPs can decide to live up to (or deny) only those expectations that they believe their selectors hold.

20. Although for most representatives local public office constitutes a consider-

able time-consuming activity (on the average six hours per week), it is not included in Table 2.5 since corresponding selectors' preferences are nearly absent.

References

Bochel, John and David Denver (1983) 'Candidate Selection in the Labour Party: What the Selectors Seek', *British Journal of Political Science*, 13 (1): 45–69.

Ceuleers, Jan (1978) 'De Verruimingsgedachte in de BSP: De Locale Weerstanden', *De Nieuwe Maand*, 23 (1): 36–40.

Ceuleers, Jan and Lieven De Winter (1986) 'De Samenstelling van de Kandidaten-lijsten in de Vlaamse Partijen', *Res Publica*, 28 (2): 197–212.

Debuyst, Frédéric (1967) *La Fonction Parlementaire in Belgique: Mécanismes d'Accès et Images*. Bruxelles: CRISP.

Dewachter, Wilfried (1967) *De Wetgevende Verkiezingen als Proces van Machtsver-werving in het Belgisch Politiek Bestel*. Antwerpen: Standaard Wetenschappelijke Uitgeverij.

De Winter, Lieven (1980) 'Twintig Jaar Polls, of de Teloorgang van een Vorm van Interne Partijdemocratie', *Res Publica*, 22 (4) 563–85.

Epstein, L.D. (1980) *Political Parties in Western Democracies*. New Brunswick, NJ: Transaction Books.

Fenno, Richard (1978) *Home Style. House Members in Their Districts*, Boston, MA: Little, Brown.

Hand, G., J. Georgel and C. Sasse (eds) (1979) *European Electoral Systems Handbook*. London: Butterworths.

Holvoet, Luc (1980) 'De Stemmingen over het Investituurdebat in Kamer en Senaat', *Res Publica*, 22 (1–2): 35–76.

Irving, R.E.M. (1979) *The Christian Democratic Parties of Western Europe*. London: Allen & Unwin.

Langerwerf, Etienne (1980) 'Het Stemgedrag in het Parlement. Onderzoek in de Kamer van Volksvertegenwoordigers voor de Periode 1954–1965', *Res Publica*, 22 (1–2): 177–88.

Obier, Jeffrey (1974) 'Intraparty Democracy and the Selection of Parliamentary Candidates: The Belgian Case', *British Journal of Political Science*, 4 (2): 163–85.

Ranney, Austen (1981) 'Candidate Selection', pp. 75–106 in D. Butler, H.R. Penniman and A. Ranney (eds), *Democracy at the Polls. A Comparative Study of Competitive National Elections*. Washington, DC: American Enterprise Institute for Public Research.

Sartori, Giovanni (1976) *Parties and Party Systems*. Cambridge: Cambridge University Press.

Smits, Jozef (1982) 'De Standenvertegenwoordiging in de Christelijke Volkspartij en de Parti Social Chrétien', *Res Publica*, 24 (1): 73–127.

Vanpol, Ivo (1983) 'Mortologie van de Vlaamse Politieke Partijen', *Res Publica*, 25 (2–3): 417–73.

Vanpol, Ivo (1984) 'Morphologie des Partis Politiques Francophones in 1983', *Res Publica*, 26 (4): 503–40.

3

Britain: centralized parties with decentralized selection

David Denver

From 1945 to 1970 the British party system was widely regarded as the archetypal class-based two-party system. The Conservative and Labour parties, loyally supported by the middle and working classes respectively, alternated in government and opposition, won the support of the overwhelming majority of voters in general elections and held all but a tiny minority of seats in the House of Commons. During the 1970s and 1980s, however, this duopoly began to break down. Single-party government remained the norm (although in the late 1970s Labour had to rely on Liberal support to stay in office) but nationalist parties established a permanent presence in Scotland and Wales, the Northern Ireland parties detached themselves from the major British parties and fragmented and, most important of all, the Liberals together with the Social Democratic Party (SDP), which was founded in 1981, made spectacular electoral advances. After the 1983 general election ten parties had representatives in the House of Commons – Conservative, Labour, Liberal, SDP, Scottish National Party (SNP), Welsh Nationalist Party (Plaid Cymru) and four Northern Ireland parties.[1]

In this chapter, however, partly for reasons of space but mainly because they alone put forward candidates across the whole country, the focus is on selection in the four major British parties.[2]

The importance of candidate selection

In Britain, as in most democratic political systems, the selection of party candidates to contest national elections is a process which is purely private and internal to the political parties themselves. Each party in its constitution or set of 'model rules' for local branches prescribes the procedures to be followed, defines who may participate and sets out rules governing the process. The four parties considered here differ in various ways in how they select candidates but in one fundamental respect they are the same. Although British parties have the reputation of being highly centralized and the rules governing selection are in all cases centrally determined, the process itself is decentralized. In theory and in practice all British parliamentary candidates are selected by relatively small groups of party members in each parliamentary constituency.[3] All aspiring Members of Parliament (MPs), from the humblest backbencher to a potential Prime Minister, must first be selected as a candidate by a local party. In normal circumstances there is no mechanism whereby the national party organization can directly nominate a candidate for a local constituency.[4] Although it predates mass parties, constituency-level selection is a concomitant of the organizational structure of the parties and of the electoral system. Each constituency elects a single MP by the simple plurality method and constituency associations or parties form the bases of party organization.[5]

In part, the importance of local selection derives from the fact that most constituencies are 'safe' for one party or another. Between 1955 and 1970, a period in which there were five general elections, three quarters of the seats in Britain never changed hands and a further 13 percent were held by one party in four out of the five elections. Even in the electorally more turbulent 1970s this pattern persisted. In the three elections between February 1974 and 1979, 88 percent of constituencies were won by the same party on all three occasions.[6]

Clearly, then, when a local party selects a candidate for a seat which it holds, the person chosen is in most cases assured of election. It is not the voters but small groups of selectors who effectively determine who shall be MPs; it is local selectors who determine the distribution of social characteristics, abilities and ideological viewpoints in the House of Commons. In addition, since ministers and opposition spokesmen are almost invariably recruited from among MPs, local selectors are responsible for providing a pool of talent that can be called upon when a government or shadow cabinet is to be formed. In a real if indirect way selectors have influence upon the recruitment of political leaders and the personnel of governments.

The electoral status of constituencies has marked effects upon the selection process. In the first place, selections in safe seats are much less frequent than in others. Up to 1979 the selection procedures in all parties were weighted in favour of a simple readoption of incumbent MPs and, although mechanisms existed for removing an incumbent, they were rarely employed (see below). Normally only death, retirement, resignation or elevation to the House of Lords gave rise to selections in safe seats. This is illustrated in Table 3.1, which shows for six elections the number of cases in which incumbents were readopted, those in which new candidates were chosen in seats held by the party concerned and the number of candidates selected in seats not held by their party.

Table 3.1 *Selections in the Conservative and Labour parties*

	1959	1964	1966	1970	Oct 1974	1979
Incumbent readopted	546	554	571	553	585	537
New candidate selected in seat held by party	66	57	38	77	13	59
Candidate selected in seat not held by party	619	625	626	604	647	649

The table does not show figures for 1955, February 1974 and 1983 because these elections followed constituency boundary revisions and incumbency is difficult to define in such circumstances. Northern Ireland is excluded from the figures.
Source: Appropriate volumes of *The Times Guide to the House of Commons*

It is clear that relatively few 'good' seats come up for newly aspiring Conservative or Labour MPs at any one election, the maximum number of incumbents making way for new candidates in the period covered being only seventy-seven in 1970. The overwhelming majority of selections, as opposed to readoptions, occur in marginal and hopeless seats, especially the latter, where selections need to be undertaken before every election. In other parties, which have few MPs and even fewer safe seats, almost all constituencies go through the full selection process for each general election.

The electoral status of constituencies also affects candidate selection in more indirect ways. Local party members and aspiring candidates know whether the selected candidate is certain to win, bound to lose or in with a chance of victory. This affects the number of aspirants who seek the candidacy: safe seats attract many more applicants than marginals and these, in turn, more than hopeless seats. In all parties selections in hopeless seats more often consist of searching for a candidate than of choosing from a number of hopefuls. This was, for instance, the case in the vast majority of selections in the Liberal Party until the 1970s (see Ranney, 1965: 248–68).

The winnability of a constituency also affects the seriousness with which selectors perceive and undertake their task. When the person selected is certain or likely to become an MP, the whole business of selection is approached in a more serious vein and any intraparty conflict is more acute. It is possible, too, that selectors in different categories of seat have different concerns and apply different criteria in choosing candidates.

Variations in the electoral status of constituencies, then, make for some variations in the practice as well as the frequency of candidate selection. Nonetheless, all local parties are expected to conform to rules and procedures determined at national level. Although there are occasional examples of local deviations and eccentricities, this means that in any one party the vast majority of selections follows a common pattern which is outlined below for each of the four major British parties.

Selection procedures in the British parties

The Conservative Party

The Central Office of the Conservative Party, the party's professional organization, is responsible for supervising and co-ordinating the selection of parliamentary candidates. A vice-chairman of the party organization is in charge of this aspect of the party's activities and is responsible for compiling and maintaining a list of approved candidates. All aspirants for candidature must be nationally approved and if a candidate is selected who is not on the list then he or she must subsequently be endorsed. Until recently, getting onto the approved list was not difficult. Applicants supplied basic personal information together with references and were then vetted by the vice-chairman in charge and briefly interviewed by a panel of MPs. Very few people were excluded at this stage (see Ranney, 1965: 27–8). In 1980, however, the Conservatives instituted a rather more rigorous screening procedure (see Holland, 1981) requiring applicants first to be interviewed by an area agent and then to be considered by a Parliamentary Selection Board in 'a modern group selection process' (Conservative and Unionist Central Office, 1981) which includes debates, interviews, group discussions and so on during a weekend residential session. Under this new procedure Criddle (1984: 266) reports that 'over a quarter' of aspirants were rejected at this stage between 1980 and 1983 on the basis of an assessment of their intellectual and practical potential, character and personality. The remaining aspirants still have to satisfy the vice-chairman in charge of candidates, however, and Criddle estimates that only about 40 percent of the original field make it to the list. An even lower estimate of 30 percent is given by Holland (1986: 34). It seems clear, therefore, that applicants for the Conservative list are now much more rigorously vetted than was the case before 1980. Although the approved list is pruned from time to time and everyone made to re-apply, it normally contains upwards of 500 names.

Constituencies which have an incumbent Conservative MP who

wishes to continue do not normally invoke the selection procedure but rather simply readopt the sitting member by passing a resolution (usually unanimously) to that effect. When, however, a constituency association (CA) wishes to initiate the selection procedure it notifies this to the area agent, who is the regional representative of Central Office. The area agent acts as a link between CAs and the national organization and attends or is represented at all local meetings connected with selection in order to ensure fair play and advise on procedure. The agent informs the national vice-chairman of the impending selection and this is advertised to everyone on the approved list. Those who are interested then apply directly to the constituency concerned. People not on the list may also apply but in practice most applicants for seats and the great majority of those selected are already on the approved list (see Rush, 1969: 22).

Each CA has a standing 'selection committee' consisting of the officers of the association together with representatives of party branches, women's committees, Young Conservatives and Conservative clubs. This committee usually has about twenty to twenty-five members. It reviews the applications received and selects, by discussion, a number for interview. The number of applicants varies with the electoral status of the seat. Safe Conservative seats regularly attract between two and three hundred applicants, marginal seats between fifty and one hundred and hopeless seats fifteen to thirty. At this first stage the majority of aspirants are eliminated. The initial field is reduced to about twenty on the basis of biographical details and letters of application. This process is highly informal and variable but committees normally proceed by excluding those they consider obviously unsuitable – those too old or too young, for example – and then agreeing on a range of suitable candidates. The criteria for judging 'suitability' may or may not be explicitly discussed but usually it seems that committee members simply have a set of vague ideas about the kind of background characteristics that make someone a likely candidate.

Those remaining in contention after this first sifting are invited to attend a 'listing meeting' with the committee. Applicants are interviewed for about half an hour and the committee then chooses a shortlist of three or four by a series of ballots in which the aspirant with most votes is successively put on the list and removed from the ballot.

Aspirants who have been shortlisted finally attend a special meeting of the executive council of the association. This is the governing body of the local association, comprising representatives of ward committees, women's committees, etc. Depending on the nature of the constituency, it varies in size from about sixty to two hundred or more people. Before this meeting a social gathering is usually organized at which aspirants and their partners mingle informally with the selectors for about forty-five minutes. In the meeting itself, aspirants speak and answer questions for half an hour. The meeting then votes by exhaustive ballot until one person has a majority of votes. This person is then recommended to a general meeting of members of the association at which the choice is usually formally endorsed. The executive council may recommend more than one person to the general meeting and the general meeting may refuse to endorse the recommendation of the executive council but in practice both of these are very rare and the general meeting is a formality with attendance often being smaller than at the crucial meeting of the executive council.

The Labour Party

Candidate selection in the Labour Party became a matter of considerable controversy during the 1970s both within and outside the party itself. Conflict between left and centre/right factions as they struggled for control of the party was increasingly expressed in battles over constitutional matters including candidate selection and the rules relating to it (see Kogan and Kogan, 1982; Williams, 1984). The left appeared to be seeking to alter the political balance of the Parliamentary Labour Party (PLP) and to make Labour MPs more accountable to party activists. 'Moderate' MPs were alleged to be threatened with removal by left-wing activists and Constituency Labour Parties (CLPs) were increasingly choosing left-wingers to replace retiring MPs (see Berrington, 1982). In 1980 the left succeeded in getting selection rules altered so that all incumbent MPs would have to face a full selection process before each election rather than being (almost) automatically renominated. All parties have procedures for removing incumbent MPs but this relatively new feature of the Labour Party distinguishes it sharply from other parties and it continues to be controversial. Reselections frequently give rise to intraparty conflict and help to sustain the image of the party as suffering from incessant left-right feuding. Whether a constituency is undertaking a new selection or a reselection, however, the selection process is the same.

As in the Conservative Party, Labour's national party organization keeps a record of suitable potential candidates, but in this case there are two lists. The 'A' list contains the names of people (usually around 100) nominated by trade unions whom they are willing to 'sponsor', which means that if one of these is selected the union concerned will pay most of his or her election expenses and make a contribution to the local party's running costs. This is a major attraction for constituencies but only in a few are financial considerations decisive (see Denver, 1985). The second or 'B' list contains the names of between 200 and 300 other people who are willing to be candidates but these must be nominated to the list by CLPs and cannot apply directly. Nominations to both lists are vetted by the National Executive Committee (NEC) and, although exclusions are sometimes made on political grounds, such cases are rare (see Ranney, 1965: 154). The lists are intended only as guides to assist CLPs and people are frequently selected who do not figure in them. In all cases, however, selected candidates must be endorsed by the NEC. The NEC has used its power to withhold endorsement only very sparingly and in unusual circumstances.[7] Although this in itself does not mean that the endorsement power is without significance, the NEC has not often attempted to overrule local parties if it is satisfied that procedures have been properly followed.

When a CLP wishes to initiate the selection process it must first seek the authorization of the NEC. This gives the party organization, through its regional representatives, the opportunity to schedule selections so that safe and winnable seats have a wider choice by selecting before those unlikely to return a Labour MP. A timetable is agreed and party membership and delegations to the constituency general management committee (GMC) frozen in order to prevent the packing of meetings by aspirants or their supporters enlisting new members.

Aspirants do not apply directly to the CLP. Rather they must try to be nominated by one of the local bodies entitled to do so – trade union branches, party branches, socialist societies, etc. A pre-scribed form is sent to each of these and each is allowed to nominate one person. Thus party and trade union branches carry out the first local screening process in Labour selections. The number of people seeking nomination varies. Ranney (1965: 170) quotes two cases of safe Labour seats where fifty and thirty-five people respectively sought nominations, but unpublished data from Bochel and Denver's (1983) study show that six hopeless seats attracted a total of only twelve applicants. While some of the nominating bodies interview applicants others, especially trade union branches, frequently do not (see Denver, 1985).

The nominees, who usually number about a dozen (but often fewer) are then reduced to a shortlist of four to six by the constituency executive committee, a small body usually of around twenty people. In many constituencies the process of drawing up the shortlist is characterized by factional conflict as groups sometimes try to exclude aspirants even though they may have obtained a number of nominations. In others, however, the procedure is more consensual and executive committees try to compile a list which gives a reasonable choice to the local party. The shortlist is agreed by a series of ballots without interviewing the nominees and is put to the GMC for approval. The GMC is the governing body of the CLP and comprises delegates from party branches and affiliated organizations, although delegates may not be mandated by their organizations to vote for a particular aspirant. At this stage the GMC may add to or delete from the shortlist, which is then sent to the NEC for validation, which involves checking that those short-listed fulfil the basic conditions of candidature.[8]

Finally, the GMC meets at a special 'selection conference' meeting where the aspirants speak and answer questions for about thirty minutes. Without discussion the meeting then proceeds to vote by exhaustive ballot until someone obtains a majority of votes. Customarily this is followed by a unanimous vote approving the choice and, as noted above, the name of the candidate is sent to the NEC for endorsement.

Candidate selection in the Labour Party is characterized by a high degree of rigidity and formality. Strict adherence to the rules is ensured by the presence at all meetings of a full-time staff member of the regional party organization. Small infractions of the rules – such as a delegate temporarily leaving the room between the aspirants' presentations – can be used as grounds for appeal by a disgruntled candidate and can result in the selection being declared invalid. Canvassing is strictly forbidden and contact between most delegates and aspirants (other than those who are local) except in formal meetings is rare.

The Liberal Party
There are relatively few seats which can be generally described as good prospects for the Liberal Party and even fewer which could be considered 'safe'. The maximum number of seats won by the Liberals in the whole post-war period was fifteen, in 1983. As a consequence almost all Liberal selections involve choosing a new candidate and the party is not flooded with applications for candidacy. During the 1950s and 1960s, indeed, local Liberal Associations were more likely to be involved in searching for a suitable candidate than choosing among contenders. The national party organization actively discouraged some associations from contesting seats – for fear of losing the election deposit – and many seats had no Liberal candidate. On average, between 1955 and 1970 only 40 percent of seats were fought by the Liberals.

In the 1970s, as electoral support for the Liberals increased, so did the number of seats contested but it was not until the 1983 election that the Liberals, in alliance with the SDP, had a candidate in every seat in Britain. It seems likely, given the current good electoral prospects for the Alliance, that Liberal selections for the next election will involve more choosing and less searching.

Candidate selection in the Liberal Party is less centralized than in other parties but even so the party constitution prescribes the procedures that local associations should follow and the national Candidates Committee compiles a list of approved candidates after each election. Individuals apply to be 'panelled' at regional level and are interviewed by members of the Candidates Committee. The list usually has around 400 names.

When a local party wishes to proceed with selection it notifies the Candidates Committee. Regional party officials are not involved and no one other than local party members attends meetings connected with the selection. If they did, this would be regarded as interference with the business of the local association. The Candidates Committee notifies approved candidates and local associations also usually advertise in the party's newspaper. Any member of the party can apply directly to the local party but the maximum number of applications one informant could recall was twenty, in a promising seat at a good time for the party.

At constituency level, a 'search' or 'selection' committee is set up to prepare a shortlist of three or more aspirants on the basis of letters of application. These are invited to address a general meeting to which all party members in the constituency are invited. Normally forty or fewer people attend although in very exceptional cases this may rise to eighty. The meeting selects a candidate using the alternative vote method. The name of the selected candidate is notified to the Candidates Committee but there is no national veto power. If the national leadership disapprove of the choice of candidate or even of the decision to contest a particular seat they can only try to persuade the local association involved to change its mind. If the local association insists, then there is little the national organization can do beyond refusing to provide any financial and other support (see Kavanagh, 1983).

The formation of an electoral alliance with the SDP in 1981 caused some problems for the Liberals. Candidates who had already been selected in constituencies allocated to the SDP (about seventy) were asked to stand down but, as noted above, the national party had no authority over local associations in this matter. Local associations had to be persuaded to comply and in the event three Liberal candidates stood against SDP candidates in seats which had been nationally allocated to the SDP.

The Social Democratic Party

The SDP is the most recently arrived 'major' party on the British political scene, having been founded in 1981, and its selection procedures exhibit a combination of traditional and novel features. Most of the leaders of the SDP were former Labour MPs who had vigorously opposed the introduction of mandatory reselection of MPs and had supported wider participation by party members in selections, on the grounds that selection in the Labour Party was falling under the control of small, ideologically motivated and unrepresentative groups. The selection procedures adopted reflect a desire to minimize this danger in the new party.

Like the other parties, however, the SDP's National Committee is charged with maintaining a list of approved candidates. Any member may apply for inclusion and there is an interviewing process to screen out unsuitable people. Just before the 1983 election there were 1100 people on the SDP's list.

Selections are made by local parties, known as 'area' parties, which regularly cover more than one constituency. All members of the area party may participate in the selection of a candidate for any constituency within their area allocated to the SDP by agreement with the Liberals. Thus a member may be able to help select a candidate in one or more constituencies in his or her area without actually residing in them. This is a unique feature of SDP selections.

As in the Labour Party, when an area party wishes to select a candidate it must first obtain the permission of the National Committee to proceed. When this is granted, the vacancy is advertised in the party newspaper and the chair of the area party is supplied with the list of approved candidates. Consideration is not, however, restricted to people on the list and anyone may apply. Applications are made directly to the area party and the local committee, without interviewing, prepares a shortlist. In order to minimize the 'rigging' of shortlists (a common criticism of Labour selections) SDP rules state that a shortlist must contain between six and nine people, two of whom must come from outside the area concerned. There must also be at least two men and two women on the shortlist. This provision, which is unique among British parties, is clearly intended to modify the supposed bias against women of those who select candidates and to increase the number of women selected.[9] When complete, the shortlist must be approved by the National Committee.

Those shortlisted are invited to a 'hustings' meeting where they address party members and answer questions but no vote is taken. All members of the local party, whether or not they have attended the hustings meeting, are sent postal ballots and the single transferable vote system is used to select a candidate.

This experiment in wider participation in selection has not been without problems. In the first place it is expensive. All party members have to be sent biographical details of the aspirants before the hustings meeting and then a ballot paper. With even a moderately sized membership postal bills quickly mount up. Secondly, most party members do not attend hustings meetings and aspirants or their supporters are forbidden to canvass or campaign in any way. Votes are cast, therefore, on the basis of little evidence of aspirants' ability or personality. Worries of this sort have led to calls for voting to be restricted to those who attend the meeting but so far these have been unsuccessful.

The SDP has experienced only one full set of candidate selections, prior to the 1983 general election. In the current round there have been a few cases in which Liberals have participated in SDP selections and vice versa, but the SDP leadership has generally frowned upon such joint selections, viewing them as undermining the distinctive separate existence of the SDP.

An overview of selection in Britain

National–local relationships
Although the local nature of candidate selection in Britain has been emphasized, selections involve an interaction between the local and national organizations of the parties. Both have clear and direct interests in the nature of the candidates selected and there may be some tension between the candidate needs of the party nationally and the desires of selectors locally.

The central organization of all four parties considered here tries to exercise some control over selection. All maintain a list of approved candidates and require confirmation of some kind of those selected. The central organizations of the Labour Party and the SDP have more formal control over selection than is the case in the other two parties. In both, central authorization has to be obtained before selection can commence, both prescribe procedures in detail, both require central validation of shortlists and both consider appeals arising out of selection. There is, then, some variation in the extent of central control but all the parties have some powers which they could use to try to block the selection of some candidates or to 'place' others.

All available evidence suggests, however, that such formal powers as do exist are rarely used and that the ability of central party organizations to influence who gets selected is very limited. Ranney

(1965: 42) found only one case of a locally selected Conservative being refused endorsement and there has been only one other case since 1964.[10] As we have seen, only ten Labour candidates were refused endorsement on clearly political grounds between 1945 and 1964 (Ranney, 1965: 164) and there has been only one such case since then.[11]

As noted above (note 4), Labour's central organization has special powers over candidate selection in by-elections, but they have been sparingly used. Ranney (1965: 147–53) found only two cases of candidates being 'placed' by the NEC in by-elections, and in each case the local party concerned was co-operative. In late 1986, however, the potential power of the NEC was starkly demonstrated when, on the grounds that there had been procedural irregularities, it forced a candidate upon an unwilling local party in the Knowsley North constituency, a safe Labour seat. The Labour vote in the by-election was little different from the vote at the 1983 general election, even though a significant part of the local organization refused to participate in the campaign. This remains a very exceptional case, but it is possible that the intense media attention that by-election candidates now attract will encourage the NEC to take a more active role in by-election selections.

Local party activists tend to be suspicious of their national organizations and jealously guard their right of selection. Any attempt by party headquarters to influence their choice is likely to diminish rather than increase the chances of any centrally favoured candidate.[12] Despite the promptings of their respective head-quarters Conservative selectors have not chosen more women or trade unionists in winnable seats and Labour selectors have not reversed the trend towards more middle-class candidates. Even the SDP's elaborate shortlisting arrangements have made little differ-ence to the proportion of women selected (see Table 3.2).

Overwhelmingly, parliamentary candidates in Britain are selected according to the desires and preferences of local selectors. If the selection process fulfils the requirements of the leadership and of the parliamentary parties, then this is more by chance than design.

Participation in selections

A common criticism of candidate selection in Britain is that it is the prerogative of small, unrepresentative groups (see, for example, Paterson, 1967). They are unrepresentative of the electorate and of their party's voters both in social terms – being more middle class and better educated, for example – and by the very fact of being political activists.

There is no doubt that the selectorate is small. The final choice of candidate is made in the Conservative Party by the executive council of the CA and attendance ranges from 200 or more in safe seats to sixty or less in hopeless seats. In the Labour Party Bochel and Denver (1983) found a median attendance of forty at selection conferences. Here again the status of the seat was important. The smallest number of delegates encountered was nine in a hopeless seat and the largest ninety-one in a safe seat. The differential interest of party members in selection is illustrated by the fact that the turnout of eligible delegates was 85 percent in safe seats, 69 percent in marginal seats and 43 percent in hopeless seats (Denver, 1985). The nebulous nature of the concept of membership in the Conservative Party and the unreliability and variability of CLP membership figures (especially of affiliated members) make it difficult to be precise about the proportions of party membership that these figures represent but some indication of the levels concerned is given by Rush's (1969: 279) estimate that only about 1 percent of Conservative members are involved in selection. In all parties selectors constitute a tiny fraction of party voters.

About forty people usually attend selection meetings in the Liberal Party and although no figures are available for participation in the SDP's postal ballots the smaller membership of the SDP means that the actual numbers of participants are probably no greater than in the other parties. Defenders of the Labour system argue that there is wider participation via the nominating process but since even candidates with a number of nominations can be kept off the shortlist the value of this sort of participation is limited.

Focusing on the arena of final choice exaggerates the extent of participation, however. Most aspirants for candidacy are rejected by much smaller bodies since in all parties a committee of about twenty-five people reduces what may be a large field to a shortlist. Only in the Conservative Party is this a formal two-stage process allowing some applicants to put their case before being eliminated, although Labour's nominating process also allows local party members an opportunity to form an impression about the candidates before the shortlist is compiled. In all parties, however, many applicants are turned down purely on the basis of an initial letter. If the selection process is viewed as a series of gates through which aspirants must pass, then the few people who determine shortlists guard the narrowest gate of all.

There has to be some mechanism for whittling down the field of candidates, however, and in the absence of primary elections the most that proponents of wider participation can hope for is that all party members be allowed to vote at the final stage. In 1984, however, the Labour Party conference rejected a modest proposal to extend voting rights, although this was to be confined to selections involving incumbent MPs. The view persists in the Labour Party and to a lesser extent among Conservatives that the right to participate in the choice of candidate is a prerogative of party activists. In part this reflects a view about the nature of intraparty democracy as involving delegation and representation rather than 'mass' participation, but the right to be a selector is also seen as some reward for the hours spent in the mundane tasks involved in maintaining the party machine at local level, a burden shouldered by the most active party members.

The position of incumbents
Given the decentralized nature of candidate selection and the value attached to the link between an MP and his or her constituency it is clearly important that there should be some procedure whereby local parties could remove unsatisfactory MPs. Such an opportunity presents itself to local parties before every general election when a candidate must be formally adopted and nominated but procedures in all parties except Labour explicitly favour the simple readoption of incumbent MPs.

As noted above, in the Conservative Party an incumbent who wishes to remain simply indicates this to his or her association. A resolution to this effect is put to a general meeting and almost invariably carried. If it is not, the association may start to look for a new candidate.

In the Labour Party up to 1980 incumbents were similarly favoured. If a CLP wished to get rid of its MP, the local GMC had to vote at a special meeting to put the replacement procedure in operation then at a subsequent meeting to pass a vote of no confidence in the MP. MPs also retained a right of appeal to the NEC. In the SDP, whose leaders defected from the Labour Party partly as a result of the controversy over reselection, incumbents are readopted by the passing of a resolution at a party meeting. Should the resolution fail there is a special procedure whereby a reselection is instituted (see Denver, 1984: 88).

Despite the existence of such procedures, refusals of readoptions have been rare. Butler and Sloman (1980: 221) report that there were only thirty-three cases of Conservative or Labour MPs being denied their party's renomination between 1950 and 1979 and suggest that the great majority of these cases involved personal failings of the MP (such as laziness, drunkenness or scandal) rather than political disagreements between the MP and the local party.

Most local parties are perfectly satisfied with their MP, but even where problems arise they rarely lead to attempts to dump an MP. Dickson (1975) suggests four reasons why this is the case. Firstly, public conflict between an MP and his party may be electorally damaging and so is avoided by party activists. Secondly, dissatisfaction with an MP is often sorted out informally. Thirdly, party activists tend to share a view that an MP is not simply their delegate but a representative of the whole electorate so that political differences are not thought sufficient to warrant an attempt to remove him. Fourthly, national bodies, again concerned about electoral repercussions, normally try to reconcile differences informally, usually in the MP's favour.

When, however, the Labour Party introduced mandatory reselection of incumbents in 1980 many in the party anticipated a 'purge' of centre/right MPs. In fact only eight Labour MPs were refused readoption in 1983, although some probably 'jumped' before being pushed, by resigning or defecting to the SDP, and many others survived only narrowly (see Criddle, 1984). In the 1986 round, with all but five reselections completed at the time of writing, six MPs have so far been deselected and at least five others have withdrawn from the contest when facing certain defeat. A number of other cases have excited much conflict and controversy.[13]

Mandatory reselection and the problems (and benefits) that it brings will continue to be a distinctive feature of the Labour Party. It is worth emphasizing, however, that the great majority of incumbent Labour MPs have been readopted and that in the Labour Party, as in other parties, a candidate once selected for a safe seat can usually look forward to a career in politics that will only be terminated by his or her own choice.

The preference of selectors

As has been indicated, it is the choices made by local selectors which ultimately determine the qualities, characteristics and attitudes of parliamentary candidates and consequently of MPs. We have, however, little direct evidence of selectors' preferences about candidates and such survey evidence as does exist (Bochel and Denver, 1983) is restricted to the Labour Party and already somewhat outdated.

Before the 1970s Labour selections were frequently characterized by much politicking, bickering and allegations of undue trade union influence but conflict was more concerned with the personal qualities, characteristics and connections of candidates than with their political position. Commentators noted the 'astonishingly non-ideological grounds' on which selections were made (Butler and Pinto-Duschinsky, 1971: 293). In their survey study of Labour selectors Bochel and Denver (1983) report that in the late 1970s their respondents displayed a mixture of ideological, electoral and personal concerns. Those on the left tended to be more ideologically orientated, having internal party considerations in mind when judging a candidate, but almost all selectors paid at least some attention to the political and personal acceptability of a candidate among the electorate. Apart from ideology, however, there was no clear pattern among respondents concerning the kind of qualities and characteristics they looked for or avoided. A wide range was mentioned and the qualities sought, such as 'sincerity' or 'an attractive personality', were exceedingly vague.

There was some evidence, however, that selectors had a distinct preference for a candidate who was a local person, a good public speaker and well-educated. The local focus of many selectors is emphasized by the fact that overall they placed 'potential as a government minister' decisively last in importance from a list of qualities they might seek in a candidate.

Since 1980 Labour selections appear to have become much more politicized. Organized groups within local parties seek to mobilize support for their preferred candidate, especially in safe seats; MPs who feel threatened with deselection devote much energy to securing support among GMC delegates. There is a danger in over-emphasizing ideological conflict, however. In many selections, ideological considerations are muted and more traditional concerns of delegates – with personality, electoral appeal and so on – are decisive.

We know little directly about the candidate preferences of Conservative selectors. Both Ranney (1965: 117) and Rush (1969: 100–2) suggest, however, that ideology or party orthodoxy play little part in Conservative selections and this is confirmed by informal interviews with participants. As yet there is no evidence that the more ideological atmosphere generated in the Conservative Party by Mrs Thatcher has significantly affected the role of ideology in selections. Likely service to the constituency, on the other hand, is said to weigh heavily together with personal qualities of decency, honesty and so on. Central Office guidance notes for selectors remind CAs that the party needs more women and trade unionists as MPs but this advice appears to go unheeded, especially in winnable constituencies.

Until recently, the Liberals had a minor role in British electoral politics and the SDP was formed relatively recently and so not a great deal is known about selections or selectors in these parties. It seems likely, however, that selections proceed in a fairly informal way on the basis of discussion among active party members. It seems likely, too, that ideological considerations play little part in these deliberations. Rather selectors have vague notions of what would make a good or even acceptable candidate and, again, these mostly relate to personality, speaking ability, sincerity and the like.

To sum up, the ideological orientation of aspirants has increased in importance as a factor influencing selectors in the Labour Party but in other parties it plays little part. In all parties, however, the same admixture of vaguely defined personal qualities are favoured by selectors. All want someone who is presentable, reasonably articulate, honest, decent, etc., and evidence suggests that many hanker after a candidate who is from the locality (Ranney, 1965: 110; Rush, 1969: 74; Bochel and Denver, 1983; author's interviews).

The initial preferences of selectors are not, however, translated directly into outcomes. Rather preferences are mediated by the selection process itself. In the first place, as we have seen, most aspirants are excluded by small committees and there is some evidence (though for European rather than parliamentary selections) that those excluded may have different characteristics from those who proceed to shortlists (Holland, 1986: 193–8).

In the second place, when it comes to the final selection meeting selectors – many of whom will be seeing the aspirants for the first time – have to form a judgement on the basis of a thirty-minute speech and question-and-answer session. In this formal context the emphasis is clearly upon some particular qualities – oratorical ability, demeanour before an audience, 'presence' – while no clues are given about others such as integrity, assiduousness, ability to communicate with voters and skill in handling informal social situations, for example. Only in the Conservative Party are selectors encouraged to encounter and observe candidates in an informal setting.

In many ways this is surprising, since the skills which are at a premium in selection meetings are now needed less by election candidates and MPs. Local public meetings play a small part in campaigns (and are poorly attended) with more emphasis being placed on doorstep canvassing, walkabouts and other forms of informal contact between candidates and voters. An average MP spends more time attending to constituents' problems and attending social functions than in making speeches. But selection processes allow little opportunity for these sorts of skills to be assessed and, indeed, while some informal canvassing does take place, it is actively discouraged in selection rules.

This is particularly surprising in the case of the SDP, given its postal ballot system. Allowing candidates to campaign would give some indication of their commitment and energy while more informal contact might help selectors to make a more considered judgement. The chance for this new sort of approach was not taken by the SDP, however, and the process of selection in all parties, at least in safe and winnable seats, continues to be highly formal, with an air of conspiracy and secrecy. Some imaginative changes in procedures might result in fewer 'identikit' candidates and broaden the range of characteristics and experience represented in the House of Commons.

Consequences

The characteristics of candidates

There are obvious problems in inferring backwards from an analysis of the characteristics of candidates to the preferences of those who have chosen them. What such analysis does reveal, however, is the kinds of people selected after selectors' preferences have been modified by other factors – ideology in the Labour Party, shared ideas about what makes a good candidate for the local constituency, the platform performances of aspirants, the needs of the local party and so on.

Some characteristics of the candidates of the four major parties are shown in Table 3.2. Candidates in all four parties are overwhelmingly male, and although the Conservatives and Labour have slightly increased their proportions of female candidates over the past few elections, this increase has been concentrated in non-winnable seats. Some commentators (Vallance, 1981) attribute male predominance to an erroneous belief among selectors that women are a bad electoral risk. while others (Ranney, 1965: 96, 198) suggest that it reflects a more generalized bias against women. Denver (1982), however, finds no direct evidence of bias against women and argues that the underrepresentation of women should not be 'blamed' on selectors but reflects wider social conventions about the role of women in politics. There are simply fewer women than men willing to contemplate a political career. In that case, the proportion of women candidates is likely to increase only very slowly.

The age distributions shown in Table 3.2 are unsurprising. The bulk of candidates are in their thirties or forties and the younger age profile of the Liberals and the SDP simply reflects the fact that these parties had many fewer incumbents than the others. It is interesting to note, however, that in both the Conservative and Labour parties there has been a trend towards younger candidates. Politics, it

Table 3.2   *Characteristics of candidates, 1983 (in percent)*

	Con	Lab	Lib	SDP
Sex				
Male	94	88	90	86
Female	6	12	10	14
Age:				
20–29	9	9	13	10
30–49	63	62	69	73
50–59	21	22	16	15
60+	7	7	3	2
Education:[a]				
State School Only	19	45	28	20
State School & University	22	44	40	53
Public School Only	15	—	6	3
Public School & University	44	12	26	24
University:				
Oxford/Cambridge	58	22	30	39
Other	42	77	70	61
(*n*)	(415)	(360)	(215)	(239)
Occupation:				
Professions				
Barrister/Solicitor	18	7	12	13
University Teacher	1	4	4	8
Other Teacher	7	28	19	21
Other Professional	17	10	24	14
Business				
Company Director	7	—	4	4
Company Executive	16	1	8	7
Other	13	8	9	9
Miscellaneous White Collar	18	21	21	21
Manual Worker	2	21	1	3
(Total *n*)	(633)	(633)	(322)	(311)

[a] Confusingly for those unfamiliar with English education, 'public' schools are in fact private schools which charge for education. The occupation data refer to 'first or formative' occupation.
Source: Criddle (1984)

seems, is increasingly regarded as a profession for relatively young men.

Parliamentary candidates are sharply distinguished from the

electorate by their level and type of education. Only about 5 percent of the electorate have attended universities while 65 percent of major party candidates have done so, ranging from 56 percent of Labour candidates to 77 percent of SDP candidates. While not quite a *sine qua non* of candidature, degree-level education appears to be considered an important qualification for candidacy by selectors. Moreover, this appears to have increased over the last thirty years since the proportion of university-educated candidates was 49 percent in 1955, 56 percent in 1966 and 55 percent in October 1974.[14] Part of the explanation for this trend may be the greatly expanded opportunities for higher education that have existed since the 1960s, but it also appears that selectors increasingly expect candidates to be highly educated.

More striking differences between the parties appear when type of school and specific universities are considered. The Conservatives seem to have a marked preference for candidates who have attended public schools and Oxford or Cambridge, and this is accentuated in seats won by the Conservatives (53 percent of elected Conservatives had public school/Oxbridge education). In all parties, however, public school/Oxbridge educated people are heavily overrepresented compared to their numbers in the electorate as a whole. Selectors, it seems, want to be represented not by 'people like us' but by people whom they think can represent their party effectively.

Somewhat similar considerations apply in the case of candidates' occupations. As noted above, the selection procedures used tend to suit people skilled in self-presentation in a formal meeting and in particular the 'talking professions'. This and the desire of selectors to have an articulate, well-educated candidate almost inevitably means that candidates will have middle-class occupations. There are some differences between the parties in that there is a stronger representation of business people in the Conservative Party while professionals predominate in other parties, but only in the Labour Party is there a significant proportion of manual workers (21 percent). Even so, this is far short of the proportion of manual workers among Labour voters (about 70 percent in 1983).

Evidence about the local connections of candidates is given by Ranney (1965) and Rush (1969). Ranney finds that about one-third of non-incumbent candidates in both the Conservative and Labour parties from 1945 to 1964 had some local connections. Rush, with a wider definition of 'local connections' reports that from 1950 to 1966 just over 60 percent of candidates selected to replace retiring Conservative MPs and over 80 percent of Conservatives selected in non-incumbent seats had such connections. In Labour's case the figure in both incumbent and non-incumbent seats was over 70 percent.

Given that there is no local residence qualification for candidature in Britain, candidates with local connections, however tenuous, clearly have a much greater than random chance of being chosen. Outsiders are not excluded, of course, and are frequently chosen where there are two or more local aspirants since victory for one of the latter might give rise to divisions within the local party. Nonetheless, the willingness of British parties to accept 'carpetbagger' candidates has been rather exaggerated. Despite a number of examples to the contrary, selectors' preference for a local candidate – broadly defined – is a powerful force in British selections.

Only a handful of people from ethnic minorities have been selected as candidates, the maximum being eighteen in 1983. This may be because of simple racial prejudice among selectors but it is also partly due to electoral calculation. Selectors believe, rightly according to the evidence, that being coloured is an electoral handicap (see Bochel and Denver, 1983). This may also be changing, however, as some constituencies have come to contain large numbers of black and Asian voters and as blacks and Asians have become more active in the Labour Party. In the 1986 round of selections Labour had at the time of writing chosen eight ethnic minority candidates, three of them in safe seats and three in winnable seats.

Ideology and mandatory reselection in the Labour Party

While local selectors in all parties have the potential to shape the ideological orientation of their party, ideological conflict has come to be an important feature of selections only in the Labour Party. During the 1970s and after, left-wing Labour activists appear to have come to recognize the truth of Ranney's (1965: 11) dictum that 'Properly understood, selection conferences that pick parliamentary candidates constitute far more significant battlegrounds than annual conferences that adopt resolutions.' Since then, and especially after 1980, many Labour selections have been to some extent local engagements in the continuing intraparty war between left and right and have been interpreted as such.

The outcomes of these battles have slowly shifted the Labour Party to the left. This reflects the increased influence of the left in CLPs and is partly a consequence of the 1980 change in party rules, promoted by the left, to require the reselection of incumbent MPs. Although the number of MPs actually deselected has been small and hardly suggests a purge, the tendency has been for centre/right MPs to be replaced by left-wingers.[15] In addition, a number of centre/right MPs have decided to retire rather than face a tough reselection battle. Mandatory reselection has had other effects. It makes Labour MPs more cautious about expressing centre/right opinions in the House of Commons and on internal party matters; it affects MPs' decisions about whom to support in party leadership elections since their individual votes are recorded; it has forced MPs to devote much energy to cultivating their local party activists sometimes to the detriment of their parliamentary duties (see Denver, 1986).

The increased influence of the left is also visible more generally in recent Labour selections. An analysis of candidates selected in the 1986 round suggested that whereas about 45 percent of current Labour MPs can be regarded as on the left, the figure would reach about 58 percent if Labour won a parliamentary majority.[16]

Ultimately, the ideological character of the Labour Party and possibly, therefore, its future role in the British party system will be determined by the decisions made by local selectors.

Conclusion

The selection of parliamentary candidates used to be regarded as 'the secret garden of British politics' (Howard, quoted in Ranney, 1965: 3). Commentators concentrated their attention upon the glamour of election campaigns and the drama of election nights rather than on the diffuse and drawn-out process by which small local groups of activists determined the range of choices electors would face. This is less true today. Mainly due to developments within the Labour Party there is much greater media and public awareness of the importance of candidate selection. This has not, however, given rise to any serious demand for wider participation in the selection process. And, although there are occasional exceptions, whoever is chosen by the local selectorate is normally dutifully supported at the polls by most of the party's supporters. The recruitment of MPs and thus of party leaders and government ministers is, therefore, controlled by local selectors. This is the inevitable consequence of decentralized selection procedures largely impervious to central control.

Locally based selection has never been seriously questioned in any party. Party leaders have, however, recognized the risk that local parties might increasingly choose candidates more suited to the back- rather than the front-benches and turn the parliamentary parties into collections of mediocrities. Thus Lord Kilmuir, a prominent Conservative, described the majority of the intake of new Conservative MPs in 1955 and 1959 as 'obscure local citizens with obscure local interests, incapable – and indeed downright reluctant – to think on a national or international scale'[17] and believed that this was a major problem for the party. But there are unlikely to be any successful attempts to increase central influence over selection. British parties are mass parties, relying on activists and members in the localities to raise finance, supply local council candidates, organize election campaigns and so on. Any diminution of local control of candidate selection would be strenuously resisted by party members.

Despite the importance of candidate selection for the nature of the parties, most candidates in all parties have thus far been selected for their personal characteristics and qualities rather than their political views. This helps to explain what Paterson (1967: 5) calls 'one of the minor miracles of British politics' namely, 'that MPs chosen by zealots should compose themselves into well-balanced, unextreme groupings'.

Given the increased importance of ideology in Labour selections and the emergence of ideological divisions in the Conservative party – even though these do not yet appear to have affected selections – it remains to be seen whether Paterson's comforting comment will continue to hold good.

Notes

I am grateful to Gordon Hands, John Bochel and the editors for comments on an earlier draft of this chapter and to Michael Mumford of the Liberal Party and to a Conservative area agent for informal interviews on candidate selection in their respective parties.

1. These are Official Unionists, Democratic Unionists, Social Democratic and Labour Party and Provisional Sinn Fein. The representation of the last is purely formal since their single MP has refused to take his seat.

2. Very brief accounts of candidate selection in the Ulster Unionist Party and the SNP are given in Rush (1969: 290) and Brand (1978: 280–1).

3. There are currently 633 constituencies in Britain with a further seventeen in Northern Ireland.

4. The Labour Party's National Executive Committee may, in emergencies, suspend normal procedure and appoint a candidate. But this is rarely invoked. The last time the NEC chose a candidate was in 1966, although in 1979 one constituency (Newham North-East) was forced to choose between three NEC-nominated candidates. Similarly, the SDP has a provision allowing the National Committee to select a candidate where there is no local organization. Labour's NEC also has special powers in by-elections.

5. Except in the SDP where 'area' parties may include more than one constituency.

6. The periods 1955–70 and 1974–9 are used because between these dates there were no revisions of constituency boundaries.

7. Ranney (1965: 164–5) finds only ten cases of endorsement being withheld in the period 1945–64 and there have been only a few cases since the publication of his study. In the current round, the NEC has endorsed the reselection of two MPs and the selection of one new candidate who are closely associated with the *Militant* newspaper despite at the same time conducting a campaign against *Militant* and its supporters.

8. Candidates must have been members of the party for at least two years prior to selection, be members of an appropriate trade union and accept and conform to the constitution and programme of the party.

9. A proposal to institute a similar system in the Labour Party was heavily defeated at the party's 1985 conference.

10. This was in October 1974 when the candidate selected in Liverpool Scotland/ Exchange (a safe Labour seat) was rejected because of his extreme right-wing views on immigration.

11. A candidate selected in Croydon North-East in 1966 was rejected on the grounds that he refused to accept party policy on a variety of issues.

12. Rush (1969: 23) dismisses rumours of Central Office influence in Conservative selections as a case of 'smoke without fire' and concludes on the Labour Party that 'the very suspicions that the NEC has a protégé is often sufficient to ensure the unfortunate nominee's defeat'.

13. In two of these outstanding cases MPs are expected to have a very tough fight to survive. The other three have been held up because of the unconstitutional involvement of black sections in the selection process.

14. These figures refer to Conservative, Labour and Liberal candidates and are calculated from data given in the appropriate volumes of the Nuffield series on British general elections.

15. Criddle (1984) reports that of the eight deselections before the 1983 general election five were unequivocally cases of this kind. In the current round there are three clear examples of the same pattern.

16. *Guardian*, 8 July 1986.

17. Quoted in Ranney (1965: 109–10).

References

Berrington, H. (1982) 'The Labour Left in Parliament', pp. 69–94 in D. Kavanagh (ed.), *The Politics of the Labour Party*. London: George Allen & Unwin.

Bochel, J. and D. Denver (1983) 'Candidate Selection in the Labour Party: What the Selectors Seek', *British Journal of Political Science*, 13: 45–69.

Brand, J. (1978) *The National Movement in Scotland*. London: Routledge & Kegan Paul.

Butler, D. and M. Pinto-Duschinsky (1971) *The British General Election of 1970*. London: Macmillan.

Butler, D. and A. Sloman (1980) *British Political Facts*. London: Macmillan.

Conservative and Unionist Central Office (1981) *Notes on Procedure for the Adoption of Conservative Parliamentary Candidates in England and Wales* (revised, 1981).

Criddle, B. (1984) 'Candidates', in D. Butler and D. Kavanagh, *The British General Election of 1983*. London: Macmillan.

Denver, D. (1982) 'Are Labour Selectors Prejudiced Against Women Candidates?', *Politics*, 2 (1): 36–8.

Denver, D. (1984) 'The SDP–Liberal Alliance: The End of the Two-Party System?', in H. Berrington (ed.) *Change in British Politics*. London: Frank Cass.

Denver, D. (1985) 'Trade Unions and the Selection of Parliamentary Candidates in the Labour Party', paper presented at the ECPR joint sessions of workshops, Barcelona.

Denver, D. (1986) 'Great Britain: From Opposition with a Capital "O" to Fragmented Opposition', in E. Kolinsky (ed.), *Opposition in Western Europe*. London: Croom Helm.

Dickson, A.D.R. (1975) 'MPs Readoption Conflicts: Their Causes and Consequences'. *Political Studies*, 23 (1): 62–70.

Holland, M. (1981) 'The Selection of Parliamentary Candidates: Contemporary Developments and the Impact of the European Elections', *Parliamentary Affairs*, 34 (1): 28–45.

Holland, M. (1986) *Candidates for Europe*. Aldershot: Gower.

Kavanagh, D. (1983) 'Organisation and Power in the Liberal Party', in V. Bogdanor (ed.), *Liberal Party Politics*. Oxford: Clarendon Press.

Kogan, D. and M. Kogan (1982) *The Battle for the Labour Party*. London: Fontana.

Paterson, P. (1967) *The Selectorate*. London: MacGibbon & Kee.

Ranney, A. (1965) *Pathways to Parliament*. Madison and Milwaukee, WI: University of Wisconsin Press.

Rush, M. (1969) *The Selection of Parliamentary Candidates*. London: Nelson.

Vallance, E. (1981) 'Women Candidates and Elector Preferences', *Politics*, 1 (1): 27–31.

Williams, P. (1984) 'The Labour Party: The Rise of the Left', pp. 26–55 in H. Berrington (ed.), *Change in British Politics*. London: Frank Cass.

4
France: the impact of electoral system change

Jean-Louis Thiébault

Examining candidate selection in France offers a valuable opportunity to assess the influence of the electoral system on the selection
process. From the beginning of the Fifth Republic up to 1986,
France practised the two-ballot system in single-member constituencies (Georgel, 1979). But a new electoral system was adopted
for the legislative elections of 1986, namely proportional representation (PR) using the 'highest average' rule. PR had been part of
the ruling Socialist Party's platform since 1971, but the immediate
motivation for introducing it was to limit the party's anticipated
losses at the forthcoming elections. The new system was based on
rigid party lists (voters were not able to alter the order of
candidates' names). Each territorial department was made a
separate constituency, which meant that there were relatively few
seats in each constituency: in metropolitan France there were 555
seats and 96 constituencies. Moreover, no party could qualify for a
seat in any department unless it had won at least 5 percent of the
votes there (Knapp, 1985). One of the first acts of the new right-
wing government upon coming to power after the election was to
abandon PR and revert to the two-ballot single-member constituency system.

This chapter will concentrate particularly on the impact of the
change in the electoral system, but of course this is not the only
factor to take into consideration. The evolution of the French party
system is also important. Its main feature has been the emergence of
two distinct blocs: a left-wing coalition comprising primarily the
Parti Socialiste (PS) and the Parti Communiste (PC), and a right-
wing coalition composed chiefly of the Gaullist Rassemblement
pour la République (RPR) and the Giscardian Union pour la
Démocratie Française (UDF).

The existence of these two big coalitions has profoundly
influenced the selection of candidates for legislative elections. Once
they emerged, the parties' national organizations had to start
controlling the nomination of candidates and reserving the right to

intervene actively to impose their decisions. This tendency was in a way paradoxical because the two-ballot single-member constituency system seems to favour both local establishment of deputies and a strengthening of the parties' local and department organizations vis-a-vis the central organizations. Candidate selection was thus the result of a complex balance of national and local influences.

The candidate selection process

There are no laws in France regulating candidate selection. It is considered to be the internal affair of the parties and is provided for in their statutes. We shall examine the selection process within each party, dealing with the topics of centralization and participation.

The Rassemblement pour la République

In the RPR, the candidate selection process shows the domination of the national organization, which wields most of the decision-making power in this area (article 24 of the RPR statutes). During the period in which the two-round majority voting system was used, a nomination commission, composed of the general secretary, the presidents of the parliamentary groups and some electoral experts of the central organization first solicited proposals from the departmental organizations. Then, after studying and perhaps eventually modifying these proposals, the commission presented the candidates' names for nomination to the Central Committee. The RPR could thus be classified as a case of selection by the national organization after taking into account the proposals of the departmental organizations.

However, the national organization constantly had to take into account the demands of its parliamentary group, its local leaders and even, in some cases, party activists (Schonfeld, 1985). The parliamentary group wanted to obtain an assurance of renomination for all outgoing deputies who wanted it. Local leaders, who were very powerful in the department or in one electoral constituency, intervened in order to obtain a nomination for themselves or for a protégé. There was, therefore, a complex system under which the power of the centre was less absolute than it might at first seem (Lacorne, 1980).

This same complex system appeared during the period of preparation for the legislative elections of 1986. The introduction of PR gave the national party organization the opportunity to try to secure a better hold.

The national organization's greater power to intervene first showed itself in the creation, during the congress of 1 June 1985, of a commission empowered to distribute the nominations. The general secretary of the RPR presided over this commission, which was composed of the presidents of the parliamentary groups (National Assembly and Senate), the national secretary of elections and some other electoral experts (*Le Monde*, 22 June 1985). This nomination commission regularly received proposals from the deputies and party leaders in each department. After numerous negotiations, the lists it drew up were passed on in October 1985 for ratification by the Central Committee of the RPR (*Le Monde*, 22 October 1985). The greater involvement of the national organization was manifested in the 'parachuting' of numerous candidates into the RPR lists, in the departments of Hautes-Alpes, Ariège, Côtes-du-Nord, Creuse, Essonne, Eure-et-Loir, Nord, Haute-Savoie, Seine-Saint-Denis and Val d'Oise.

Nevertheless the influence of outgoing deputies, local Gaullist leaders and local heads of the party remained significant. In numerous cases the departmental organizations, under the direction of an outgoing deputy or an important local leader, were able to agree on a leading name for the list, and on the names and the order of the other candidates. When the departmental organizations were able to reach agreement in this way, the power of the national organization was reduced to a supervisory role. Moreover, certain local leaders responded to the decisions imposed by the centre by threatening to make up dissident lists, or by resigning in protest against these decisions. In the event eight dissident RPR lists were put forward, but none won a seat. The RPR had to resort, more often than in the past, to disciplinary measures, even including expulsions.

Party member participation in the candidate selection process is very limited. The adoption of PR, by reinforcing the centre's power, certainly did not increase membership participation.

Even when the majority ballot system operated, RPR members' participation was always very low. However, there were many cases in which the departmental organizations, and then the national committee, ratified a candidate chosen by the activists (*militants*) in a vote in the general assembly of a given electoral constituency. The activists themselves chose, in most of these cases, between several aspirants.

With the change in voting system, party member participation in the Gaullist movement was reduced virtually to nothing. In most cases, unlike in previous elections, no vote was held in the branches (*sections*) or in the general assemblies of the electoral constituencies. Such a situation seemed to lead to members becoming less active and, on a wider scale, to an absence of motive for activism, if one considers the opportunity to choose candidates as one of the principal motivations for membership.

The Union pour la Démocratie Française

In the UDF the power of the national organization is considerably limited by the influence of outgoing deputies, leaders of the local organizations and even party activists. Generally, the national organization takes into account local circumstances and situations. Also, local organizations within the party, no matter how weak they are, never subordinate themselves completely to the decisions of the centre. The change in voting system did not fundamentally alter this general picture, but it reinforced the tendency towards more centralization.

The UDF is a confederation of parties. It is a loose alliance of centrist groupings: Parti Républicain, Centre des Démocrates-Sociaux (CDS), Parti Radical, Parti Social-Démocrate (PSD) and Perspectives et Réalités clubs. It also has direct members. In the UDF, as in the RPR, a commission was convened to prepare candidate nominations for the 1986 elections. This commission, which was under the authority of the president of the UDF's parliamentary group in the National Assembly, was composed of a representative of each component of the UDF (*Le Monde*, 22 June 1985). This commission convened regularly to examine the electoral situation in each department, keep tabs on the aspirants and take into account particular demands of the local leaders and the departmental organizations. This process took a long time, and it was only on 6 November 1985 that the political committee of the UDF was in a position to ratify the first list prepared by the commission (*Le Monde*, 9 November 1985).

In fact, the UDF experienced more difficulty than the RPR in making up its lists. The UDF departmental organizations' deliberations were often protracted because of the demands of the six components and those of local leaders. The departmental organizations were perhaps able to agree on the head of the list, or on the order of the candidates, or on the political balance between the different components, but rarely on all three, and so they had to ask the nomination commission to resolve the impasse.

The UDF nomination commission responded by directly placing certain candidates on the lists, while respecting a balance arrived at by the political committee. Indeed, in order to avoid too many conflicts, the UDF political committee decided to establish a quota of elected representatives for each component, which the selectors had to attain through negotiations. Under this agreement ninety-seven seats were given to the Parti Républicain, fifty to the CDS, twelve or thirteen to direct members, eleven to the Parti Radical, four to the PSD and four to the Perspectives et Réalités clubs (*Le Monde*, 9 November 1985). Each departmental organization was given a detailed guideline as to how many candidates from each component should be picked on its list.

Conflicts arose in certain departments (Ardennes, Indre, Nord, Pas-de-Calais, Landes, Pyrénées-Atlantiques, Seine-et-Marne and Seine-Saint-Denis). Some local leaders resigned from the UDF in protest and threatened to draw up dissident lists. Such lists were established in ten departments, and in three a candidate was elected. However, in many cases the departmental organizations, under the auspices of a national political leader or a powerful local leader, came to an agreement on forming a list and thereby limited the national organization's power.

When it comes to the extent of party member participation in the candidate selection process, the choice of UDF candidates was achieved under the two-ballot system by a vote among members of the departmental committee. However, very often a prior consultative vote was held in general meetings of all members in a given electoral constituency to ascertain members' views. The new electoral system brought about changes in 1986. Ballots of party members were rarely held. The departmental committees were, more often than not, consulted by the commission without there being any vote within the local party, and members were often presented with a fait accompli.

However, some of the parties and the clubs which constitute the UDF are more concerned with member participation than others. Constituency assemblies sometimes suggested names for candidacies to the departmental committees of the party. Their members then had some say in the choice of candidates in their constituency. In other parties and clubs, with fewer members, suggestions are essentially the work of the departmental committees or even of a group of local leaders within the organization. The necessity of making up lists at the departmental level, under the 1986 voting system, considerably reduced the already limited role of UDF members, as members were not consulted, at least in a formal vote, on the composition of lists.

The tendency towards centralization within the two right-wing political parties (RPR and UDF) was also the result of electoral agreements between them, reached to present common candidates in elections from 1967 to 1981 or common lists for the 1986 elections. The need for arbitration between these parties gave birth, on a national level, to co-ordinating organizations which were expected to establish common candidatures or to achieve a balance in the common lists. They were not, though, expected to choose the candidates, a task reserved for the respective nomination commission within each party. However, the allocations always provoked conflicts at local level because they ruined the chances of numerous local leaders.

The Parti Socialiste
In the PS selection under the old electoral system was concentrated at the departmental level of the party, but even so local party members seemed to control candidate selection. However, the national organization was sometimes decisive in cases of conflict and in attaining national objectives (Schonfeld, 1985). The change in electoral system maintained the general pattern, but the national organization's power was also considerably reinforced.

During the majority ballot period, candidate selection began at constituency level. Candidates for legislative elections were chosen at a local convention by all the members of the branches of a constituency, and the nominations were then ratified by the departmental organization. The central organization of the party, however, had very important supervisory powers. A national convention (a party mini-congress) empowered it to resolve the conflicts and to overcome the possible resistance of any departmental organization or tendency which might threaten party cohesion (article 49 of the party statutes). So prior to 1986 the selection process of the PS can be considered as essentially a decentralized one, despite the supervisory power conferred on the national organization by the convention.

In the run-up to the legislative elections of 1978 and 1981 the delegates to the national convention ratified the departmental organizations' voting in most cases. They solved some difficult cases (though there were few of them) involving conflicts between majority and minority tendencies (supporters of François Mitterand versus supporters of Michel Rocard), and they also imposed the nomination of some female candidates as well as some members of the Mouvement des Radicaux de Gauche (MRG), a centre-left party allied to the Socialist Party. In addition, in 1981 the national party organization nullified the nomination of some locally chosen candidates in punishment for initiating and supporting the candidature of Mme Huguette Bouchardeau, general secretary of the Parti Socialiste Unifié (PSU), in the presidential election, or to break their grip on a constituency reserved for an outgoing MRG deputy (*Le Monde*, 9 November 1977 and 6 May 1981).

The introduction of PR brought about some changes in 1986. The departmental organizations were given responsibility for making up their lists, which were only then submitted to party members. The members could, however, propose alternative lists during voting in the branches. The national convention ratified the lists, after final modifications. The candidate selection process thus remained decentralized, but a more vigorous power of national intervention on the party of the national organization appeared. In fact, a new degree of national intervention was achieved on 6 July 1985 with a national agreement on dividing up seats in future among the different tendencies (*courants*). This agreement, established on the assumption that PS candidates would win approximately 170 seats, reflected the balance within the outgoing parliamentary group, and so it provided for eighty-one seats for the Mitterand tendency, twenty-nine for the Mauroy tendency, twenty-seven for the Rocard tendency, nineteen for the Chevènement tendency and two for the neo-Rocardian line. The remaining seats were reserved in order to solve particular cases, especially those of ministers, women and non-party figures. The departmental organizations prepared their lists within the framework of this national agreement. As in the UDF, the central apparatus gave detailed instructions to each departmental organization as to the required balance between tendencies on its list; this breakdown was based on the strength of each tendency within each departmental organization, as measured by the vote taken prior to the preceding party conference.

This national agreement was particularly important because it reinforced the power of the centre when it came to the winnable positions at or near the top of the lists. It also had the consequence that Socialist lists generally appeared as a succession of representatives from different tendencies. When the distribution between tendencies had been decided, each had to present its own candidates. Before the adoption of PR, less heed was taken centrally of the balance between tendencies; the national organization concerned itself less about how many candidates each tendency had. Each tendency had to take responsibility itself for positioning its candidates to its best advantage, which usually meant getting involved in the candidate selection process only in constituencies where it was strong.

The national convention of 9 and 10 November 1985, which was convened to draw up the final Socialist lists of candidates for the 1986 legislative elections, ratified most of the choices made in the departmental organizations and in the branches, since they conformed to the national agreement. However, choices made by certain departmental organizations were altered, either in order to respect the agreement between the tendencies or to resolve deferred nominational problems in relation to ministers or non-party figures. The national convention reinstated candidates who had been eliminated or demoted by party activists in the departments of Haute-Loire, Manche, Ardèche, Haute-Savoie, Mayenne, Marne, Pyrénées Orientales, and Indre et Loire. It also forced acceptance of ministers despite some departmental hesitations in the departments of Loir-et-Cher, Yonne, Cher, Calvados, and Doubs. Finally, it offered open seats to MRG members in the context of a national agreement for common lists in nine departments (*Le Monde*, 12 November 1985).

Inevitably, the decisions made by the national organization generated some conflicts. Certain local leaders refused to recognize the national decisions and threatened to make up dissident lists (in the departments of Tarn-et-Garonne, Mayenne, Orne and Manche). Some finally bowed to the national direction's pressure, but about a hundred, who persisted in refusing to obey and who constituted dissident lists, were expelled (*Le Monde*, 14 March 1986). Dissident lists were put forward in eight departments, and a candidate was elected from four.

As for membership participation, under the two-ballot electoral system there was first a call within each constituency for candidates, in response to which at least two or three aspirants usually came forward. Members, voting at branch level, then chose between them. After the members had voted, the departmental organizations ratified the branches' choice in the vast majority of cases. Under PR in 1986 party members still voted, but this was now the second stage in the process. The first stage, after the initial call for candidates, was that the departmental organizations drew up a provisional list which was voted on by party members. They could either accept it or reject it en bloc; modification was not possible. Alternative lists could be, and quite often were, presented for members to choose between, but sometimes there were few differences between the alternative lists: only the order of names was different.

In most departments party members accepted the list proposed by the departmental organization. However, difficulties arose in some departments (Mayenne, Marne, Ardèche, Indre et Loire, Vienne), where members rejected the proposed list for one reason or another. In four of these departments the members eventually did accept the proposed list, but in Mayenne they put up a dissident list, from which one candidate was elected. Participation by members was high. In certain branches 80 percent of members voted, even though the average attendance at branch meetings was rarely more than 40 to 50 percent of members. The high turnout was facilitated by the voting booths remaining open for several hours.

The adoption of PR, then, generally reduced the role of Socialist Party activists in candidate selection. An exception occurred in the department of Pas-de-Calais, where the departmental organization was unenthusiastic about the methods prescribed by the national organization, preferring to give the members a more active role. The Pas-de-Calais members chose between eighteen aspirants, spread over five geographical sectors, for a list of sixteen candidates, from which five were eventually elected. The departmental organization attached great weight to this non-binding vote and, when deciding on the order of the list, awarded the candidatures to those aspirants who obtained the largest number of votes in each geographical sector. No further vote among the members was held. The national organization of the Socialist Party did not veto this method of choosing candidates, which was specifically limited to the Pas-de-Calais.

The Parti Communiste

Candidate selection in the PC seems on paper to be very decentralized. The departmental organization first suggests the name of a candidate, then this proposal is submitted for discussion and voting by activists in the cells. Finally, the candidatures are submitted for ratification to the Central Committee (article 54 of the statutes). But in reality this nomination mechanism is conducted on the principle of democratic centralism and amounts to co-option. The party's central apparatus controls the selection process in its entirety, and only lets the departmental organizations nominate people of whose political reliability it is already certain. Communist candidates are experienced activists, with a record of total loyalty to the party. They usually occupy positions of responsibility at some level within the party apparatus. Even so, the national organization can be flexible enough to accommodate local feeling. It can choose to acknowledge the existence of the local power base of some Communist mayors, well established in their own area (Lacorne, 1980).

The adoption of proportional representation has not brought about any great changes in the PC's candidate selection process. Thus the final decisions of the national organization in 1986 corresponded, in practically all cases, to the wishes of the department organizations (even to those of the *rénovatrice* organization of the department of Haute-Vienne organized by the former minister, M. Rigout). The national leadership of the Communist Party has not made use of the technique of 'parachuting' candidates, a source of some conflict in other parties. There have only been two exceptions. Charles Fiterman was well received in the Rhone, even though it was not at the request of the departmental organization that he went there initially. In the same way, M. Gayssot was imposed on the department of Seine-Saint-Denis with no prior discussion (*Le Monde*, 15 November 1985).

The adoption of PR did not alter the rate of membership participation in candidate selection. Party members continued to vote in their cells on the proposals made by the departmental organizations. However, their choice was reduced; they could only accept or reject these proposals en bloc, without the possibility of voting on suggested alternative lists. This constraint did not prevent members from accepting the suggested list most of the time without difficulty, but sometimes only after numerous discussions. In most cells, membership participation is nevertheless high because, as in many other parties, choosing electoral candidates constitutes one of the most important moments in party life.

The Front National

At the 1986 elections, for the first time in its fourteen-year life the extreme right-wing Front National (FN), headed by Jean-Marie Le Pen, a Poujadist deputy in the 1950s, emerged as a significant party. Its anti-immigrant and strong law-and-order views were the major elements in its platform, and it was aided by the introduction of PR for the 1986 elections. Its candidate selection process displayed the domination of the national organization and especially of Le Pen. He, together with the FN's general secretary M. Stirbois, was the effective selector. To try to broaden the party's appeal somewhat, Le Pen made overtures to some local political leaders, usually centre-right elected representatives, and to some interest group leaders such as small businessmen, farmers or professionals. But conflicts arose in many departments, and criticism of this centralized process came from many new local party leaders.

Participation in candidate selection: a summary

Participation by party members varies considerably between the parties. On the left, between 50 and 80 percent of members are involved in the process to some degree, but in the right-wing parties the figure is in the region of 10–20 percent. In each case, this represents a negligible proportion of party voters, of the order of 0.05 to 0.1 percent.

One qualification that should be made to this is that, under the two-ballot electoral system, newspapers have been prone to speak of the first round of voting as a 'primary' election comparable with an American primary. From 1967 onwards, each party in both of the two main blocs often presented a candidate in the first round.

Whichever party's candidate won most votes was then the sole flag-bearer of the bloc in the decisive second round. The left-wing parties used the first round systematically as a primary in this fashion. The right-wing parties, though, often came to an agreement on a common candidate for the first round; they used the first round as a primary in only fifty constituencies in 1969, sixty-one in 1973 and eighty-six in 1981, though the figure rose to 344 in 1978 (Frears and Parodi, 1979). This practice provided a certain degree of voter participation in the selection process. But in 1986, under the rigid-list PR system, this disappeared.

What the selectors are looking for

Party rules in France, as elsewhere, give only a partial picture of what the selectors are looking for. For example, party statutes prescribe a party membership, but the left-wing parties sometimes, and the right-wing parties very often, pick people not hitherto members of the party. Moreover, party statutes, except those of the PC, prescribe only a minimum length of time for which candidates must have been party members. The selectors are looking in fact for two other elements: being an incumbent and having a local base. These two factors are important under both electoral systems.

Outgoing deputies
All incumbents must face reselection: no nomination is formally guaranteed in advance. But all political parties have a tendency to renew the candidature of outgoing deputies. They do not 'rotate' their deputies by preventing them from serving more than a certain number of terms.

Under the two-ballot system the selectors generally regarded outgoing deputies as better candidates than newcomers. They were better known to the voters, and often had great influence in the departmental or national organizations of their party. So, for the most part, those who did not obtain renomination had voluntarily stood down. The deselection of incumbents was rare. Under PR, too, outgoing deputies still constituted the best candidates the selectors could possibly choose. Even if not as well known to all the voters of the new larger constituency, their influence was still to be reckoned with. For the 1986 elections, 379 outgoing deputies (about 80 percent of all members of the National Assembly) were reselected.

Outgoing deputies are in a strong position to achieve reselection regardless of the level at which the decision is taken. If the decision is taken at national level, the presence of deputies on national bodies offers them some protection against any threat to deselect them. Deputies can make their experience and connections count. But if the decision is taken at local level, the deputies can use the fact that they generally exercise considerable power within their party's departmental organization. Moreover, local activists do not seem to expect more from their deputies than conformity with the general line of the party and an active presence in the constituency.

Thus deselections are infrequent. The rejection of their outgoing deputies by PS members in two constituencies in the department of Nord before the 1978 election (*Le Monde*, 7 October 1977) was exceptional. In the same year the RPR's national organization declared its intention to 'renew' the parliamentary group. Many deputies vented their displeasure at this idea, and in the event the scope of the renewal was very limited. Only two deputies were deselected (*Le Monde*, 8 November 1977). Similarly, it was a newsworthy event when the writer Maurice Druon, a Gaullist deputy, ceded his Paris seat, under pressure, to the RPR's general secretary, M. Pons, in 1981 (*Le Monde*, 31 May and 1 June 1981).

The adoption of PR in 1986, though, made effective (if not formal) deselections inevitable in areas where one party had been dominant in 1981. In such departments the selection was cruel and the choice of victims difficult. For example, in Pas-de-Calais the PS had twelve outgoing deputies but could expect, under PR, to win only five seats. The PS faced this problem more often than the other parties, but it occasionally arose for the latter too. In Paris, the RPR held fifteen seats but knew it could retain at most eight. Those deputies not selected for a safe or hopeful position on their party's list reacted in different ways. Some were given safe places on the lists for regional elections; some stood down voluntarily in the hope of being compensated with a seat in the next Senate; others sought a winnable position on a list in another department.

Local roots

The factor to which the selectors pay most attention, after incumbency, is the degree of the aspirants' local roots. The importance of these local roots was especially highly regarded by the selectors under the two-ballot system, when all parties looked for local elected representatives to represent them. An aspirant enjoyed an even greater electoral advantage if he already held several local elected positions (*mandats*). Influence in national political life is often based on local influence. Moreover, numerous members of parliament accumulate local and national *mandats* so only a minority of candidates hold no elected position (Frears and Parodi, 1979).

Among this minority, special mention must be made of the practice of *parachutage*, i.e. dispatching outsiders to new territory where the party's chances look promising. In these cases local roots do not exist. This practice has been employed most notably by the Gaullist movement, from the start of the Fifth Republic. It assisted ministers, as well as secretaries of state, who did not represent any electoral constituency and so were not in Parliament when they became government ministers. They were induced to seek a parliamentary seat, with more or less success, usually in electoral constituencies regarded as winnable.

Parachuting was also practised for young members of ministerial cabinets in constituencies regarded in advance as lost causes, but where the Gaullists had to show the flag despite their weak local presence (one example was Jacques Chirac in 1967). However, this phenomenon was not unique to the right-wing parties. It has also been used to the advantage of certain Socialist leaders, such as MM. Hernu, Mermaz and Dumas (Mabileau, 1972).

In 1978 and 1981 parachuting still took place, even though the parties wanted to encourage candidates who were already well-established locally. Some ministers or leaders of the right-wing coalition tried their luck in a constituency where they had never campaigned before (for example, MM. Barre, Deniau, Stoleru and Haby). On the other hand, genuine parachuting has become rare in the Socialist Party. New candidates, seeking a nomination in a particular constituency, establish themselves locally before putting themselves forward at a legislative election (examples being Michel Rocard and Laurent Fabius).

With the adoption of PR, strong local roots remained a key asset in obtaining a nomination. As well as favouring local elected representatives, the selectors aimed to represent equally all geographical sectors within a department. However, this often did not happen, and failure to produce a geographical balance produced numerous conflicts. Moreover, the list system enabled the selectors to pick, in addition to those candidates who had local roots and local *mandats*, other candidates, local or national party leaders, who lacked a local electoral base, and so PR increased the practice of parachuting. While imposed candidates with some local connections were usually well received, complete outsiders, even if national leaders, encountered more difficulty. In fact, parachuting has its rules and its risks. Certain aspirants did not succeed in their efforts. This is why, for instance, M. Delanoe, national Socialist Party secretary, had to withdraw, despite his involvement with the departmental party organizations, from the contest in Vaucluse in the face of the hostile reactions of the outgoing deputies. In the same way, in the UDF, the parachuting of a national leader provoked open hostility from local leaders in the department of Pas-de-Calais, especially from the mayor of Le Touquet, who announced his intention to set up a dissident list. In many departments, national leaders had to exert pressure on departmental leaders, sometimes without any results.

Under PR in 1986 the selectors aimed, in principle at least, to compose lists which balanced geographical areas within each department. But it was clear that this factor was less important than reselecting incumbents and preserving a balance between parties or tendencies, and thus it was not always heeded. It was practised more for the hopeless positions on the list than for the winnable ones.

Influences on the candidate selection process

In order to understand the different characteristics of candidate selection in France, several factors need to be considered: the electoral system, the political situation, and the nature of the political parties.

The electoral system

Each of France's two recent electoral systems has had its impact on the selection process (Goguel, 1981). The two main characteristics of the two-ballot single-member constituency system are the small size of the constituencies and the personal character of the voting. The former has had a strong impact on the candidate selection process, making the parties feel they must choose a candidate with strong local roots. This partly explains the selectors' preference for recent former deputies, who were well known in their constituencies, and for aspirants who already had accumulated several local *mandats*. This was particularly important in marginal constituencies.

The second characteristic, the personal character of the voting – even if it is impossible to separate a vote for the party from a vote for the candidate – is one reason why the candidate's personality often looms larger than the party in the minds of the voters. This helps explain the influence of the parties' departmental and local structures on the candidate selection process, even in those parties with a highly centralized structure. In fact, the departmental organizations are, in general, in the hands of local political leaders who are well known in their area.

PR also had two aspects: the larger size of the constituency, based as it is on the department, and the more partisan character of the vote itself. The decision was made by the Socialist government to use PR not at national but at departmental level, where local personalities count for a lot. The first aspect, large constituency size, induced the parties to draw up lists under the direction of a powerful departmental leader, who acted as the driving force in putting the list together. The adoption of PR increased the complexity of the selectors' task, as they had to come up with a list respecting a balance between outgoing deputies and new candidates, between geographical sectors, between men and women and/or between tendencies.

The more partisan character of the vote explained the tendency towards centralizing the selection process. Once it was decided that seats would be awarded to candidates strictly on the basis of list order, the parties' national organizations sought to exert influence on the order of candidates, downgrading the preferences expressed by the departmental organizations. Before the voters had even voted in 1986, at least 450 out of 577 seats were certain to go to particular parties, with most of the best-known politicians from right and left already assured of election. The voters decided the final balance of forces between the political parties, but the parties themselves decided the composition of their future parliamentary group.

The political situation
Ever since 1967 French legislative elections have involved constitutional provisions along with the normal electoral issues. There was always the possibility that the election results might modify constitutional practice and/or question presidential powers, as happened in 1986. The fact that so much is at stake may be an additional factor in explaining why the political parties' national organizations felt they had to control candidate selection very closely, constituency by constituency, rejecting certain candidates in favour of others for reasons of electoral effectiveness, and reserving the ultimate right to impose their decisions. Practices reinforcing the influence of national agencies developed in each party before the appearance of deals between parties. Within the right-wing majority, from 1967 to 1973, the Prime Minister himself presided over the majority's liaison committee which was endowed with the power of nominating candidates (Masclet, 1979).

The nature of the political parties
French political parties have certain characteristics which are related to the noticeable variations between them in the candidate selection process (Duverger, 1951).

The RPR is characterized by strong centralization around its president, Jacques Chirac, by a lack of democratic ideology when it comes to running its internal affairs, and by its parliamentary group's independence. Centralization has led to control of the departmental organizations by the national organization; for example, it is the RPR's general secretary who appoints the departmental secretaries, the departmental committee merely ratifying this. On the other hand, it is the departmental committee, which comprises constituency delegates and deputies, which elects the departmental president. The RPR is thus an extremely centralized organization, but one where local Gaullist leaders can influence the departmental organizations. This explains the complex balance between national and local influences in designating RPR candidates. The absence of a democratic ideology tends to exclude ordinary members from any sort of participation in the selection process. Finally, the independence of the parliamentary group in relation to the party's national organization means that the latter seeks to control the candidate selection process in order to ensure the loyalty of the RPR's future deputies (Schonfeld, 1985).

The UDF, as we have seen, is a confederation of parties and groups characterized by a centralization which is necessary in order to deal with and resist the RPR's strength. It too is characterized by a lack of democratic practice and by the independence of its parliamentary group. Centralization here also leads to a control of the departmental organizations by the national organization but, as in the RPR, the departmental president is elected by a departmental council in which local notables dominate. Centralization in the UDF is necessitated also by the need for arbitration between its different components on matters including the nomination of common candidates. This helps explain the national organization's difficulties when it is faced with the double pressure of the different components and of the departmental organizations, which explains in turn the length of the candidate selection process in the UDF. Here too, as in the RPR, the absence of democratic ideology excludes most of its members from any sort of participation in the process. Finally, the independence of its parliamentary group in relation to the national organization leads the latter, again as in the RPR, to try to control the candidate selection process so as to ensure the discipline of the future members of the group.

The Socialist Party is characterized by a pronounced decentralization; by an organizational pluralism which gives it the appearance more of an alliance of tendencies than a homogeneous organization; by a desire to ensure internal democracy; and by the dependence of its parliamentary group. The departmental organizations, and ordinary branch members, play essential roles in the candidate selection process. But one should not overestimate the role of ordinary members, in that they are often expected simply to approve their local leaders' preferences. Moreover, as these local leaders are often in a position of dependence with respect to national leaders, the latter have the means of applying pressure to gain influence when candidates are being chosen. Finally, the national leadership of the Socialist Party exercises, in some cases, a decisive influence (Schonfeld, 1985) which was especially evident in 1986. The division of the PS into tendencies obliged the national organization to intervene closely in the affairs of the federations in order to ensure an equitable distribution of seats in the future parliamentary group. Up to now the national organization has kept a tight rein on the positions taken by the parliamentary group and has kept it in a state of subordination.

The Communist Party is a highly centralized party, but with a desire to ensure a certain degree of internal democracy. Its parliamentary group is dependent on the central party apparatus. In the Communist Party the principle of democratic centralism underpins the candidate selection process. Candidates are in theory designated by the departmental organizations, but the central apparatus's control of these organizations is so strong that they only nominate candidates whom they know will be approved by the central apparatus. Similarly, the principle of democratic centralism aims at ensuring the participation of party members in the selection process, but they only have the possibility of accepting or rejecting proposals made by the party organization. Finally, the complete control of the national organization over the positions taken by parliamentary group explains why the former does not need to have complete direct control of the selection process and can ratify, without modification, the lists proposed by the departmental organization.

Consequences of candidate selection

The candidate selection process within the different political parties has consequences for the nature of their parliamentary groups, with respect to both their background and their behaviour.

The background of the parliamentary groups

When selecting candidates, the selectors of the different parties give priority to certain social and political characteristics which have a marked impact on the backgrounds of the different parliamentary groups. In general, the candidates picked by the selectors reflect the social and professional backgrounds of members and supporters of the different political parties. Every study concerning the social composition of parliamentary groups shows a close relation between the two.

In the right-wing parties, the selectors have a preference for candidates of high socio-economic status, such as top civil servants, businessmen, managers, engineers or members of the liberal professions. The most striking feature of right-wing candidates is the high proportion of top civil servants, especially former students of the Ecole Nationale d'Administration (ENA), showing the advantage of belonging to the parties in power for the members of this administrative elite.

Socialist selectors prefer candidates from the liberal professions (11.3 percent in 1978; 11.6 percent in 1981), white-collar workers (17.7 percent in 1978; 18 percent in 1981) and, above all, teachers (39.8 percent in 1978; 39.7 percent in 1981). Of these teachers, about a third in both 1978 and 1981 were university lecturers or secondary-school teachers. The proportion of high civil servants among Socialist candidates is always low (4.3 percent in 1978 and 2.7 percent in 1981).

Communist selectors were the only ones to have clear preferences for working-class candidates (33 percent in 1978 and 27.3 percent in 1981). They also recruited candidates from secondary-school teachers (17.3 percent in 1978 and 16.9 percent in 1981) and primary-school teachers (10.2 percent in 1978 and 12.2 percent in 1981). In 1981 teachers were the best-represented social category among Communist candidates, with 30.4 percent as against 27.3 percent for working-class candidates (Fabre-Rosane and Guédé, 1978; Guédé and Rozenblum, 1981).

The French parties reserve only a small space for female candidates. Under the traditional single-member constituency system, being a women often constituted an obstacle to nomination, since the selectors nearly always seemed to find a male candidate whom they deemed better. Female candidates represented only 6.7 percent of the total number of major party candidates in 1978, 7.4 percent in 1981 and 7 percent in 1986. The Communist Party was the only major party to present a significant percentage of female candidates. In 1986 the Socialists failed even to respect the 20 percent candidate quota written into the party statutes. The national organizations of the major political parties have occasionally urgently recommended departmental organizations to nominate female candidates, virtually forcing them to do so by threatening to impose the women concerned (Fabre-Rosane and Guédé, 1978; Guédé and Rozenblum, 1981). The change in electoral system did not make life easier for female aspirants. Members of Parliament such as Mmes E. Cresson, E. Roudy, G. Dufoix and H. Bouchardeau experienced difficulty making the head of their lists, and some of them had to be content with second place.

The selectors favour local elected representatives, and hence do not create a genuinely national political class (Aubert and Parodi, 1980). The proportion of locally elected representatives is high among candidates of all parties. Since French deputies do not relinquish their local mandates, but rather add them to their parliamentary one, French parliamentary groups have a large number of locally elected representatives (Masclet, 1979). For example, in 1981 only 38 percent of RPR deputies, 35 percent of PS deputies and 38 percent of PC deputies did not hold a local 'mandat' (Guédé and Rozenblum, 1981: 991).

The behaviour of the parliamentary groups
One might expect to find a relationship between the nature of the candidate selection process and the discipline of the parliamentary group. When candidate selection is in the hands of the national party organization the discipline of the parliamentary group might be expected to be tighter. This is indeed so in the case of the Communist Party. However, the examples of the UDF and RPR show that centralization of the decision-making process does not necessarily limit the parliamentary group's independence, despite the often-expressed desire of the party leaders to bring about stricter control. Indeed, the statutes of these parties do not even mention the existence of their parliamentary group. The parliamentary groups retain a fair degree of autonomy – manifested in issues like whom the deputies should elect as president of the parliamentary group – because they contain powerful figures who may be rivals of the party leader. This is most obvious in the RPR, in whose parliamentary group Gaullist 'barons' like MM. Debré, Chaban-Delmas and Guichard wield considerable influence. The tendency within the UDF and RPR to centralize the decision-making process is limited by the pressure exerted by the parliamentary groups and by the presence, which they insist upon, of their presidents within the national selection committees (Schonfeld, 1985).

On the other hand, when candidate selection is in the hands of the departmental party organization one might expect to find less discipline in the parliamentary group because of the influence of local factors or the ideological preferences of local activists. However, this is contradicted by the example of the Socialists, where decentralization of the decision-making process has not succeeded in eliminating the subordination of the parliamentary group to the national party organization. The statutes of the PS state that deputies must respect the rule of voting en bloc in their group (article 54) and that the parliamentary group may not commit the party without its agreement (article 52). Moreover, group members must pay a monthly contribution to the party.

Deputies also know they would have little chance of being reselected if they have a record of indiscipline. Obviously, one breach of the party rules does not necessarily mean banishment, but repeated infringements might. It is noteworthy that most cases of indiscipline by the parliamentary group do not concern the party's policy stands, but rather stem from economic and social problems which concern the dissident's constituency, such as difficulties connected with the steel industry, wine-growing or the closing of a coal mine.

This relationship between the nature of the candidate selection process and the behaviour of the parliamentary group extends also to the type of activities in which deputies engage. Under the two-ballot system most deputies have tended to spend more time, and be more active, in their constituency than in Parliament. By carrying on in this way, they became spokesmen for the particular interests of their voters and assumed the role of local brokers. They ran one or several offices in their constituencies to receive voters' complaints about the administration. This approach was, as we have seen, in accordance with the expectations of the selectors, who almost invariably looked for candidates who were well-established locally (Masclet, 1979). The adoption of PR, even if it had lasted for a prolonged period, was never likely to alter this type of attitude, which is a deeply embedded part of the traditional practices of the French local political and administrative system.

Conclusion

Candidate selection in France is the result of an interplay between local and national factors. Locally rooted candidates are preferred, but the evolution of the selection process has also shown a tendency for the central organizations to achieve greater control over the choices of departmental organizations, partly due to the more structured nature of the party system, with the emergence of two large blocs. If anything, the adoption of proportional representation in 1986 reinforced this tendency.

The selection process is important in two ways. First, it is important in the recruitment process, since becoming a deputy is a usual step on the ladder to becoming a minister. Although it is not possible to hold both positions simultaneously, so that deputies appointed to government must resign their seat in the Assembly, it remains the case that most ministers (on average about three-quarters in each government since 1974) have previously been deputies.

Second, it has become more important in terms of the mechanisms used to gain supremacy within party organizations and parliamentary groups in the context of the presidential election. Aspiring future presidential candidates within each party cannot ignore this battle. Within the PS the procedure adopted for distributing seats between tendencies before the 1986 election was proposed by the majority (Mitterand) tendency so as to preserve its control and to keep the Rocard tendency within acceptable bounds. Within the RPR control of candidate selection was kept in the hands of those who were loyal to Jacques Chirac. It was within the UDF that candidate selection was most important. The allies of former president Valery Giscard d'Estaing put all their weight in the scales to tip them towards candidates favourable to him rather than to those favourable to Raymond Barre, the former prime minister (*Le Monde*, 15–16 December 1985).

France's next parliamentary elections are due in 1991, though they may take place before then. It will be interesting to see whether candidate selection practices revert to the pre-1986 pattern, or whether the short-lived adoption of a PR electoral system has a lasting impact.

References

Aubert, Véronique and Jean-Luc Parodi (1980) 'Le Personnel Politique Français', *Projet*, 147: 787–800.

Duverger, Maurice (1951) *Les Partis Politiques*. Paris: A. Colin.

Fabre-Rosane, Gilles and Alain Guédé (1978) 'Sociologie des Candidats aux Elections Législatives de Mars 1978', *Revue Française de Science Politique*, 28 (5): 840–58.

Frears, J.R. and Jean-Luc Parodi (1979) *War Will Not Take Place. The French Parliamentary Elections, March 1978*. London: Hurst.

Georgel, Jacques (1979) 'France', pp. 87–120 in Geoffrey Hand, Jacques Georgel and Christoph Sasse (eds), *European Electoral Systems Handbook*. London: Butterworths.

Goguel, François (1981) *Chroniques Electorales. La Quatrième République*. Paris: Presses de la Fondation Nationale des Sciences Politiques.

Guédé, Alain et Serge-Alain Rozenblum (1981) 'Les Candidats aux Elections Législatives de 1978 et de 1981. Permanence et Changements', *Revue Française de Science Politique*, 31 (5–6): 982–98.

Knapp, Andrew F. (1985) 'Orderly Retreat: Mitterand Chooses PR', *Electoral Studies*, 4 (3): 255–60.

Lacorne, Denis (1980) *Les Notables Rouges*. Paris: Presses de la Fondation Nationale des Sciences Politiques.

Mabileau, Albert (ed.) (1972) *Les Facteurs Locaux de la Vie Politique Nationale*. Paris: Pedone.

Masclet, Jean-Claude (1979) *Le Role du Député et ses Attaches Institutionnelles sous la 5ème République*. Paris: Librairie Générale de Droit et de Jurisprudence.

Ranney, Austin (1981) 'Candidate Selection', pp. 75–106 in David Butler, Howard R. Penniman and Austin Ranney (eds), *Democracy at the Polls*. Washington, DC: American Enterprise Institute.

Schonfeld, William R. (1985) *Ethnographie du PS et du RPR*. Paris: Economica.

5

The German Federal Republic: the two-lane route to Bonn

Geoffrey Roberts

There are only four significant parties in the German Federal Republic, each now represented in the Bundestag.

The Social Democratic Party (SPD) has nearly one million members, and obtains about 37–45 percent of the votes at federal elections. Like the Labour Party in Britain, the SPD embraces a wide range of orientations, from marxist socialism to the more centrist and pragmatic social democracy of former Chancellor Helmut Schmidt. The SPD has close links to the trade unions; however, since under the Party Law of 1967 only individuals can be members of political parties, unions cannot formally affiliate to it.

The Christian Democratic Union (CDU), and its Bavarian sister-party, the Christian Social Union (CSU), together form a single parliamentary and electoral party: the CDU does not present candidates in Bavaria, nor the CSU outside Bavaria. The Christian Democrats are the conservative party of the German Federal Republic; they have affinities to the Christian churches, and the Catholic church in particular has retained considerable influence in the party. There are about 90,000 members of the CDU-CSU, and the Christian Democrats poll about 45–48 percent of the vote at federal elections.

The Free Democratic Party (FDP) is the liberal party of the German Federal Republic, with about 70,000 members. It occupies a central position in the party system, but is oriented towards the left or the right at different times, and thus usually determines whether the SPD or the CDU-CSU will, in coalition with the FDP, form the government in Bonn. This crucial role in forming governments contrasts with the marginal electoral position of the FDP: it polls usually between 6 and 8 percent of the vote at federal elections, and is thus often dangerously close to falling below the 5 percent level that qualifies it for seats in the Bundestag.

The Green Party is a new addition to the party system, which obtained representation in the Bundestag for the first time in 1983, polling 5½ percent of the votes in that federal election. The Green Party represents especially the ecology, peace and feminist movements in the Federal Republic, and is basically a left-wing party, though on several issues differs markedly from the SPD. It is difficult to estimate its membership, since many of its supporters do not acquire formal party membership. No other party has even 1 percent of the vote at federal elections, and none has seats in the Bundestag or in Land legislatures.

The process for the selection of candidates for the Bundestag – the elected chamber of the bicameral West German legislature – is characterized by three significant features.

It is, first, a very democratic process, in formal terms at least, because of the strict minimum legal requirements imposed by the Party Law and Electoral Law. Second, it possesses an unusual duality because of the 'hybrid' nature of the electoral system. It is, thirdly, often tantamount to election because of the numbers of safe seats which normally exist. This third feature has provoked much criticism since it is regarded as derogating from the democratic influence of the electorate and transferring undue power to the party 'selectorates'. Though increased electoral volatility has kept the number of such safe seats within bounds, estimates still suggest that well over half the members of the next Bundestag will be known at the selection stage, irrespective of the swings of electoral opinion revealed by the election itself (Kaack, 1969: 16; Rapp, 1976).

To appreciate the procedures, motivations and consequences involved in candidate selection in the Federal Republic of Germany, it is essential first to understand the way in which the electoral system operates.

Although some minor amendments and adjustments of procedure have been adopted since 1949, the basic features of the West German electoral system have remained unchanged since the 'Founding Fathers' drafted the Basic Law and designed an electoral system to elect the first Bundestag in 1949.

At present the Bundestag normally consists of 496 MdBs (Mitglieder des Bundestages, i.e. members of the Bundestag). On occasion, as explained below, that number may be exceeded very slightly. Of the 496 seats, 248 are filled from single-member constituencies, where each voter has one vote, and the candidate with the largest number of valid votes (irrespective of whether that candidate's votes constitute an absolute or a relative majority) is declared elected. The remaining seats are filled from party lists. Each voter, in addition to the 'first' vote for a constituency candidate, also has a 'second' ('list') vote for a party list. The voter is free to 'split' the two votes by voting for a constituency candidate of one party (or even a non-party candidate, though these are extremely rare), whilst giving the 'second' vote to the list of a different party. The crucial point is that the *overall* composition of the Bundestag depends upon the total of list votes which each party obtains. Once that total number has been calculated, the number of constituency seats won (if any) is deducted for each party, leaving the remainder to be filled from the party's lists in the Länder (provinces). Two significant points of qualification must be made:

1. A party only qualifies for a distribution of *list* seats if it has *either* obtained 5 percent of all list votes, calculated nationally, *or* won three constituencies (though any party winning one or two constituency seats of course retains them).

2. If a party wins more constituency seats in one Land than its calculated total allocation of seats for that Land, the normal size of the Bundestag is increased to accommodate the extra MdBs, by having additional seats (*Überhangmandate*) for the period of that Bundestag. Thus in the 1983 federal election two such additional seats were needed, because the Social Democrats had won all seven constituency seats in Hamburg and all three in Bremen, though entitled on the basis of list votes to only six and two seats respectively.

Apart from the slight distorting effect of the 5 percent/three seats requirement referred to above, the West German electoral system is completely proportional. It can be termed a 'hybrid' or 'mixed' system only in that candidates may be elected in either of two different ways, and are selected in two different ways also. (For further details of the electoral system of the Federal Republic, see Roberts, 1975; Pulzer, 1983; Jesse, 1985).

Table 5.1   *Result of the 1987 federal election*

	Constituency 'first' votes (percent)	Party list 'second' votes (percent)	Constituency seats won (number)	List seats won (number)	Total seats won (number)
CDU/CSU	47.7	44.3	169	54	223
SPD	39.2	37.0	79	107	186
FDP	4.7	9.1	—	46	46
Greens	7.0	8.3	—	42	42
Others	1.4	1.6	—	—	—
Total	100.0	100.2	248	249	497

Source: Official provisional results as published in *Das Parlament*, 31.1.1987

There is no provision for by-elections to take place for the Bundestag (except in the extremely unlikely case of a non-party MdB vacating a seat through death or resignation). This means that a vacant seat – whether previously occupied by a candidate elected for a constituency or one elected from a party list – is filled by the next available non-elected candidate from the Land Party list of that party to which the MdB vacating the seat belonged. This has relevance for the selection process in two ways: (a) no selection procedure is necessary to fill vacancies between federal elections, either in constituencies or for list candidates; (b) however, the selection of candidates for party lists – even for those places unlikely to secure seats at the federal election itself – becomes important, because those selected for places just below places that are successful at the federal election may well be invited to fill vacant seats in the course of the legislative period. On the basis of past experience, some thirty to forty vacancies (equivalent to 12–15 percent of list seats) can be expected to arise in each legislative period through death or resignation. This excludes the vacancies artificially created following the 1983 election by members of the parliamentary party of the Greens, who are required by the party in almost all cases to serve for only two years, and then, through the principle of 'rotation', to vacate their seats in favour of successors. This means that nearly twice the number of candidates originally elected to the Bundestag for the Green Party will serve during the four-year legislative period.

The regulative context

The extreme self-consciousness towards Germany's anti-democratic past and the need to ensure a democratic future, coupled with the tendency of German politicians to look for statutes and regulations to provide a legal context for social institutions and processes of all kinds, have meant that candidate selection occurs within a more rigorously defined regulative context than is the case in many other democratic states.

The starting point is the Basic Law of 1949 (the Grundgesetz), which is the constitution of the Federal Republic. It contains, unusually, a very specific article relating to the role and obligations of political parties, article 21, which requires, among other things, that the internal organization of parties 'must conform to democratic principles'.

This constitutional requirement that parties be democratic in their internal arrangements is a principal reason for the existence of the Party Law of 1967. The Party Law (section 1 (2)) includes the presentation of candidates at elections among the formal defining functions of a political party, and section 17 requires that parties select their candidates by secret ballot, but leaves further details of the selection process to the Electoral Law and the statutes of the parties.

The Electoral Law also includes legal provisions relevant to the selection process. Constituency candidates (paragraph 21) must be nominated by either a meeting of the membership of the constituency party or by a meeting of delegates elected by the membership of those local party branches which are located in the constituency. Where several constituencies are located completely within the area of a county-level (Kreis) party organization, a single meeting of party members or their elected delegates can select all the candidates for those constituencies at one meeting. Under the provisions of the Electoral Law, the party executive of the Land organization (or its nearest lower equivalent if no such organizational unit exists in a party) can object to a selected candidate and require the repetition of the selection process, but the decision of the reconvened selection meeting will then be decisive.

Paragraph 27 provides guidance for the selection of list candidates. Lists can be presented only by officially recognized parties. List candidates are selected by meetings of delegates of local party organizations within each Land. The Electoral Law leaves details concerning the selection of these delegates to the statutes of the parties, though such statutes must conform generally to the provisions of the Party Law. Parties not already represented in the Bundestag with at least five representatives require the signatures of either one in every 1000 voters, or of 2000 voters (whichever is the lesser number). No person can be nominated on more than one Land list at any federal election.

Paragraph 30 states certain requirements concerning the ballot paper. Constituency candidates appear in the left-hand column, with their name and party given; party lists appear in the right-hand column, with the name of the party and the first five names on the list. Party lists are placed in order according to: (a) the order in which parties obtained votes in that Land for their lists in the previous federal election, *if* their lists qualified for representation in the Bundestag; (b) then all other parties in alphabetical order. Constituency candidates are placed opposite their party list on the ballot paper (or a blank space is left if no constituency candidate has been nominated by a party presenting a list).

Finally, the modalities of the selection process are further regulated by party statutes, within the regulative contexts of the Party Law and Electoral Law. Frequently, federal party statutes will provide only very broad guidelines for selection procedures (as is the case with the CDU and FDP), leaving it to the statutes of the Länder party organizations to give more detailed rules. The CSU in

Bavaria is a party which only exists in that Land, so its provisions may be offered as a good illustration, since they combine the 'national' and Land elements which in other parties would be found in federal and Länder statutes separately. For selection procedures in the CSU, its statutes make the following provisions:

1. Meetings of sixty delegates of local parties take place within each Bundestag constituency, to select the candidate for that constituency, and to choose four delegates to the Land delegate conference.

2. The Land delegate conference consists of four delegates from each Bundestag constituency meeting, together with the members of the party praesidium, the chairmen of the regional (Bezirk) party organizations and the chairmen of party working groups (Arbeits-gemeinschaften), though only the constituency delegates have the right to vote for candidates. This delegate conference elects the candidates for the CSU list. All delegates must themselves be in possession of the right to vote in federal elections. Delegates must not be chosen earlier than two years prior to the date of the federal election.

The selection process: constituency candidates

The procedure for selecting candidates in constituencies, as pre-scribed by the Electoral Law and party statutes, is straightforward. *Either* a meeting is held, open to all the members of the party within a Bundestag constituency (feasible for smaller parties, such as the Green Party or the Free Democrats, in some areas of the Federal Republic where their membership strength is low), *or* there is a meeting of delegates who themselves have been elected by meetings of members at the level of the local branch party. The delegate meeting, at which attenders decide by secret ballot which aspirant is to be the party's candidate, is the more usual mode. Usually an absolute majority of votes is prescribed for obtaining nomination on the first ballot, but on the second ballot (if one is necessary) a simple majority will suffice. Such delegate meetings, it has been estimated, consist of about twenty to twenty-five members on average, representing eighty to a hundred active members who have elected them: a proportion of about 25 percent (Zeuner, 1971: 165). This would represent about 25 percent of active members, but a much smaller proportion of the parties' total membership. In 1985 the three main parties (excluding the Greens, who have less formal notions of membership) had about 1,900,000 members between them. If in each constituency about twenty-five people attend delegate meetings of the SPD and CDU-CSU, and about twenty attend FDP meetings, then the total number of delegates across the country is around 17,000, only about 0.9 percent of the total membership.

As indicated in the preceding section, where a city party (in Köln or Düsseldorf, for instance) wishes to meet to select candidates for all the constituencies in the city at one meeting, it may do so. Cases exist where – especially following constituency boundary revision – Bundestag constituency boundaries cut across the territorial boundaries of party organization; in such cases, the relevant *branches* that fall within the constituency area (perhaps from two or more local party organizations) send delegates on a proportional basis to a selection meeting, or else all the members of those branches meet to make the selection themselves. For example, Hamburg Nord constituency contains the SPD area party of Hamburg Nord *and* part of the area party of Hamburg Wandsbeck.

The selection of constituency candidates normally precedes the selection of party list candidates, and preliminary procedures concerning nomination of aspirants and the election of delegates for selection meetings may occur even two years prior to the next federal election. It is desirable that the decisions of the Land selection conferences concerning selection of list candidates be made with full information about the choices made in constituencies; to give a favourable place to a prominent candidate rejected by a 'safe' constituency, for example. If time permits, and if more than one aspirant seeks the nomination, potential candidates may visit party branches to make themselves known and to seek the support of members and delegates. The idea of instituting American-style primary elections has sometimes been suggested, but rarely, if ever, has such an experiment been instituted for the selection of Bundestag candidates (though the Rhineland-Pfalz CDU experimented with primaries prior to the Land legislative elections in 1971).

The principal parties now tend to present candidates in all 248 constituencies, as the 1983 federal election demonstrated (see Table 5.2).

The selection process: list candidates

Parties may present lists of candidates in any Land. They can combine their Land lists so that the calculation of seats occurs nationally, rather than on a Land-by-Land basis (which might be a disadvantage because of remainders), and this facility is normally adopted by all national parties. There is no restriction on the size of a list within each Land.

Candidates already selected for constituencies may also be selected for a party list. These 'double candidates' who win constituency seats are then removed from the party list before the allocation of list seats is made. Such double candidatures act as a form of insurance for politicians whom the party wishes to ensure will obtain a seat – one way or the other – in the Bundestag (prominent figures in the party, experts, potential ministers, interest representatives and so on), or provide constituency candidates, even in safe seats, with a very high place on the list as a gesture.

Table 5.2 *Number of candidates in the 1983 federal election*

	Constituency candidates	Land list candidates	Double candidacies[c]	Total candidacies[d]
Social Democrats (SDP)	248	447	235	695
Christian Democrats (CDU)[a]	203	405	148	608
Christian Social Union (CSU)[b]	45	45	18	90
Free Democrats (FDP)	248	318	213	566
Green Party	244	204	95	448

[a] The CDU does not present candidates in Bavaria.
[b] The CSU presents candidates only in Bavaria.
[c] Number of candidates on party lists who also contested constituencies.
[d] Number of list candidacies plus number of constituency candidacies.
Source: Statistisches Bundesamt (1984)

List candidates are chosen either by a special meeting of delegates of the local party organizations in the Land, or by the Land party conference itself acting in this special capacity, subject to delegates being in possession of the franchise for federal elections. The composition of such delegate meetings or party conferences is left as a matter for each party, provided that it abides by the democratic procedures required by the Party Law. Typically, allocation of delegates among local party branches will be based upon a mixture of membership strengths and electoral support for the party in each area or constituency in the Land. On average, each party's Land congress or selection conference is likely to have approximately 250 delegates, though this number varies considerably from party to party and from Land to Land. Since there are ten Länder, a total of about 7500 delegates attend the list selection conferences of the three main parties combined. This represents about 0.4 percent of their total membership, but around 10 percent of their active membership. Adding these figures to those for constituency selection conferences, and ignoring the possibility of overlap between the two groups of selectors, suggests that altogether around 25,000 of the three main parties' 1.9 million members take part in candidate selection, i.e. about 1.3 percent of them. This represents only about 0.07 percent of these parties' voters.

Voting, by law, must be by secret ballot. Each place on the list is voted on, in descending order. Any number of aspirants may contest any place (though most contests, if they occur at all, are between two, or at most three, aspirants). Defeated aspirants for any specific place are free to challenge for lower places. Especially for those places likely to be successful in the election, the Land party executive will normally propose a carefully constructed list of nominees (see below), but it is always open to delegates to make additional nominations from the floor. Unlike constituency selection procedures, there is no provision, in the Party Law or in party statutes, for the Land or national party executive to exercise any form of post-selection veto.

Each nomination, to be successful, must obtain an absolute majority of votes of the total number of delegates (not just those who use their vote). This applies even to unopposed nominations for a specific place. In a contest between two or more nominees, run-off elections may be necessary. Especially for lower places on the list (and particularly where these are extremely unlikely to have any chance of being elected) nominations may, by agreement among the delegates, be grouped into blocks of, say, five places to be voted on collectively by the delegates. There is no uniformity concerning the instruction of delegates by their local party organization. Some will have instructions, others will be given full discretion, or instructions regarding a few candidates only (perhaps those from the local or area party which the delegate represents).

Factors in the selection process: constituencies

Various factors operate, positively or negatively, to influence the selection of candidates in West German federal elections.

The parties tend not to have eligibility requirements, and do not insist on prior party membership. In each of the main parties there are cases of prominent newcomers being selected. Erhard was not even a member of the CDU when he became Minister of Economics, and Dahrendorf stood for the FDP only a few weeks after joining the party. In 1982 Verheugen and other 'renegades' from the FDP after that party's switch of coalition partners were given secure seats by the SPD only weeks after becoming members.

Generally speaking, an incumbent MdB in a constituency, and even an unsuccessful candidate at the previous election (especially one who nevertheless became an MdB by means of the party list), may expect reselection, and frequently without a formal contest (Zeuner, 1971: 176). In the 1976 federal election, for example, the Christian Democrats had the same candidate in 65.5 percent of constituencies, the Social Democrats in 74.6 percent of constituencies (Kaack and Roth, 1976: 430). In some cases, there is a tendency to look more closely at *second* reselections of candidates: a kind of feeling that perhaps 'eight years are sufficient', and a dislike of older 'sitting tenants' as candidates, but this is less pronounced than the tendency to retain successful – and therefore relatively well-known – candidates (Rapp, 1976). Sitting MdBs have greater prestige than new or previously unsuccessful aspirants, which may be an influential factor both for the party and the electorate. The power of incumbency was demonstrated, for example, by the difficulty which Hans Koschnick, the former Lord Mayor of Bremen and federal deputy chairman of the SPD, experienced in trying to secure selection for a Bundestag seat for the 1987 election. Despite his prominence in the party and his strong local reputation and political influence, none of the incumbents for the three constituency seats in the Land of Bremen was willing to step down in his favour (and the SPD, by winning all three constituency seats in the Land comfortably, had no hope of claiming even a single list seat in Bremen) (*Frankfurter Allgemeine Zeitung*, 29 October 1985). Faced with the possibility of Koschnick being adopted for a constituency outside Bremen, the Bremen SPD persuaded all three Bremen MdBs to agree to put their seats at the disposal of the party, and the party then decided which seat Koschnick would be offered. In this way the SPD were also able to ensure that Koschnick would be the first name on the Land list, and thus would spearhead the SPD campaign in Bremen (*Frankfurter Allgemeine Zeitung*, 22 and 26 November 1985).

Nevertheless, efforts are made from time to time to unseat sitting MdBs, though such attempts are always newsworthy. In 1979 in one Hamburg constituency, for example, a protégé of Herbert Wehner (the then chairman of the SPD parliamentary party), the incumbent MdB Glombig, lost the nomination to Duve, a left-wing Social Democrat, by sixty votes to fifty-nine. Attempts, ultimately unsuccessful, were made in 1985 to unseat Hans Apel in another Hamburg constituency which Apel had represented for twenty years – in which he had been Minister of Finance and Minister of Defence, had led the West Berlin SPD in the city elections of 1985, and was currently spokesman for his party in the Bundestag on finance matters. His constituency had become dominated by left-wingers, and they seemed determined to deny him reselection for the 1987 federal election, preferring instead a local left-wing Hamburg city councillor (*Frankfurter Allgemeine Zeitung*, 23 August 1985). Certainly, for reselection the attitude of the local party will be more important than the record of the MdB in Bonn – or elsewhere outside the constituency. Accusations of neglect of the constituency may result either in deselection or in a decision by the incumbent not to enter a hopeless contest. The changes of political orientation of the Free Democrats (in 1969–72 and in 1982) meant that incumbent FDP candidates opposed to the change of coalition partner which had resulted were unlikely to be reselected, at least without a challenge – though, of course, no candidate of the FDP has a realistic chance of winning a constituency seat. Putting a figure to the number of MdBs deselected is difficult, given that some will resign or stand down voluntarily if they believe they have little chance of reselection. In addition, some of those rejected by a constituency organization might still be picked for a safe or combative place on a list. Actual deselections of MdBs are rare, and amount to at most five to ten cases for each of the SPD, CDU-CSU and FDP per election.

Factors influencing choice of candidate, in addition to the possibility of incumbency, are numerous. Commentators on the selection process tend to emphasize the importance for selection of the aspirants' reputations within the constituency, especially in terms of party office-holding and local service (Rapp, 1976; Kaack, 1969: 68 and 71; Fishel, 1972: 64 and 69) as well as conformity with the 'trend' within the party nationally or locally. Other factors noted as potentially important are the personality and the attractiveness of aspirants for voters (especially groups of electors who might be newly attracted to the party, such as young voters or professional people) (Rapp, 1976; Kaack, 1969: 72). Expertise, a record of political achievement in Bonn or internationally and a reputation for non-political attainments tend not to be positive advantages for an aspirant. For example, the incumbent CDU candidate in Oldenburg-Ammerland, Broll, was defeated in his constituency selection meeting by a challenger, Kossenday. Broll had apparently given too much time to his Bonn activities, at the expense of his constituency engagements (*Frankfurter Allgemeine Zeitung*, 5 August 1986). Certainly, if coupled with an accusation of devoting insufficient attention to constituency affairs, these other attributes may be positively harmful to the hopes of an incumbent being reselected (Rapp, 1976). Gender seems to be a factor; very few female aspirants are selected to fight constituency seats (other than in the Green Party), and even fewer are chosen in winnable constituencies (see Table 5.3).

Table 5.3 *Female candidates, 1983 federal election*

	Constituencies	Party lists	Total candidacies	Elected	Female candidates as percentage of total: Constituencies	Lists
SPD	21	65	86	20	8.5	14.5
CDU	14	78	92	13	6.9	19.3
CSU	0	5	5	3	0	11.1
FDP	29	43	72	3	11.7	13.5
Green Party	40	45	85	10	16.4	22.1

Source: Statistisches Bundesamt (1984)

Intervention – or suspicion of intervention – by regional or national party leaders or officials in favour of a particular aspirant will usually be dangerous to the aspirant's chances of selection, unless such intervention is undertaken very discreetly indeed, but even then is not guaranteed to be successful. Constituency parties tend to be very jealous of their independence, especially in selecting their candidates (Zeuner, 1971: 178).

Contested selection meetings have become more frequent since the 1950s and early 1960s (Niess, 1980: 20). Such contests may be reflections of the desire to unseat an incumbent, or may (perhaps in addition) be an attempt to exert influence on behalf of a particular party section or faction (left-wingers in the SPD; progressive youth organizations in all major parties; the left-leaning 'Social Committee' in the CDU). Or they may be competitions among different local party organizations within the same constituency to have the honour of presenting the successful aspirant.

Delegates to selection conferences tend mostly to be middle-level office-holders in the party, chosen as delegates more often because of their prominence or activism in the party than because they represent some particular political trend (though the fact that delegates often hold party office may itself demonstrate that one or other wing or orientation in the party is dominant locally). In any case, delegates are often faced with the product of informal discussions among the party oligarchs within the constituency, in terms of support for a favoured aspirant or a proposal to renominate an incumbent (Zeuner, 1971: 177–8). The *formal* process of selection in a constituency is therefore not surprisingly often merely the benediction bestowed by the party on the outcome of *informal* discussions and decisions which have occurred well before the selection meeting takes place, though the formal procedures guard against undemocratic 'railroading' of selection decisions, and may be very significant in a contested selection process.

Factors in the selection process: party lists

Rapp (1976) has written: 'Land list selection conferences become colleges of surprising, fluctuating formations of groups, unexpected ballot outcomes, an arena for skilled tacticians and a nightmare for the Land party chairman.' In theory (as described above) the Land party conferences which select the candidates for party lists do so as democratic organs, with free choice and total power concerning whom they select and in what order. However, the Land party leadership will normally propose a list of nominations covering at least the top five places on the list, which appear printed on the ballot paper, and, in larger Länder, most of the 'hopeful' places after the top five as well. This is done so as to make the selection process comprehensible and to give it structure and order, and also to take account of the numerous factors which have to be considered and the informal agreements or long-standing conventions which provide for various forms of balance or compromise among the 'interests' involved. For example, in 1961 the CSU Land Executive in Bavaria decided on places 1–5 in order, and the nominees for places 6–10, though these were not placed in any specific prescribed order. The selection conference then endorsed these decisions (Mintzel, 1980: 28–30). Any changes to such proposals which the selection conference wishes to make may thus upset a carefully constructed set of agreements and compromises, and the executive's proposals may 'unravel' entirely (Kaack, 1969: 85).

A major problem facing the Land party executive committee in drawing up its nominations, the aspirants, and the delegates who select or endorse the list at the conference, is to forecast not only the likely percentage vote for the party in that Land (which determines to a large extent the total number of seats available to the party in the Land), but also: (a) how many of those seats will be won by constituency candidates; and (b) how many such victorious constituency candidates will be on the list, and thus have places which they then vacate. Even for the larger parties (the CDU and the SPD) it is possible that no seats in a Land will come from the list, because they win all the constituencies in a Land and qualify for no additional seats from the list: this happened to the SPD, for instance, in Hamburg and Bremen in 1976, 1980 and 1983, in Schleswig-Holstein in 1980 and in Bremen in 1987, and to the CDU in Saarland in 1961 and 1965, in Schleswig-Holstein in 1961 and in Baden-Württemburg in 1987. The number of list seats won by the SPD in North Rhine-Westphalia between 1957 and 1972, a period in which its share of the vote, both nationally and in that Land,

Table 5.4   *Seats won by the SPD in North Rhine-Westphalia, federal elections 1957–72*

	1957	1961	1965	1969	1972
Total number of seats won by SPD	54	60	66	73	75
of which:					
constituency seats	13	25	35	47	52
list seats	41	35	31	26	23
SPD percentage share of 'list' votes in North					
Rhine-Westphalia	33.5	37.3	42.6	46.8	50.4

Source: Schindler (1983: 48–52)

increased at every federal election, is shown in Table 5.4. An increased share of the vote led to a *decline* in the number of successful list places at each election, because extra votes (in constituencies as well as for the list) were converted into constituency seats by winning constituency seats that, at the previous election, had been narrowly lost. Thus place 30 (after elimination of successful constituency candidates on the list) on the SPD list in North Rhine-Westphalia was 'safe' in 1957 and 1961, 'marginal' in 1965, but 'hopeless' in 1969 and 1972. Fluctuations between elections are, of course, common for all parties. Thus matters of 'balance', insurance and other factors are difficult to arrange since they depend on the accuracy of forecasts of how many list places will ultimately be successful.

Generally speaking, sitting MdBs from list places can count on reselection for safe places on their party's list, especially if they are also contesting constituencies, though practice varies with regard to candidates reselected for safe constituency seats, and political factors may cause exceptions to be made even for sitting list MdBs (see below).

Because a party list – in contrast to the selection of a single nominated candidate for a constituency – is a collective selection of candidates, more numerous factors come into play than in constituencies, and more complex balances among factors can be accommodated.

The insurance both of prominent politicians (whether contesting constituencies or not) and sitting MdBs contesting marginal or hopeless constituencies is a principal factor in constructing a list (Kaack, 1969: 62–3). Some parties – and especially the SPD – insist that almost all candidates for promising places on the list already be constituency candidates. Other parties (especially the FDP) regard willingness to contest constituencies as a positive recommendation for aspirants for list places. The number of double candidacies is therefore very high. Where a candidate has some realistic hope of winning a constituency, but it is by no means certain, then a double candidacy acts as insurance, in other cases a double candidacy offers the only possible route to the Bundestag, since the candidate has no chance of winning the constituency which he or she contests (and this applies to all FDP and Green candidates, of course, as well as to some SPD candidates in rural Bavaria, or CDU candidates in parts of the Ruhr or in Bremen). The value of such insurance was illustrated by the SPD list in North Rhine-Westphalia in the 1983 federal election. Thirty-one list places were successful (extending down to place 33, as two names had to be removed because they had already won constituency seats). Only three of the thirty-one successful list candidates had not also contested a constituency; for many of the twenty-eight other candidates their insurance on the list was vital, because the vote for the SPD was very much below expectations, and in more 'normal' elections several of these candidates would have had hopes of winning their constituencies.

Of course, combined with the insurance and 'double candidacy' factors, parties seek, when constructing their lists, both to satisfy different interests and tendencies within the party and to present the most attractive list possible to the voters (since not only are the first five names printed on the ballot papers, but the media and opposing parties will publicize any deficiencies of the list, such as a shortage of younger candidates or of women candidates in hopeful places).

Group interests are one important factor in the composition of party lists. The SPD especially will ensure that trade union representatives are given prominent places (Adolf Schmidt, a trade union chairman, was given place 4 on the North Rhine-Westphalia list in 1983, for example). Commercial interests in the Land will expect to have a representative among the hopeful places, perhaps even among the top five: shipping in Bremen or Hamburg, wine-growing in Rhineland-Pfalz, farming in Bavaria and Schleswig-Holstein, for instance; these will mainly be included on the Christian Democrat or Free Democrat lists. Some of these representatives may also be adopted for safe constituency seats, but their placing on the list will be an indication of concern by the party that these interests are regarded highly by the party, if only in terms of ensuring voting support from trade union members, farmers or wine-growers, and perhaps to encourage financial support for the electoral campaign as well (Rapp, 1976; Zeuner, 1981: 180; Kaack, 1969: 88–9).

Regional balance is an important consideration in most Länder: between Bremen and Bremerhaven in Land Bremen; among the regions of Bavaria or North Rhine-Westphalia; between Baden and Württemberg in Baden-Württemberg; and so on. Such balance has sometimes attained the status of a semi-official distribution rule in some Land parties, so that – with extremely rare exceptions – each region knows that it is allotted, say, every fourth place on the list for its nominees, though with regard to other factors of balance, of course. In 1980, for example, in North Rhine-Westphalia the thirty-four successful places on the SPD list were divided as follows: twelve went to West Westphalia (the Ruhr area), ten to Lower Rhine, eight to Middle Rhine and three to East Westphalia. This distribution reflected relative party strengths in those four party regions. Brandt, the leader of the national party, had not been counted within this proportional division (*Frankfurter Allgemeine Zeitung*, 13 December 1982).

The social composition of the list is also important. Most parties will include a female candidate among the top five places in each Land, and female aspirants have more success in winning election to the Bundestag through list places than through constituency selection. This is because Land parties deliberately seek a degree of balance in selecting candidates for their lists, a balance that cannot be attained in constituency seats where a series of discrete choices is made, and where constituency parties are reluctant to select women for safe or marginal seats – even where female aspirants present themselves. Since 1953 the ratio of women elected from constituencies to those elected from party lists has varied from 1:6.5 in 1972 to 1:3.5 in 1965 (Schindler, 1983: 190). The Green Party insists on achieving as near to parity between men and women as it can get on its Land lists as a consequence of a decision of its first party congress in 1980 concerning parity of representation of men and women on committees and as candidates for office. Indeed, in 1987 it introduced a scheme for almost every Land whereby women should be selected for every odd-numbered position on the list. Consequently, the newly elected Green parliamentary party is 57 percent female, compared with 37 percent in 1983 (other parties for comparison: SPD up from 10 percent in 1983 to 16 percent; FDP up from 8.5 percent to 12.5 percent; CDU-CSU up from 6.5 percent to 8 percent) (Hocker, 1987: 5).

Age is another relevant factor; a fair representation of different generations will often be sought, and, if not attained, the youth organizations of the parties will indicate their dissatisfaction, perhaps by contesting early places on the list with their own nominated candidates. However, there are indications in advance of the 1987 federal election which suggest that incumbency is likely to outweigh the 'age' factor with party executives in drawing up recommended lists of nominees. With the exception of the Green Party, no party has indicated that it will ensure that leaders of party youth organizations will receive promising list places. For instance, Westerwelle, chairman of the Young Liberals, was promised the hopeful 11th place on the North Rhine-Westphalia FDP list, but has since been warned that he will probably be offered place 15 – a place only likely to be successful if the FDP do unusually well (*Der Spiegel*, 28 April 1986).

The matter of political balance can also be significant in the composition of the list. In particular, the Free Democrats faced problems in 1972 and 1983 as a result of their earlier decisions to change their coalition partners (in 1969, after a period in opposition, and in 1982). Opponents of the change of orientation were either eliminated completely from the Land lists or given places that were extremely unlikely to result in election to the Bundestag. In 1983 in Baden-Württemberg, for instance, the first six places on the FDP list were divided equitably among those who had supported and those who had opposed the 1982 change when it occurred; *but* no aspirant who continued to oppose Genscher (the party leader) and the change of coalition which Genscher had brought about, after the party congress in November 1982 had confirmed the coalition change and re-elected Genscher as party chairman, was chosen for the first eight – hopeful – places (the FDP in fact won seven seats from their Baden-Württemberg list) (*Frankfurter Allgemeine Zeitung*, 6 and 8 January 1983).

Finally, parties may decide to choose as many candidates as they please for their list, even though most places will have no chance of qualifying for election, even with a relatively favourable result. Such selections may have a symbolic function, however, for individuals or for party 'interests' (Mintzel, 1980: 33). This freedom of Land parties to select as many candidates as they wish accounts for the FDP in Hessen selecting eighty-four candidates in 1983, yet in the much larger Land of North Rhine-Westphalia only fifty-four, or thirty-one candidates in Rhineland-Pfalz, yet in the much more favourable situation of Baden-Württemberg only thirty-seven.

Attempts at intervention by national party authorities or by interest groups are more common than at constituency level, though not very much more successful (Niess, 1980: 22). This intervention may be to produce a more balanced list or to correct some potential deficiency, to secure the election of an expert or prominent politician, or to defend a loyal incumbent. Genscher, for example, campaigned within the North Rhine-Westphalia FDP to try to ensure that his former ministerial colleague, Baum, who had been elected from place 3 on the North Rhine-Westphalia list in 1980, was given a secure place in that Land for the 1983 election, despite Baum's opposition to Genscher's engineered change of coalition

(*Frankfurter Allgemeine Zeitung*, 20 December 1982). The party congress, displeased by what they saw as Baum's disloyalty and also mindful of the disastrous consequences of returning opponents of the previous change of coalition on their list in 1969, compromised by giving Baum place 9 – by no means a secure placing (*Frankfurter Allgemeine Zeitung*, 17 and 21 January 1983). In fact, Baum's was the next-to-last place to qualify for the Bundestag from that list in 1983. Matthäus-Meier and Verheugen – prominent renegades from the FDP after the change of coalition – were both given places likely to be safe on SPD lists in North Rhine-Westphalia and Bavaria respectively, as a result of the influence of national and Länder party leaderships. Interest-group intervention has to be subtle to be effective; resentment otherwise will render it counter-productive, whether intervention is linked with promises of financial support for the campaign or not (Zeuner, 1971: 181–2).

The development of party organization (even in the Christian Democratic parties since their ejection from government in 1969) and the availability of 'careerist' politicians for selection, have more or less eliminated the possibility of interest groups being able to demand that their nominees be given safe seats or secure list places. In addition, various developments, including the financial provisions of the Party Law and more recent legislative restrictions on contributions to parties, have made parties less dependent upon the donations of specific interest groups, hence less open to financial 'persuasion' by the threat of withholding such donations, a tactic which, in the 1950s and 1960s, may have secured nominations for some interest groups in safe seats or to high places on Land lists.

Interest-group representation on party lists is therefore most usually achieved because the party wishes to demonstrate its association with, or support for, the group concerned. The most obvious example is the SPD and trade unions, where a union official or leader is given a prominent place on a Land list (as was Adolf Schmidt on the North Rhine-Westphalia list in 1983), and without the normal requirement of having to contest a constituency seat also. The Christian Democrats do the same for representatives of business interests and farmers, and the Free Democrats for the professions and 'white-collar' unions. It is, though, extremely difficult to quantify this phenomenon. Many candidates in constituencies or on Land lists will have formal association with at least one 'interest'. All SPD candidates will be expected, if possible, to be members of an appropriate trade union, for instance, and farmers, doctors, lawyers and civil servants will all be members of appropriate associations or professional bodies. But it is impossible to state that their selection as candidates indicates 'interest group penetration'. One indicator, counting paid employment or paid or unpaid office-holding in an association (including trade unions, cultural and religious organizations, etc.) by MdBs, suggests that over 50 percent of MdBs elected in 1980 came into this category of interest-group representatives (an approximate figure, as the number of offices held was counted, and some MdBs held more than one). The Christian Democrats had the largest number of such offices or interest-group employees, followd by the SPD, then the FDP (Schindler, 1983: 204).

Despite the importance of carefully negotiated composite nominations for the chief places on the list produced by the Land party executive, challenges and contests do take place frequently, and are sometimes successful. Mende, former chairman of the FDP, beat off a challenge from Professor Klug (an exponent of the 'new image' FDP) for second place on the North Rhine-Westphalia list in 1969 (*Die Welt*, 9 June 1969). Matthäus-Meier, then a leading member of the Young Democrats (the FDP youth organization), having been promised place 12 on the party's North Rhine-Westphalia list in 1972, challenged for place 11, as a result of which she was defeated both for that place and for place 12 (*Der Spiegel*, 16 October 1972). The 1980 FDP list in North Rhine-Westphalia produced contests for all places from number 11 onwards, overthrowing the agreements reached by the Land executive (*Frankfurter Allgemeine Zeitung*, 2 June 1980). In Bavaria in 1983 Hamm-Brücher, an outspoken opponent of the Genscher strategy of changing coalition partner in Bonn, was defeated for place 2 on the FDP list (Englehard, a right-winger and Minister of Justice in the Bonn coalition, obtained the place by 215 votes to 195), but was elected to place 3. There were contests for the first two places – the only places likely to be successful – on the Rhineland-Pfalz list of the FDP in the same year.

So list selection is by no means a 'cut-and-dried' process, even though the choices organized by the Land executive usually prevail. Certainly the charges made by, for instance, opponents of proportional representation in Britain, that list selection in the Federal Republic provides the central or provincial bureaucracies of parties with undemocratic and undesirable power over the choice of candidate for the Bundestag, cannot be sustained.

Consequences of the selection process

The nature of the selection process in the Federal Republic of Germany may be seen as having consequences for the composition and organization of the parliamentary parties (*Fraktionen*), for the national, regional and local levels of party organization, and for the electorate.

The existence of party lists alongside single-member constituencies as a second route to the Bundestag enables the parties to undertake a certain amount of implicit planning of the composition of parliamentary party groups. Such planning has its limits: as indicated above, too-blatant 'interference' – in constituency or list selection processes – by national or regional party headquarters can be self-defeating. Nevertheless, lists are constructed to balance a variety of characteristics and qualities of candidates, both those of relevance to the party itself, as explained above, and those of relevance to the electorate it is hoped to attract (inclusion of women candidates; spread of age groups; occupational representatives, such as farmers, the self-employed and those from the learned professions; and so on). Insurance enables parties to guarantee that potential ministers, policy experts and others whom parties want at all costs to be returned to the Bundestag can be assured of electoral success, even if they contest constituency seats unavailingly.

However, two main features of the selection process – the tendency to select incumbent MdBs, and the insurance feature of the lists – have meant that there has been a trend towards increasing the number of 'careerist' MdBs (those who see membership of the Bundestag as their new profession, and for whom failure to be reselected, or electoral defeat, would mean the loss of their profession). In turn, this means a reduction in 'new blood' MdBs, a recent tendency towards an ageing Bundestag and a loss of opportunity for younger, talented politicians to make their way in elective politics at the national level. Some find consolation in Länder politics, others in employment by the parties, but others leave politics for private sector employment or for public service occupations in the civil service, teaching or other fields. This may be a contributing factor to the phenomenon of *Parteiverdrossenheit* – the tendency for established parties to become unresponsive, inflexible and impervious to change, and is one of the features of the established parties which the Green Party seeks to avoid, by rotation of MdBs, for example.

The influence of local and regional elites over candidate selection, especially of list candidates, does reinforce party discipline. Persistent rebellion, at least against decisions or policies of the Land party, will lead either to the Land party executive withdrawing a proposal for a hopeful seat for the rebel or (unless the rebellion is widely supported) to the Land congress refusing to endorse the aspirant for any place likely to result in election to the Bundestag. The case in North Rhine-Westphalia of Gerhard Baum, the FDP left-wing opponent of the 1982 change of coalition, has already been described.

The predilection, especially of constituency selection meetings, for local candidates does mean that a large proportion of MdBs will hold, or will have held in the past, local party office and perhaps previous elective office at local government or Land level. The existence of the list system allows parties to correct tendencies towards an 'over-provincial' Bundestag by ensuring that nationally known politicians, or those with special expertise or a previous career outside party politics, can acquire seats in the Bundestag.

There is practically no difference – once elected – in the status or behaviour of constituency candidates and list candidates. Constituency candidates may have certain additional engagements and duties in the constituency, but, since most list candidates have contested constituencies – and perhaps hope to do so again – they, too, will 'nurse' constituencies and undertake engagements there. The close links that exist in Britain between an MP and constituents do not manifest themselves in the Federal Republic anyway, in part because of tradition, in part because the problems taken up by British MPs on behalf of their constituents will usually be matters for Land politicians or for local government representatives rather than for MdBs.

The readiness of parties to nominate candidates who possess links to interest groups means that such candidates, once elected, can serve usefully on relevant committees of the Bundestag (farmers on the agricultural committee, for instance). Their expertise and their links to interest groups may both be valuable assets to their parties. However, only in the very broadest terms can it be suggested that interest groups benefit directly from such committee membership. Party discipline, the cross-party nature of committee membership (which will constrain or counter any partiality exercised in favour of affected interests), the overt nature of interest-group links – whether based on paid employment or honorary office-holding – required by Bundestag regulations, all limit such possibilities of interest-group benefit from securing the election of favoured candidates to the Bundestag. Interest-group influence on Bundestag committees is exerted more effectively by giving evidence and making representations to such committees, rather than by hoping to use MdBs to win votes in committee, votes which in any case may then be reversed in plenary session of the Bundestag.

Consequences for party organizations at national, regional and local level are more diffuse. The duality of selection procedures complicates party organizations to an extent; for example, the suggested nominations from the Land party executive for hopeful list places may have to await the outcome of constituency selection procedures before they can be finalized. Certainly the existence of two different types of selection, and the strict legal preconditions which form the context for both sets of procedures of selection, promote opportunities for participation by members and enhance the level of intraparty democracy in formal terms. Such formal intraparty democracy can serve to protect the autonomy of the party vis-a-vis external, and especially interest-group-related, pressures (Mintzel, 1980: 37). However, the rather low levels of participation by members in the selection process (whether directly or through the selection of delegates to selection meetings) has led to suggestions that primary elections should be instituted, US-style, to allow members (and perhaps even all party supporters, by means of a system of registration) to have a direct vote in the selection process (Zeuner, 1971: 166).

Regarding the consequences of the selection process for the electorate, two points must be made. First, the voter is little affected by the existence of two different types of candidate, selected by two different processes. The widespread ignorance of the voter concerning the relative importance of first and second votes has been well-documented (Jesse, 1983). Similarly, research has established the relative unimportance of the 'personality factor' of constituency candidates. Few – and never a majority of – respondents in surveys can name their constituency MdB; parties tend to capture the same safe seats over several elections irrespective of the candidate whom they present in them, and, in most cases, constituency first votes and list second votes are closely similar and co-vary at elections (Jesse, 1985: 291). True, for the FDP and the Greens there is a greater proportional difference between first and second votes than for the larger parties, but tactical splitting, rather than the negative effect of the personalities of their constituency candidates, explains this. Other research has shown more directly that party rather than personality matters in constituencies. A survey in 1976, for example, showed that 57 percent said that party loyalty would lead them to vote even for a constituency candidate whose personality they disliked; only 29 percent said they could vote for a constituency candidate on personal grounds, if the candidate belonged to a party other than that favoured by the respondent (Noelle-Neumann, 1976).

The general 'invisibility' of the list in terms of details of candidates in places beyond the first five, and the inability of the voter to change the ordering of the list at the election, mean that selection of particular persons or types of candidate perhaps has less relevance for the elector than generalized party loyalty in determining voter choice of a party list. Composition of the list can be important to the elector if some omission or deficiency (with regard to regional imbalance or insufficient prominence of some local interest representative, for instance) is publicized, leading the voter to reject the party list. It can also be important to party members, who might react to list choices which they felt were imbalanced or unwise by withholding assistance in the campaign.

Proposals to allow the electorate to change the order of candidates on the list through their votes have not found support (Jesse, 1985: 219).

Conclusion

The selection of candidates for the Bundestag elections in the Federal Republic has always been regarded, in formal terms, as an important element of the party-based democracy that was designed to replace the dictatorship of the Third Reich and the unstable conditions of the Weimar regime. The evidence available suggests that the selection process *is* as democratic a procedure – both in constituencies and in Land delegate conferences – as one could reasonably hope to have, given that most party members do not choose to participate in the selection process, and that initiatives by local and regional elites (and, less frequently, by national leaders) are required to give structure to the selection process, by sounding out possible candidates, calculating balances among different groupings or interests in the party, arranging compromises, and so forth. It is open for all electors to join a party, and for all party members to participate in the selection process, at first- or second-hand. One might speculate as to whether higher rates of membership participation would be electorally rewarding (in that aspirants favoured by local or regional elites on grounds of imbalance, or preferred on the basis of the long experience of electoral campaigns possessed by party elites, might be rejected in favour of more superficially attractive, locally known or radical candidates), or whether cohesion – of individual parties or of the party system – would necessarily benefit.

Certainly the dual nature of the selection process seems to make hardly any difference to the composition of the Bundestag compared to that which would be produced by an electoral system based only on regional lists. Candidates in constituencies are usually also selected for places on the party list – especially if they are likely to be defeated in their constituencies. A purely list-based proportional system of election, implying only one mode of candidate selection, would not therefore introduce much alteration to the composition of the Bundestag parties, other things being equal.

Finally, the greater homogeneity of the Bundestag membership in recent years (increases in those with public-sector occupational backgrounds; increases of those with trade union membership – including white-collar unions; increases in those who are academically qualified; greater clustering around the 40–60 age groups, etc.) is reinforced, but not caused, by the modes of selection that operate. (Though here, as in many other respects, the Green Party is the exception. Its parliamentary group is decidedly younger on average, more equally balanced in terms of male and female MdBs, and certainly less 'bland' in terms of occupational background, and so on, than the other, 'established', party groups in the Bundestag. The decision at the 1986 national party congress of the Greens to abandon mid-term rotation for Bundestag representatives will make little difference, since the rule is now that no MdB should serve for more than four years in succession, which will ensure circulation of personnel.) Such homogenization seems to be a near-universal phenomenon in Western parliamentary democracies, and is also a consequence of the parties in the Federal Republic becoming more professionalized and more established since the 1950s.

The selection process in the Federal Republic is important; it is influential with regard to the composition and behaviour of the parliamentary party groups, local, regional and national party organizations, and the political system as a whole. It is also important in the political recruitment process, since almost all federal government ministers are also members of the Bundestag, even though it is nowhere prescribed that they must be. It is also – in formal terms – exceedingly democratic. But one must avoid the danger of loading too much responsibility onto the selection process. It is but one of numerous functions which, for good or ill, help to shape party democracy in West Germany.

References

Edinger, Lewis J. and Paul Luebke, Jr (1971) 'Grass-Roots Electoral Politics in the German Federal Republic', *Comparative Politics*, 3 (4): 463–98.

Fishel, Jeff (1972) 'Parliamentary Candidates and Party Professionalism in Western Germany', *Western Political Quarterly*, 25 (1): 64–80.

Geisler, Christiane (1973) 'Kandidatenaufstellung nur durch Wahlberechtigte? Bundes- und Landeswahlgesetze solten Klarheit schaffen', *Zeitschrift für Parlamentsfragen*, 4 (4): 470–9.

Hocker, Beate (1987) 'Politik: Noch immer kein Beruf für Frauen?', *Aus Politik und Zeitgeschichte*, 9–10: 3–14.

Jesse, Eckhard (1983) 'Sie haben am 6 März zwei Stimmen', *Frankfurter Allgemeine Zeitung*, 28 February 1983.

Jesse, Eckhard (1985) *Wahlrecht zwischen Kontinuität und Reform*. Düsseldorf: Droste Verlag.

Kaack, Heino (1969) *Wer kommt in den Bundestag? Abgeordnete und Kandidaten 1969*. Opladen: C.W. Leske Verlag.

Kaack, Heino (1971) *Geschichte und Struktur des deutschen Parteiensystems*. Opladen: Westdeutscher Verlag.

Kaack, Heino and Reinhold Roth (1976) *Parteien-Jahrbuch 1976*. Meisenheim-am-Glan: Verlag Anton Hain.

Mintzel, Alf (1980) 'Kandidatenauslese für den Bundestag über die Landeliste', *Zeitschrift für Parlamentsfragen*, 11 (1): 18–38.

Niess, Wolfgang (1980) *Über die Wahl hinaus*. Reinbeck bei Hamburg: Rowohlt Taschenbuch Verlag.

Noelle-Neumann, Elisabeth (1976) 'Der unbekannte Wahlkreiskandidat', *Frankfurter Allgemeine Zeitung*, 2 October 1976.

Pulzer, Peter (1983) 'Germany', pp. 84–109 in Vernon Bogdanor and David Butler (eds), *Democracy and Elections. Electoral Systems and Their Political Consequences*. Cambridge: Cambridge University Press.

Rapp, Alfred (1976) 'Vorwahlen zum Bundestag', *Frankfurter Allgemeine Zeitung*, 8 April 1976.

Roberts, Geoffrey K. (1975) 'The Federal Republic of Germany', pp. 203–22 in S.E. Finer (ed.), *Adversary Politics and Electoral Reform*. London: Anthony Wigram.

Schindler, Peter (ed.) (1983) *Datenhandbuch zur Geschichte des Deutschen Bundestages 1949 bis 1982*. Bonn: Presse- und Informationszentrum des Deutschen Bundestages.

Statistische Bundesamt (1984) *Fachserie 1. Bevölkerung und Erwerbstätigkeit: Wahl zum 10 Deutschen Bundestag am 6 März 1983*. Stuttgart und Mainz: Kohlhammer Verlag.

Zeuner, Bodo (1971) 'Wahlen ohne Auswahl – Die Kandidatenaufstellung zum Bundestag', pp. 165–90 in W. Steffani (ed.), *Parlamentarismus ohne Transparenz*. Opladen: Westdeutscher Verlag.

Note: Any translations from German are by the author of this chapter.

6
Ireland: the increasing role of the centre

Michael Gallagher

There are no legal provisions relating to the selection of candidates
at elections to Dáil Eireann (the lower house of parliament in
Ireland). The existence of parties is neither mentioned in the
constitution nor assumed by the electoral system, and only since
1963 have candidates' party affiliations even appeared on the ballot
paper at elections. Parties or other groups are thus free to select
parliamentary candidates in whatever fashion they wish.

The selection process

The main parties
The mechanics of candidate selection in the main parties differ in
details but are similar in essentials.[1] Candidates are selected at
constituency level, by a selection conference or convention consisting of delegates from all the party branches in the constituency. The
party's national executive has the right to veto the candidate(s)
selected and/or to add a name to the panel selected locally; it also
has, in most cases, the power to determine the number of candidates the convention may select.

Fianna Fáil is the largest party in Ireland, with an average
electoral strength of around 47 percent of the votes. It is a party of
the centre-right, allied in the European Parliament with the French
Gaullists (RPR) in the European Democratic Alliance. Its support
is cross-class, though strongest among small farmers. It differs from
Fine Gael in that it takes a more traditional nationalist line on
Northern Ireland, and, in recent years, has emerged as more
conservative on issues like the liberalization of laws on contracep-
tion and divorce and on the general question of the role of the
Catholic Church in society (for details of the Irish parties see
Gallagher, 1985a). Fine Gael is Ireland's second largest party. It
draws its strength mainly from the middle class and large farmers,
but has reasonable support from all social groups. Its electoral
strength has been around 35–40 percent at recent elections,
dropping to 27 percent in February 1987. It too is a centre-right

party, which belongs to the Christian Democratic group in the European Parliament. The Progressive Democrats (PDs), founded in 1985, have a generally similar outlook to Fine Gael, and won 12 percent of the votes on their electoral debut in 1987. The Irish Labour Party is a trade-union-backed party of the moderate left. Its support has declined in recent years and it won only 6 percent of the votes in 1987, mainly from the working class. Since 1970 Labour has been deeply divided over whether or not to join coalitions, the left generally being anti-coalition.

We shall look at the selection process in these four parties, examining how they deal with five questions: how many candidates to select; who attends the convention; the eligibility requirements of candidature; how the convention selects the candidates; and the powers of the national executive. We shall then discuss some informal features of the reality of the processes.

In the three centre-right parties the candidate selection procedure is prescribed in the party constitution, so that changes cannot be made without the approval of members voting at an annual conference, but in Labour it is decided by the national executive. Candidates used until recently to be picked only on the eve of elections, but since the start of the 1980s parties have increasingly selected them up to two years in advance of an election, partly to give new candidates more time to get themselves known in the constituency. One disadvantage is that a TD (member of the Dáil) deselected some time before an election has no incentive to remain loyal to the party line.

The number of candidates to be nominated needs some thought because of Ireland's electoral system (see the discussion below); there are both advantages and disadvantages in a party picking more candidates than it expects to win seats. The national executive in Fianna Fáil appoints the convention chairman, and recommends the number of candidates to be selected, though the convention sometimes disregards its recommendation. Fine Gael's national executive lays down the minimum and maximum number (which are almost always the same) of candidates the convention may select; so does the PD's national executive, 'in consultation with' the party leader. In Labour the convention itself decides how many candidates to select. In Fianna Fáil, Fine Gael and the PDs the national executive may stipulate that one or more candidates must come from a particular part of the constituency, as it sometimes does where a constituency is composed of readily distinguishable geographic units. In all parties the number of aspirants putting their names before the convention is rarely more than four more than the number of candidates to be selected.

Fianna Fáil conventions are attended by three delegates from each branch in the constituency (for details of the parties' organizational structures see Gallagher, 1985a: 121–30), and the youth organization also sends delegates. This gives the average convention about 220 delegates, the largest (in Clare) having about 440 delegates, and the smallest (in Dublin South-East) only about forty. Labour conventions, too, are attended by a fixed number (four) of delegates per branch; the average convention would be attended by about 50 delegates, the range being from twenty or fewer to about 200. PD conventions are attended by one delegate per ten branch members. Candidate selection in Fine Gael is unique in that a branch's representation at the convention is related, under a 'model system' introduced in 1978, to the size of the electorate in its 'functional area' rather than being fixed. This removes the incentive for aspirants to create a plethora of inactive 'paper branches', packed with their own supporters, around their home base. Each branch, outside Dublin, sends a mean of five members to the convention, which on average has about 320 delegates, the range nationally being from approximately 120 to 450. In all parties, delegates may be given instructions by their branches as to how to vote, but these are unenforceable since voting is by secret ballot, and moreover the full range of aspirants may not be known until the convention actually meets.

There are few restrictions on eligibility in the major parties. In neither Fianna Fáil, Fine Gael nor the PDs is any minimum period of party membership prescribed. Each party demands a 'pledge' from aspirants. In Fianna Fáil they must undertake that, if elected to parliament, they will resign their seat if the National Executive, by a majority of two-thirds of its members, calls on them to do so. Aspirants may not be convention delegates, nor – a curious stipulation – may they even attend the convention until the selection has been completed. Fine Gael and PD aspirants must promise that, if elected, they will 'contribute to the Party such sums as the Parliamentary Party shall have determined or may from time to time determine'. Labour aspirants must have been party members for at least six months (on one occasion in 1977, when a centrally favoured aspirant's eligibility was challenged on the ground that she had been a member for only five and a half months, the national executive ruled that this was enough as it amounted to six lunar months).

Voting at Fine Gael, PD and Labour conventions is by the same electoral system as that used at national elections, i.e. the single transferable vote (which becomes the alternative vote if only one candidate is to be picked). Fianna Fáil, though, uses elimination voting for *each place* on the panel, so that the names of all the aspirants are placed before the convention for the first place on the panel. If none wins a majority of the votes the lowest-placed candidate is eliminated and a further vote takes place, this process continuing until one aspirant wins a majority of votes. The remaining aspirants then go through the same process for each of the remaining places on the panel.[2] Fianna Fáil conventions are 'expected to give preference to Irish-speaking nominees provided they are otherwise properly qualified' (rule 46(f)). The names of the selected candidates are forwarded to the party's national executive, which, in all parties, has the power to refuse to ratify one or more of the candidates selected, or to add a name to the panel selected at the convention.

The party constitutions, of course, do not give a complete picture of candidate selection. In Fianna Fáil it is common at conventions, though not universal, for a proposal to be put and passed that incumbents be declared selected by acclamation, without needing to fight for a place. The national executive's powers to conduct the selection itself (which it can take, in exceptional circumstances, under rules 46 and 52 of the party constitution) and to call on deputies to resign their seats have always lain dormant, and it has very rarely vetoed a candidate. It does, though, sometimes add candidates of its own to those selected locally, and there are signs that its interventions are on the increase. At the 1977 election it added a record sixteen candidates to the 116 selected at conventions (Marsh, 1981b: 273). In November 1982 it added only three to the 129 selected locally (the Fianna Fáil general secretary commented that this showed how well the conventions went), and eight were added in February 1987. Another token of the centre's increased interest in candidate selection came in July 1984 when it was announced that the party had set up a 'high-powered committee', chaired by the party leader, to identify strong potential candidates and attempt to promote their prospects, by discussions with the relevant constituency organizations, in advance of the selection conferences.

In Fine Gael there is no question, as in Fianna Fáil, of incumbents being selected automatically; indeed, one of the main reasons behind the introduction of the 'model system' was precisely to prevent incumbents dominating the nomination process via captive branches. Fine Gael practice resembles that of Fianna Fáil in that while the national executive quite often adds candidates to a panel selected by a convention (in November 1982 it added eight to the 107 picked by conventions), it rarely if ever vetoes a candidate selected locally. The party has gone further than the others when it comes to central involvement in the process (see Mair, 1987: 94–135, for a fuller discussion). After suffering a heavy defeat at the 1977 general election it embarked on a complete overhaul of its organization, initiated and executed by the centre under the new leadership of Garret FitzGerald. Head office was expanded and began to monitor constituency organizations closely. Before each of the three subsequent elections it attempted to identify the key marginals where extra effort and attention was needed to save or win a seat. It devised detailed tactics to apply to each such constituency, which involved, among other things, identifying strong potential candidates in the constituency and attempting to smooth their path to selection by the local organization, usually by having a quiet word with influentials in the local party, especially local deputies.

In Labour too the centre has been taking an increasing interest in the process. In July 1984 a new rule was introduced to allow the party leader (who is elected by the deputies) and the party chairman (elected by annual conference), acting together, to add candidates to those selected by a convention, though in the event none was added in February 1987. In November 1984 the national executive decided that at least a quarter of candidates at the 1985 local elections should be women (the figure actually achieved was only 11 percent). Labour differs from the other parties in that it has corporate members, namely those trade unions which are affiliated to the party. The unions do not directly control any candidacies via 'sponsored' MPs as they do in Britain, and there is no requirement in the party's rules that a candidate be, if eligible, a member of a trade union. Even so, aspirants are certainly helped by belonging to a union which is affiliated to the party, not least because their union will then make a contribution to the local campaign. The sum involved will not be large, perhaps around £2000 or less, but this is still significant given the fairly low sums involved in expenditure by the local organization. Consequently, this may incline conventions to favour a union member over a non-member, but only when other things are equal; the likely contribution of the respective aspirants towards winning a seat for the party would be the main consideration. In any case, this would help only individual trade unionists rather than the trade unions themselves; there would be no question, for example, of a local Labour organization giving a nomination to a union and inviting it to fill it with the candidate of its choice.

At the time of writing, the PDs have contested only one general election, that of February 1987. On that occasion the national executive imposed quite a number of candidates, provoking open resentment from those already selected locally. The party leadership justified such intervention by arguing that since they were a new party good potential candidates had not had a chance to establish themselves locally.

Other parties

The only other parties with pretensions to a nationwide organization are the Workers' Party and Sinn Féin, which won 4 percent and 2 percent of the votes respectively at the February 1987 general election. They rarely nominate more than one candidate in any constituency.

The Workers' Party, in essence an Irish Eurocommunist party, has been through a prolonged process of transformation from the political wing of a military organization, a role it abandoned in the early to mid-1970s, to a political party seeking power via elections. Its constitution says only that candidates are to be nominated by constituency councils and are subject to ratification by the national executive; and that all candidates for any public office must meet certain criteria, namely 'continuous party membership of at least two years; active participation in internal education courses and a record of consistent and efficient work on behalf of the party'. Conventions are attended by delegates on the same basis as annual conferences: branches with up to ten members send four delegates, and those with over ten members send six. This results, with very few exceptions, in conventions of fewer than thirty delegates. The absence of detailed guidelines causes few real problems, because there are very few contests at the nomination stage. In most constituencies where the Workers' Party has an organization one individual is usually established as the party's electoral flagbearer, and is almost invariably unopposed at the nomination convention.

Sinn Féin is Ireland's only 'anti-system' party; it does not recognize the legitimacy of the Dublin regime, and although it has nominated candidates at Dáil elections, its policy until November 1986 was not to take any seats it won. The detailed rules for nomination conventions are not part of the party constitution, which stipulates merely that 'only those whose membership of the Republican Movement exceeds twelve months shall be eligible for selection and nomination' as candidates (rule 39). The 'party pledge' required from candidates prior to the abandonment of the abstentionist policy made them promise not to attend the Dáil, and acknowledge that such attendance would constitute 'an act of treachery'. Given Sinn Féin's role as the political arm of the IRA, such a pledge was not taken lightly. It seems that the Sinn Féin national executive has tended in practice to have greater power than other parties' executives to intervene in this process and, indeed, effectively to make the selection. This is because, with candidates pledged not to attend parliament, voting for Sinn Féin has been essentially a symbolic act, not influenced greatly by the identity of the candidate or by such factors as whether he had local roots. But recently, especially in Dublin, Sinn Féin has been trying to build local support by the traditional method of brokerage work, and, as in the Workers' Party, one individual generally emerges in each constituency as the party's best-known figure.

An overview
From these descriptions of the selection process in each of the parties, some general patterns emerge. First, it would be accurate to summarize the process in all parties as one of constituency-level selection, with national supervision and influence. Ranney's (1981: 82) conclusion that Ireland has 'regional selection with national supervision' is mistaken, since the parties do not have regional organizations. Second, although many of the formidable paper powers of the national executive lie dormant, it is clear that national headquarters in all parties, especially Fine Gael, are taking a closer interest in candidate selection, believing that this will bring electoral dividends. They are increasingly active at what might be termed the 'pre-selection' stage, to try to smooth the path for bright local prospects and to persuade local organizations to select them. While the national executives hardly ever veto candidates, they quite often add names to the panel selected locally.

Third, there seems to be fairly wide involvement of party members in the selection process, even though the great majority of party voters is excluded. Calculation of the proportions is difficult because of cross-constituency variations within each party, and because the parties are unable to be precise as to how many members they have. Using the most realistic estimates produces the figures given in Table 6.1. This suggests that the proportion of party members who are entitled to attend selection conferences ranges from about a tenth to something over two-fifths, while the proportion of party voters is only 1 or 2 percent. Fine Gael allows the widest involvement of members and voters, and the PDs the narrowest. Fourth, the qualities formally needed by aspirants vary somewhat: to be selected by one of the largest three parties it is not even necessary to be a party member, but the smaller parties require membership of from six months to two years.

The question of what qualities the selectors are looking for when they pick the candidates is difficult to answer definitively in the absence of extensive survey data. There is little doubt that individual selectors vote for aspirants from their own branch or locality, but the main collective desire seems to be to produce an electorally attractive ticket. The prime determinant of electoral appeal is widely regarded as the candidate's reputation in the constituency. This, naturally, gives an advantage to incumbents (who very rarely fail to be reselected), to holders of a local elective office, to aspirants who have polled respectably on a past candidacy, and to those who have, by some other method, acquired a high local profile. The potential parliamentary ability of aspirants does not seem to be a chief consideration of selectors.

TABLE 6.1   *Involvement of party members and voters in candidate selection in Ireland*

	Average attendance at selection conference	As % of party members	As % of party voters
Fianna Fáil	220	23	1.2
Fine Gael	320	44	2.0
PDs	58	10	0.9
Labour	50	34	1.3

Note: All figures are estimates.

These speculations match the findings of the only hard evidence available, reported by Katz (1980: 97–8, 125–6) from a survey conducted in the mid-1970s of twenty-eight participants in selection (deputies, defeated candidates and local party officials). He found that the most important factors in selection were perceived as local government experience, support from party branch secretaries in the aspirant's own area of the constituency, and constituency contacts. Only one respondent thought aspirants' personal views were most important. Katz concludes (p. 97) that 'these data illustrate clearly that the *only* way to secure nomination is to have an individual local base of support'.

Aspirants' political views (provided they are compatible with broad party policy) are rarely important, because the parties are not seriously divided internally along these lines, but they might occasionally be significant. Within Fianna Fáil party activists seem to attach special importance to the party's professed goal of bringing about a thirty-two county Irish Republic, so to be regarded as lukewarm, let alone hostile, towards this goal would reduce an aspirant's chances. At the elections of 1981–2, when the position of party leader Charles Haughey was under threat, aspirants' attitudes to his continued leadership may have counted with some delegates. Fine Gael in recent years has been divided between conservative and progressive wings, and for some delegates this factor would be important. Labour is divided on the coalition question, and at some of its selection conferences, especially in Dublin, it is clear that delegates attach very high significance to the aspirant's stand on this issue. The conflict can be particularly heated in Labour because often only one candidate is to be selected, so the ticket cannot reflect the balance of opinions among the membership. A protracted row in 1985–6 over the selection of a successor to a long-standing Labour deputy, Joe Bermingham, in the Kildare constituency, where the membership was split between pro- and anti-coalitionists, eventually led to Bermingham leaving the party in protest at the intervention of the party's national executive. Many local members also left, but the Labour seat was comfortably retained at the next election.

As in other countries whose electoral systems involve multi-member constituencies, a 'balanced' ticket is important. Locality is the only factor which conventions make an invariable point of balancing: this may be enforced explicitly by the national executive, as described above, and is in any case guaranteed by the proportional nature of the voting systems used at Fine Gael and Labour conventions. It is clear from numerous newspaper reports that conventions are keen, perhaps as much to satisfy the membership as to ensure the support of party voters, to nominate a panel of candidates who between them cover the constituency, rather than having candidates whose home bases are all close to one another. This is also evident from the backgrounds of those selected: Marsh (1981b: 274) shows that, within a party, a clustering of candidates' home bases is rare. Thus, for an aspirant, having a geographic base which would give the party a balanced ticket is also an asset. The other dimensions of group representation, which conventions in some other countries must bear in mind (religious, linguistic, occupational, ethnic and so on) do not have much salience. The only exceptions concern specific small areas. In the border counties, where there is a significant number (10–15 percent) of Protestants, the major parties sometimes include a Protestant on the ticket, while in the Galway West constituency they usually include a candidate from the Gaeltacht (Irish-speaking) area. Subsidiary groups, apart from the trade unions in Labour, play no part in the process for the simple reason that the parties do not have such groups, either as sections of the party or as autonomous affiliates. Parties do not try to balance the ticket with regard to gender; for example, Fianna Fáil selected only seven women among its 132 candidates in forty-one constituencies at the November 1982 election, and ten among 122 candidates in February 1987.

Influences on candidate selection

Electoral system

The single transferable vote (STV) in multi-member constituencies is designed to give a high degree of proportionality while maximizing voters' power to choose their representatives. Under the system, candidates' names are listed on the ballot paper not by party but in alphabetical order. Voters cast a vote by placing '1' by their first choice, '2' by their second, and so on. The vote is assigned to the first-choice candidate, with whom it remains unless he or she is either eliminated during the count or has a surplus above the quota necessary to secure election, in which case it passes to the voter's second choice, and so on (for descriptions of the system see Hand, 1979; Chubb, 1982: 350–3; Gallagher, 1986). STV has two main features: it is a preferential system, and voters can vote across party lines.

The fact that the system is preferential makes it especially important that a balanced ticket is presented so that, ideally, every potential party supporter can find on the ticket a candidate who attracts his or her first preference vote. Also, since the voters alone decide which of a party's candidates are elected, the latter are in intense competition with each other, competition which is liable to manifest itself at the key battleground of the nomination stage (see the section below on 'political style').

The second feature of STV, voters' power to cross party lines, forces the selectors to be sensitive to voters' wishes. STV is unique among PR systems in that a vote cannot help a candidate unless it explicitly contains a preference for him or her. Other PR systems involve party lists, and a vote cast for any candidate on the list (or for the entire list) could potentially be decisive in securing the election of any candidate on the list, even one the voter does not like. The need under STV for deputies to secure direct personal endorsement enables party voters to reject a candidate who is unacceptable to them without needing to desert the party. This, of course, would apply only to weak party identifiers; the strong ones would swallow their reservations and place attachment to the party ahead of dislike of one of its nominees. But when the number of votes separating victory from defeat is likely to be small (and in November 1982 the average margin between the last elected candidate and the runner-up was only about 1800 votes), the weak identifiers and the non-identifiers are vital. Besides, the lack of significant policy differences between the two main Irish parties means that a weak identifier of one of the parties, faced with a gap in his or her party's ticket, is likely to have little difficulty finding an acceptable candidate of the other party, such as one with a neigh-bourhood base, to fill it. Voters make wide use of their ability to cross party lines; analysis shows that from 20 to 40 percent of the main parties' supporters do not vote for the full party ticket (Gallagher, 1977: 4). This facility, then, restricts the freedom of manoeuvre of the selectors, and perhaps gives an extra boost in the selection process to those with demonstrated electoral popularity, such as incumbents and members of local councils.

At the same time there is one aspect of STV which allows a greater role for the national executive than most electoral systems permit. It is easier to add a name to a locally selected panel than under an electoral system employing single-member constituencies (where the national executive cannot put its own nominee on the ticket without displacing the local choice) or under an ordered list system (where giving someone a high place on the list means pushing everyone else down a place). Under STV the national executive can add a name without displacing anyone. If the local organization protests, the national executive can point out that it is simply increasing the choice available to the voters, and that, after all, if party voters do not like its nominee they can reject him or her. Excessive protests by any of the locally selected candidates may suggest fear that the new addition will prove more popular with the voters. Although there are dangers in a party nominating too many candidates (for discussion of whether there is an optimum number and, if so, what it is, see Katz, 1981; Gallagher, 1980: 492–5; Lijphart and Irwin, 1979), and it is possible that two candidates will fail to win a seat between them where one would have succeeded, it is nonetheless unlikely in most circumstances that nominating, say, four candidates instead of three will have any adverse effects.

Political culture
The electoral system, then, allows a high degree of expression of the voters' wishes, which raises the question of just what those wishes are. Many studies of Irish political culture (for example, Bax, 1976; Chubb, 1982: 14–17, 21; Sacks, 1976: 16–58) stress the importance of localism, and portray a population, especially in rural Ireland, which is intensely locally orientated and whose voting behaviour is strongly affected by perceptions of the respective candidates' abilities to secure grants and benefits for the local area and for individual constituents.

While this picture is not inaccurate, two qualifications must be made to it. First, party orientation is much stronger than local orientation. Far more of an eliminated candidate's votes pass to candidates of the same party whose bases lie elsewhere in the constituency than to locally based candidates of other parties (Marsh, 1981b; see also Carty, 1981: 63–9).

Second, the expectations which voters have of their parliamentary representatives should be seen not as an immutable and entirely independent input into the recruitment process but as a set of attitudes significantly affected by the way those representatives behave. It is not possible to test voters' insistence on having deputies with local roots, as the parties rarely nominate candidates without them, so Marsh (1981a) did not use local/non-local residence as an independent variable when analysing the impact of candidates' backgrounds on their performances. Voters have little choice but to vote for local candidates, since non-local aspirants rarely reach the ticket. Of course, given the closeness of most constituency contests, it is unlikely that selectors would persist in picking local candidates if they were actually less popular than the right kind of non-local candidate (such as one of apparently ministerial calibre). But it may well be that local candidates are not per se any *more* popular than such non-local candidates, and that the aversion to outsiders comes at least as much from the selectors, who want to reserve the prize of a nomination for members of the local organization, as from the electors.

If this is the case, why does the national executive make so little use of its power to add candidates to a locally selected panel, and why, when it does use it, does it add only local candidates, usually aspirants who were unsuccessful at the convention? There are two reasons. One, which applies only in certain cases, is that the imposition of such an outsider, warmly regarded by the leadership but unknown in the constituency, may have adverse electoral repercussions. If the newcomer really is unknown, he or she will have to be sold to the voters by the local organization, and if they are so resentful at the imposition that they refuse to campaign actively for him or her, a seat could be lost. But this does not apply in non-marginal constituencies, where the national executive could direct the local convention to select one candidate fewer than the number of seats the party is certain to win, and then add a centrally approved outsider, knowing that party voters will, because of the strength of their party identification, elect him or her, even if reluctantly. Why does the national executive not do this even when an incumbent stands down in a non-marginal constituency, i.e. when a newcomer can be given a seat without displacing an incumbent?

The explanation lies not in mass political culture but in the parties' own political cultures. Although such direct central involvement would be possible under party rules, it would violate the consensus on which parties operate, by creating resentment among party members. This resentment, it is true, could probably be absorbed by the parliamentary party: there is little that disgruntled members can do to deputies since the latter are not answerable to the membership except through the nomination process. But party leaderships do not wish to alienate the membership, not because the membership could take punitive retaliation but because to sweep aside the wishes of the members would violate the spirit of the organizations. In the centre-right Irish parties the membership has no effective say in the making of party policy, and its right to select candidates is the only real power it has. The centre is happy with the tacit consensus under which the membership selects candidates and policy-making is left to the leadership. The political culture of the party, which expects this state of affairs, is stronger than a legalistic interpretation of the rules, which would allow central control.

This, together with whatever degree of localism may exist among voters, greatly restricts the power of the national organization in imposing a candidate. It means that the national executive cannot add one of its protégés — an aide of the party leader, a head office researcher — to a locally selected panel, even though it has the right, under the parties' constitutions, to do so. The most that can be done by the central organization is to give a boost to one local aspirant as opposed to another, and even this must be done sensitively. It must appear that the centre is attempting to win an extra seat for the party rather than simply helping a favoured aspirant at the expense of another. To some extent this is less true in Dublin, where local roots are not a sine qua non for election, but it is a serious constraint on the central organization's power over most of the country.

Irish political style
Deputies' heavy emphasis on brokerage work for constituents, over matters like eligibility for grants and delay in social welfare payments, which is widely regarded as a characteristic of Irish political style (see Komito, 1984; Farrell, 1985; Roche, 1982), plays an important part in shaping the nature of the selection process. It means that contests at the nomination stage are largely centred on personalities, and strengthens the position of incumbents.

It does this because it leads to the creation by established and aspiring deputies of personal 'machines'. Carty (1981), outlining the process, explains how politicians aim to win control of the local party organization by a variety of means, such as installing 'personally loyal supporters, including astonishing numbers of relatives . . . as local branch officers to solidify control' (p. 130). The personal machine provides 'a steady stream of gossip and information, allowing a politician to anticipate, as well as respond to, his constituents' needs. By seeing to it that specific requests for help are channelled to their leader, rather than one of his party competitors, these local contacts help reinforce and expand their sponsor's network of supporters' (p. 130). Documenting machine-building in one particular constituency, Carty relates (p. 132) how a new deputy developed 'a network of contacts reaching into each polling area'. These people, about 120 in number, formed the deputy's personal machine, assisting him in constituency work and steering constituents in his direction. Wherever possible they 'were integrated into the formal party organization', reinforcing the deputy's 'influence and control over the constituency party'. The creation of personal machines is the weapon resorted to by all deputies in order to try to build up a strong brokerage base, partly to protect themselves against rivals in other parties but mainly to strengthen their position against rivals in their own party. Deputies in Ireland do not, and indeed cannot afford to, practise the lofty disengagement from local affairs recommended for British MPs (Barker and Rush, 1970: 208).

Consequently, a party's local organization is very often, in effect, dominated by the local party deputy or deputies. The people who select the candidates at conventions are, to a considerable extent, the very people installed by the deputies in positions of power in the local organizations. This means that local deputies have a major say in candidate selection. It does not give them complete control of it, because the political machine-building process is not a static one, and a deputy can never rest secure in the knowledge that he controls the local party organization. Other deputies are seeking to carve out larger areas for themselves; aspiring deputies are struggling to build up their own machines; and even some of the key personnel in the deputy's own machine may nurture parliamentary ambitions, and may be judging when to make a move against the deputy. Deputies' political machines, as Carty observes (1981: 133), are 'inherently unstable'. Nonetheless, while they last they are a formidable weapon, and they ensure that a lot of power in the local organization rests with the deputies.

Consequences

Parliamentary party discipline

Since TDs depend for reselection on the local party organization, which they come close to controlling, it seems that they are free to defy the party whip in Parliament without much fear of being deselected. Given the already mentioned importance of localism, one might expect deputies to be very responsive to local pressures when it comes to voting in Parliament. But in fact deputies vote solidly along party lines in the Dáil, and defiance of the whip is very exceptional. Even when contentious local issues arise, such as the closing of a county hospital, it is standard practice for the deputies concerned to voice their discontent but still vote with their party.

The main reason for this is the salience of party in binding the parliamentary group together and in determining voters' behaviour. Deputies have a loyalty to their party, an emotional identification with it, and a disposition to respect the decisions it and its parliamentary group reach. Moreover, they know that they have little chance of re-election if they lose the party label. Voting against the party in Parliament is likely, certainly if it is persistent or if it occurs in a key vote, to lead to the loss of the party whip; it will also, of course, severely damage a deputy's prospects of promotion. Repeated infringements may lead to expulsion from the party, in which case a deputy will be in no position to seek selection as a party candidate. In this eventuality his or her constituency work over the years will count for little, as all the evidence shows that this is useful primarily in attracting support only within the pool of party votes, so a deselected deputy running as an independent will find that most of his or her previous support remains with the party (this is shown for erstwhile major party candidates generally by Mair, 1987: 67–8). The point was emphasized in 1973 (Carty, 1981: 135) when a number of Fianna Fáil deputies, some with very successful electoral records, broke with their party and ran as independents. Only one was re-elected. In February 1987 two deselected Fine Gael TDs, Alice Glenn and Liam Skelly, ran as independents and polled very poorly.

Moreover, a deputy's organization, even if it is a personal machine, might be loyal to him only for as long as he remains within the party fold. Party members have a loyalty not only to their deputies but also to the party and its leader, and if the first loyalty comes into conflict with the others, many will refuse to back a deputy who has defied the leader and/or contributed to party disunity. Ambitious members of the deputy's machine will see in his expulsion an opportunity to advance their own political careers. It is also possible that a rebellious deputy, even if he is not expelled from the party and is reselected as a candidate, might be refused ratification by the national executive. This has not happened yet, but in February 1985, in the run-up to an important Dáil vote on liberalizing the law on the availability of contraceptives, two members of

Fine Gael's national executive said that they would vote to veto the ratification at the next election of any deputy who was outside the parliamentary party as a result of losing the whip over the issue. In the event three deputies opposed the bill and lost the whip (though it was restored within a year). It was not clear how widely this view was shared by other national executive members, but it clearly signalled a desire among some sections of the party to use the candidate selection process as a means of enforcing the extra-parliamentary organization's wishes on the parliamentary group.[3]

In September 1986 the party leader, Garret FitzGerald, announced that he would ask constituency organization chairpersons to try to ensure that deputies who 'stepped out of line' were deselected, and this fate subsequently befell two mavericks. One, Alice Glenn, had voted against her party on several issues, and had been deprived of the party whip for a while. She was an outspoken opponent of moves towards making the Republic a pluralist state, and of her own party leader. Her defeat at the Dublin Central convention came a few days after she had described those who favoured the legalization of divorce, including the leaders of the minority churches, as 'enemies of the people'. The other, Liam Skelly, had often criticised the party leadership and the bulk of the parliamentary party, and had threatened to vote against the party in the Dáil unless his special demands were met.

So, in Ireland, the importance of party as a voting cue, and as a unifying force for deputies and members, outweighs the dominant position which deputies normally have in the selection process, which might otherwise free them from party discipline in Parliament. The nature of the candidate selection process may work in the expected direction, but, if so, other factors outweigh its impact.

Deputies and local activists
The fact that nomination decisions are taken locally might seem to mean that deputies need to be responsive to the views of local activists. But, in practice, cases of incumbents being threatened with deselection unless they adhere to a particular line are virtually unknown. The motivations behind activists' joining and remaining within the Irish parties have not been studied in depth (though see Mair, 1975, and Garvin, 1976), but activists do not appear to demand more of their deputies than conformity to the broad outlines of party policy. Nor are activists likely to deselect a deputy on the ground that, by refusing to cross party lines in the Dáil, he or she has not been sufficiently assiduous in defending local interests, for they understand the limits of what can realistically be expected. Consequently, locally active deputies have little to fear from

activists provided they do not drift unacceptably far from the party consensus, a route few take. In the cases of Glenn and Skelly, discussed above, it was clearly the TD rather than the activists whose views were far from the party mainstream.

Members are not, then, interested in the deputy simply as a tangible representative of an abstract philosophy; instead they usually have a personal regard for and loyalty to him or her. But, as was pointed out in the previous section, this loyalty is not an unconditional one: members, like voters, combine loyalty to party with loyalty to a deputy, and might disown the latter if the two loyalties come into conflict. This could happen if, for example, a deputy was involved in an effort to displace the party leader. When a number of Fianna Fáil deputies did attempt to unseat their leader, Charles Haughey, shortly before the November 1982 general election, there were rumblings among activists in some constituencies, and suggestions that more TDs would have voted for a change of leader had the crucial vote been a secret one; they feared to do so in an open vote, it was believed, because they might be deselected by the membership, who were generally reckoned to be strong supporters of Haughey. Despite the discontent expressed by some activists, though, no deputy was deselected, and none was in serious danger of suffering this fate. A decentralized nomination process, then, far from turning deputies into puppets of local activists, scarcely restricts them at all, provided they keep within the broad confines of what is acceptable to the party.

The survival rate of incumbents
The dominant role in the nomination process of incumbent deputies could be expected to result in very few of them failing to win reselection. This proves to be the case. Instances of incumbents failing to be reselected have been very rare in the past, numbering no more than about one every two elections. Deselections generally arose only if a deputy had become old and tired, or had lost interest in remaining in the Dáil, and had no longer made the effort to keep his or her personal machine in good trim. In February 1987 there were four deselections, perhaps the most ever to occur at an election. Apart from Glenn and Skelly, the other two were simply victims of other aspirants' personal machines. One, Tom Leonard, was a Fianna Fáil TD in Dublin Central who had no organizational strength in the constituency, as shown by his derisory vote (four out of sixty) at the selection conference. The other, Dick Dowling, a Fine Gael TD in Carlow-Kilkenny, was much stronger, but was outmanoeuvred by rivals. With eighty-six votes at the convention, he fell just short of the 103 needed for a nomination (*Kilkenny*

People, 30 January 1987). Having been deselected, he refused appeals by the national executive to allow his name to be added to the ticket. At the election Fine Gael did not retain the seat he had held.

With deselections rare, it might seem that a deputy could achieve more than merely being reselected; he might be in a position to use his strength in the process to boost his re-election prospects by ensuring that the party ticket contains no one who could threaten his electoral position, such as someone whose home base is close to his own. If there are two party deputies in the constituency, they might agree to throw their weight at the selection conference behind a weak aspirant for the third place on the ticket.

Unquestionably, there are cases where this happens. For example, in the late 1960s, when the Labour Party's central organization decided that each of the party's outgoing deputies must be accompanied on the ticket by a running mate, several of these running mates were clearly just makeweights (Gallagher, 1980: 498–9). In addition, it may happen within the major parties at by-elections (held to fill casual vacancies between general elections), when incumbent deputies do not wish to boost the position of an internal party rival who could take their seat at the next general election. But it is doubtful whether the practice is as widespread as might be expected, for the evidence is that incumbents have not by any means managed to eliminate internal threats to their positions. Studying the elections of the 1948–77 period, Carty (1981: 115–16) found that incumbents of the two main parties sustained as many as 42 percent of their defeats to other candidates of their own party and concludes that 'fellow partisans' rather than candidates of any other specific party 'constitute the single most important source of competition'. At the following three elections (held in 1981 and 1982), fellow partisans proved even more of a threat, for of the fifty-one incumbents of the two main parties to suffer defeat, thirty were unseated by another candidate of their own party and only twenty-one by another party's nominee. At February 1987, though, only five of the twenty-four deputies were ousted by one of their party's other candidates.

Variations between the two main parties since 1977 in this respect are illuminating because of the different voting procedures they use at their conventions. Because Fianna Fáil conventions vote separately for each place on the ticket, a deputy or an alliance of local notables controlling a majority of convention votes could determine the composition of the entire ticket. But under Fine Gael's system all places are voted on simultaneously, and so an incumbent's supporters have to use their votes to ensure his or her selection; they cannot be reused en bloc to affect the other places. Consequently, if repelling internal threats was uppermost in incumbents' minds at convention time, one would expect to find that Fianna Fáil deputies, who can minimize the threat, are less likely to be unseated by running mates than Fine Gael deputies, who cannot.

The reverse turns out to be the case. Of the thirty-eight Fianna Fáil incumbents to suffer defeat at the elections of 1981–2, twenty-three (60.5 percent) lost their seat to a running mate, whereas in Fine Gael the corresponding proportion was seven out of thirteen (53.8 percent). In February 1987 three of the four defeated Fianna Fáil TDs, but only two of the fourteen defeated Fine Gael TDs, were replaced by a running mate. The absence of the predicted relationship, coupled with the fact that in both parties replacement by running mates often accounts for over half of incumbent defeats, suggests strongly that either they do not try to keep attractive alternatives off the party ticket, or, if they do try, they are singularly unsuccessful.

The explanation for deputies' apparent reluctance to exploit their numerical dominance of conventions in this way is simply that 'talent suppression' of this nature is not always in a deputy's own interests. The affected aspirant's camp will be alienated, and may not campaign for the panel selected, with adverse effects on the party vote. If the deputy, by placing her own interests ahead of those of the party, seems to have cost the party a seat, her standing in the party and her prospects of preferment will be reduced. In contrast, a deputy who encourages the selection of a strong running mate, putting her own seat at risk in the hope of gaining an extra seat, will improve her standing. From 1977 onwards Fine Gael made a determined effort to tackle the first type of deputy, termed a 'quota squatter', and organizational reforms, such as the 'model system' outlined earlier, were introduced to open up local party organization and take it out of the local deputy's hands. Deputies knew what the leadership wanted, and this was a factor in inducing some to encourage the selection of strong rather than weak candidates as their running mates.

The backgrounds of deputies and the nature of the legislature

If the nature of candidate selection is an important factor in the Irish recruitment process, evidence of this should be detectable from scrutiny of deputies' backgrounds. There are two ways of examining this: first by comparing the Dáil with other legislatures, and secondly by analysing interparty differences in the Dáil.

Comparing the Dáil with other legislatures throws up three main points of contrast (see Table 6.2). Of the deputies elected in November 1982, the proportion of university graduates is relatively low; small businessmen (who comprise nearly all of those in the 'business' category, and form 25 percent of all deputies) are unusually prominent; a high proportion (also about 25 percent) were related to present or former deputies. In addition, the over-whelming majority had strong local roots before they were first elected, and most were or had been local authority members, though these two characteristics are not especially unusual for parliamentarians.

Table 6.2   *Backgrounds of deputies elected in the November 1982 general election (in percent)*

Occupation	
Employee	16.3
Business	27.1
Farmer	12.7
Professional	41.6
Other	2.4
Education	
University degree	38.0
Gender	
Male	91.6
Female	8.4
Age	
Under 30	5.4
30–39	27.1
40–49	36.7
50–59	25.3
60+	5.4
Local government	
Past or present membership	77.7

Source: Gallagher (1985b)

It is striking that several of these attributes were found, in a study of the November 1982 Dáil (the most recent to be analysed), to be inversely related to the prospects of becoming a minister.[4] Most (52 percent) deputies to have been ministers had a university degree, compared with only 33 percent of other deputies. Of the deputies never to have been local authority members, 41 percent had entered the cabinet compared with only 20 percent of those who had been local councillors before entering Parliament. Both of these relationships became stronger when a control was introduced for seniority (Gallagher, 1985b: 386–7). Thus the political recruitment process, in which candidate selection plays a significant part, produces deputies who are not, by the criteria applied in ministerial appointment, well qualified for government. Carty (1981: 137) argues that the 'talent suppression' practices engaged in by incumbents, both when candidates are selected and at earlier stages of the recruitment process, 'result in the promotion of decidedly mediocre individuals, handicapping the parties' ability to provide the system with effective political leadership'.

In addition, it is often argued (see, for example, Ward, 1974, and Chubb, 1982: 205–29) that the Dáil is an exceptionally weak and ineffective parliament, due largely to so many deputies' low level of educational attainment and strong local orientation. Several surveys have been conducted into deputies' work. The most recent (Roche, 1982: 100–1), conducted in 1981, finds that deputies reported working an average of seventy-five hours per week. Of this, half was spent on constituency work and less than 10 percent on 'attending in the Dáil chamber and reviewing legislation'. Every single respondent said that constituency work occupied more of their time than any other political duty. Deputies were asked to deal with an average of 140 'representations' a week, which works out at about 100 casework contacts per week per 10,000 constituents, an exceptionally high figure (Gallagher, 1985b: 390). One result is that deputies are, not surprisingly, well known to their constituents. A survey conducted in 1976, over three years after the previous general election, found that only a quarter of respondents could not name any of the deputies in their constituency, and many (38 percent in three-seat constituencies) could name all of them (Farrell, 1985: 245–7).

In each of these points the impact of the candidate selection process is apparent. To be selected it is essential to have a strong base in the local organization, which needs to be built up over a period of time and is reinforced by acquiring a local elective office. Virtually the only way of acquiring such a base without going through this process is by inheriting one, which partly accounts for the high proportion of relatives in the Dáil. There is certainly no reason to suppose that it reflects the desires of the electorate, as there is no evidence that voters themselves penalize, through their use of preference votes, candidates of ministerial timbre and boost the success rate of candidates who have a local authority background and are non-graduates. It is true that there is no direct evidence that it reflects the selectors' values, in the sense of unsuccessful aspirants being more likely to possess 'ministerial' attributes than those picked. But it might well be the case that since the selectors' values are so well known, those without the factors which make for success, such as holding a local effective office and having a base in the local organization, do not even bother to seek a candidacy.

Finally, the candidate selection process may well have a bearing on the number of women in the Dáil. The November 1982 election returned fourteen, as did the February 1987 election (8.4 percent of the total), not markedly lower than in most competitively elected legislatures outside Scandinavia. The reasons why women are underrepresented in all parliaments are many (see, for example, Randall, 1982: 84–99, and, for Ireland, Gallagher, 1984: 253–5), and obviously extend well beyond the nature of the candidate selection process. Even so, this process may be an additional barrier in Ireland. The aspirants who are best placed to succeed are those who have spent some time building up a local base, both elective and organizational. The average deputy first stands for the Dáil when aged about thirty-six which means that this type of self-establishment is usually done in the late twenties and early thirties. This is just the period when many women are least able to participate in a political career, which requires the freedom to take time off at irregular intervals, given the persisting cultural norm that women should bear the prime responsibility for bringing up the children and running the home. Thus women find it harder than men to win selection via the creation of a 'machine' within the local organization.

In the past, at least, women have certainly needed, more often than men, to rely on central intervention to win a place on a party ticket. In 1977 six of the sixteen candidates added by Fianna Fáil's national executive were women, compared with only six among the 116 selected locally (Marsh, 1981b: 276). In November 1982, though, only one of the eleven candidates added by the two major parties' national executives between them was a woman, compared with eighteen among the 236 selected locally.

Turning to interparty variations, it should first be pointed out that Fine Gael's greater centralization does not manifest itself in a lower proportion of deputies with local roots, since, as was argued above, head office intervention can at most help one local aspirant vis-a-vis others, rather than help 'outsiders' win selection. Nor does the pledge demanded from Fine Gael and PD aspirants that they will make payments to the party if elected favour wealthy individuals, since all the parties, with the possible exception of Fianna Fáil, demand dues from their parliamentarians. There are, though, four differences between the parliamentary groups elected in November

1982 (for details, see Gallagher, 1984) which may be related to the slightly higher degree of central involvement in Fine Gael's candidate selection process. First, Fine Gael had a higher proportion of women deputies (13 percent) than Fianna Fáil (5 percent) or Labour (6 percent). This is a recent development: there was only one female Fine Gael TD elected in 1977, but nine were elected in November 1982. Some of these Fine Gael women became candidates after encouragement from the leadership, sometimes coupled with pressure on the local organization. In contrast, the other parties, which did not alter their selection processes between 1977 and 1982, had no more women TDs elected in 1982 than in 1977.

Second, Fine Gael deputies were less likely than other deputies to have been members of a local authority. Third, Fine Gael deputies, especially those entering the Dáil after the organizational reforms took place, had received most education. Fourth, Fine Gael had the youngest TDs. Each of these differences could be seen as brought about partly by the centre trying to secure the selection of relatively young people of parliamentary and ministerial ability, who have not followed the traditional route of building up a local electoral and organizational base, in preference to candidates oriented mainly towards constituency service. Admittedly, the last two could be explained by other factors. High education among Fine Gael deputies reflects the fact that the party is strongest among voters with high education, and the youth of its 1982 deputies may result simply from its having the newest parliamentary party.

The other two parties' selection processes also have unique features. Labour's gives an advantage to union-backed aspirants, and a high proportion of its deputies and candidates are union members. Many are full-time union employees: in November 1982, 30 percent of Labour candidates and 37 percent of its deputies were trade union officials, who have always comprised a high proportion of the party's parliamentary group. The unusual feature of Fianna Fáil's selection process is that aspirants are not permitted even to attend the convention, as noted earlier, whereas in the other parties they usually address the convention. Just as the British Labour Party's convention format favours well-educated middle-class aspirants because of the importance attached to the quality of the convention speech (Bochel and Denver, 1983: 58–9), so Fianna Fáil's barring of aspirants could be seen as likely to protect the inarticulate. There is, though, no evidence concerning interparty variations in deputies' articulateness. There is no sign that Fianna Fáil deputies use the Irish language more often than other deputies, despite the party's conventions' supposed preference for Irish-speaking nominees.

Conclusion

It has been argued above that in Ireland ordinary party members are quite widely involved in the selection process, but that powerful roles are played by the incumbent deputies and, within limits, the central organization. Incumbents are almost certain of reselection, as in most countries, and they may be able to minimize the challenge from internal party rivals, although empirical evidence shows that they cannot by any means eliminate it. Party head offices have in recent years become increasingly active in the process, and often add names to those selected locally. This is made possible by the electoral system, and is accepted by the local membership provided the centre respects the convention that any added candidates be local people.

The lack of central control does not produce fissiparous parliamentary parties. On the contrary, deputies are for the most part as loyal to the party line as any leadership could want, as is true of many countries where selection is under the control of the local organization. But this does not prove that the locus of control is unimportant, for even if the result in terms of legislative cohesion is much the same no matter who controls the process, there may be other consequences. It has been suggested in this chapter that, at the nomination stage, the selectors, mainly local branch members, may introduce a specific set of values into the recruitment process. They may attach greater importance than the voters would to such factors as membership of the local party organization and holding a local elective office, and less importance than the voters to factors like high education. Certain aspects of deputies' backgrounds, both collectively and with respect to interparty differences, support this suggestion. If it is accurate, then the candidate selection process is more than simply an impartial transmitter of the electorate's values; it has consequences for the calibre of deputies and, more importantly, for the calibre of government ministers. It is a key stage, one with an independent effect of its own, which enables the selectors to inject their own values into the recruitment process. These values concern candidates' backgrounds more than their views on policy matters, which suggests that, in Ireland at least, the importance of candidate selection may lie more in its role in political recruitment than in its being an arena of intraparty conflict.

Notes

I should like to thank Peter Mair and Michael Marsh for comments on earlier drafts.

1. The sources used for the following account are:*Fianna Fáil Constitution and Rules* (Dublin: Fianna Fáil, 1983); *Fine Gael Constitution and Rules* (Dublin: Fine

Gael, 1982); *Model System for Conventions and AGMs* (Dublin: Fine Gael, nd); *Labour Party Constitution* (Dublin: Irish Labour Party, 1979); *Standing Orders for Dáil Selection Conferences* (Dublin: Irish Labour Party, 1973); *Workers' Party Constitution* (Dublin: Workers' Party, 1983); *Sinn Féin Constitution and Rules* (Dublin: Sinn Féin, 1983); *Progressive Democrats' Constitution and Rules* (Dublin, 1986).

2. Reference to first and subsequent places on the panel denotes only the order in which candidates are selected. This should not be confused with selection of candidates in countries where national elections employ a list system, where decisions must be made as to who receives which place on the party list. Under Ireland's electoral system the names of all candidates, regardless of party affiliation, appear on the ballot paper in alphabetical order, so the order in which candidates are selected by the convention makes no difference whatsoever to the prospects of any of them. This means that there is no such thing as a 'safe', 'marginal' or 'hopeless' place on the ticket, so it is not possible, as it is in some countries, to compare the characteristics of individuals alloted to these three categories.

3. For the 1979 European Parliament election the Fine Gael convention in the Dublin constituency selected as a candidate a deputy who had been expelled from the parliamentary party for defying the whip, though remaining a member of the party as a whole. The national executive refused to ratify him, and this did not lead to a significant adverse reaction among members.

4. Virtually all ministers are Dáil deputies; although the constitution makes provision (in article 28.7) for two ministers per government to belong instead to the Seanad (the upper house), there have been only two such ministers since 1937.

References

Barker, Anthony and Michael Rush (1970) *The Member of Parliament and His Information*. London: George Allen & Unwin.

Bax, Mart (1976) *Harpstrings and Confessions*. Assen: Van Gorcum.

Bochel, John and David Denver (1983) 'Candidate Selection in the Labour Party: What the Selectors Seek', *British Journal of Political Science*, 13 (1): 45–69.

Carty, R.K. (1981) *Party and Parish Pump: Electoral Politics in Ireland*. Waterloo, Ontario: Wilfrid Laurier University Press.

Chubb, Basil (1982) *The Government and Politics of Ireland*, 2nd ed. London: Longman.

Farrell, Brian (1985) 'Ireland: From Friends and Neighbours to Clients and Partisans: Some Dimensions of Parliamentary Representation under PR-STV', pp. 237–64 in Vernon Bogdanor (ed.), *Representatives of the People?* Aldershot: Gower.

Gallagher, Michael (1977) 'Party Solidarity, Exclusivity and Inter-Party Relationships in Ireland 1922–1977: the Evidence of Transfers', *Economic and Social Review*, 10 (1): 1–22.

Gallagher, Michael (1980) 'Candidate Selection in Ireland: The Impact of Localism and the Electoral System', *British Journal of Political Science*, 10 (4): 489–503.

Gallagher, Michael (1984) '166 Who Rule: The Dáil Deputies of November 1982', *Economic and Social Review*, 15 (4): 241–64.

Gallagher, Michael (1985a) *Political Parties in the Republic of Ireland*. Manchester: Manchester University Press.

Gallagher, Michael (1985b) 'Social Backgrounds and Local Orientations of Members of the Irish Dáil', *Legislative Studies Quarterly*, 10 (3): 373–94.

Gallagher, Michael (1986) 'The Political Consequences of the Electoral System in the Republic of Ireland', *Electoral Studies*, 5 (3): 253–75.

Garvin, Tom (1976) 'Local Party Activists in Dublin: Socialization, Recruitment and Incentives', *British Journal of Political Science*, 6 (3): 359–72.

Hand, Geoffrey (1979) 'Ireland', pp. 121–39 in Geoffrey Hand, Jacques Georgel and Christoph Sasse (eds), *European Electoral Systems Handbook*. London: Butterworths.

Katz, Richard S. (1980) *A Theory of Parties and Electoral Systems*. Baltimore and London: Johns Hopkins University Press.

Katz, Richard S. (1981) 'But How Many Candidates Should We Have in Donegal? Numbers of Nominees and Electoral Efficiency in Ireland', *British Journal of Political Science*, 11 (1): 117–23.

Komito, Lee (1984) 'Irish Clientelism: A Reappraisal', *Economic and Social Review*, 15 (3): 173–94.

Lijphart, Arend and Galen A. Irwin (1979) 'Nomination Strategies in the Irish STV System: The Dáil Elections of 1969, 1973 and 1977', *British Journal of Political Science*, 9 (3): 362–9.

Mair, Peter (1975) 'Social Factors in the Maintenance of Party Loyalty', *Social Studies*, 4 (2): 152–61.

Mair, Peter (1987) *The Changing Irish Party System: Organisation, Ideology and Electoral Competition*. London: Frances Pinter.

Marsh, Michael (1981a) 'Electoral Preferences in Irish Recruitment: The 1977 Election', *European Journal of Political Research*, 9 (1): 61–74.

Marsh, Michael (1981b) 'Localism, Candidate Selection and Electoral Preferences in Ireland: the general election of 1977', *Economic and Social Review*, 12 (4): 267–86.

Randall, Vicky (1982) *Women and Politics*. London: Macmillan.

Ranney, Austin (1981) 'Candidate Selection', pp. 75–106 in David Butler, Howard R. Penniman and Austin Ranney (eds), *Democracy at the Polls*. Washington DC: American Enterprise Institute.

Roche, Richard (1982) 'The High Cost of Complaining Irish Style', *Journal of Irish Business and Administrative Research*, 4 (2): 98–108.

Sacks, Paul Martin (1976) *The Donegal Mafia*. New Haven: Yale University Press.

Ward, Alan J. (1974) 'Parliamentary Procedures and the Machinery of Government in Ireland', *Irish University Review*, 4 (2): 222–43.

7

Italy: local involvement, central control

Douglas A. Wertman

In the 1983 parliamentary elections about 10,000 candidates were selected by Italy's political parties to compete for the 945 seats available in the Chamber of Deputies and the Senate. Candidate selection always receives a great deal of publicity during Italian parliamentary election campaigns. This has been particularly true since 1976 because of its direct use by the major parties as part of their national political and electoral strategy in trying to project a certain image, or to create a new one.

Two aspects of candidate selection have attracted special attention. First, there is the inclusion by some parties, especially the Italian Communist Party (PCI) since 1976 and the Christian Democratic Party (DC) in 1983, of prestigious independents in their lists. Second, there is the effort made in 1976 and 1983 by the DC, whose parliamentary personnel had changed little in the 1960s and early 1970s, to increase the rate of turnover among its parliamentary delegation. In the case of the Communists this was part of their effort to project the image of a party with broad support and one fully committed to pluralist democracy. In the case of the DC, which had been continuously in power since 1945, this was part of a campaign strategy in the 1976 and 1983 elections to overcome a negative image by projecting one of a 'new DC'.[1] Nevertheless, despite the importance given to candidate selection by the parties themselves and the press, it has received little systematic attention by researchers.

The political environment

The electoral system
This chapter differs somewhat from most others in this book in that candidate selection for both the lower house of parliament, the Chamber of Deputies, and the upper house, the Senate, will be examined. This is because in Italy, unlike in most other West European parliamentary systems, the two houses have identical legislative powers and a new government must receive a vote of

confidence from both houses. Furthermore, the two electoral systems, while somewhat different, are both highly proportional and therefore produce houses with similar political compositions.[2] Both houses have always been elected at the same time, even though this is not legally necessary, because the government parties have wanted to ensure roughly the same majority in both houses. Therefore, the selection of candidates for the two houses should be considered one process rather than two.

The electoral systems determine, first, how many seats each party wins and, second, which individual candidates are awarded the seats their party has won. The imperiali largest remainder system is used to allocate Chamber seats to the parties. It is one of the most precise of proportional representation electoral systems, particularly because of the national pool of remainders which allows parties reaching the quota for a seat in even one of the thirty-one multi-member constituencies (varying in size from three seats to fifty-four seats) to qualify for their full national share of seats.[3] Therefore, parties with as little as 1 or 2 percent of the national votes can get seats in the Chamber. Because of the smaller number of seats for the Senate (315 compared to 630 for the Chamber), which creates a higher quota for a single seat, and the lack of a national pool of remainders under the d'Hondt highest average system used for the Senate, some of the smallest parties represented in the Chamber may not gain seats in the Senate. Nevertheless, the different electoral systems create only minor differences in the political composition of the two houses.

There are, however, greater differences in the second stage, the allocation of each party's seats to individual candidates, which have important implications for candidate selection. In particular, when voting for the Chamber of Deputies, the individual voter may, after choosing his or her party, cast up to three or four preference votes for candidates on the party's lists. It is these preference votes (which only about 30 percent of the voters – varying greatly between north and south and among the parties – bother to cast) rather than the order of the list presented by the party which determine who will win each party's seats in a Chamber district. Consequently, at Chamber elections there is an open battle for preference votes among the individual candidates within each party's lists, except in the Communist Party, where the preference votes are more controlled. This has a significant impact on the style of Chamber elections, in that candidates, except in the PCI, must build personal election machines to mobilize the votes necessary to win one of their party's seats.[4]

By contrast, candidate selection for the Senate elections

resembles that for a non-preferential party list system, since the parties, when selecting Senate candidates, largely determine who the winners, marginals and losers will be. There is no intraparty competition for Senate seats during the election campaign, since each Senate constituency has only one candidate per party. Determination of which individuals win each party's seats is done within each region (except for tiny Val d'Aosta, each of Italy's twenty regions elects two or more senators) in the order of the percentage vote the party receives in each Senate district.[5] As a result of this system a kind of positioning on lists clearly does take place for the Senate because each party has a good idea, from past elections, about which constituencies in each region are safe, which are marginal and which are hopeless.

The post-war political system
Italy's economy and society have undergone substantial change in the period since Second World War, while the party system and political institutions have seen little change. There has been no alternation of power as there has been in other West European democracies, primarily because the major opposition force has been the Communist Party, rather than a socialist or social democratic party. The largest party, the Christian Democratic Party (34.3 percent in the 1987 Chamber elections), has, through a series of different multi-party coalition formulae, been in every post-war government since December 1945 (forty-six up to September 1987), while the second largest party, the Communist Party (26.6 percent in the 1987 Chamber elections), has not had ministers in any government since 1947.

Furthermore, the basic choices facing voters have been pretty much the same in all elections throughout the post-war period. Italy has had a multi-party system since 1945, with at least eight parties represented in Parliament at any one time, and the changes in the party system have been very limited. Only a few small parties have gone out of existence in the post-war period, and a few small regionalist and leftist parties have been formed in the last ten to fifteen years.

There has also been very little change in Italy's political institutions, with the limited exception of the setting up of regional governments. Since the mid-1970s this lack of change, accompanied by the inability of multi-party coalitions to take strong decisions to deal with Italy's economic and social problems and the permanence in power of the DC, has sparked a widely publicized, broad-ranging debate among political elites and scholars about Italy's governability and the need for institutional reform. However, little meaningful reform of the political system is likely to result at any time in the near future.

The selection process

There is no legal regulation of the candidate selection process within Italy's parties, even though the parties are mentioned in the Constitution and receive public subsidies, and although the parties and winning parliamentary candidates are obliged to file reports (which no one ever checks) on expenditures and receipts. Furthermore, the candidate selection process itself has been mentioned only very infrequently in the debate on institutional reform, largely because the parties do not want state regulation of their internal procedures.[6] Consequently, candidate selection is entirely a matter for the parties. In fact, it is the extra-parliamentary party organizations, many of whose top leaders are also members of Parliament, which in most cases have the final word on major decisions, whether governmental, parliamentary or more strictly political. While some effort has been made in some parties over the last decade to change the outcome of candidate selection, the process itself, like the party organizations, has changed relatively little in the post-war period.

The Christian Democratic Party

Two major factors must be kept in mind in examining the DC's candidate selection process. First, a parliamentary career is crucial to achieving a top position in the DC; virtually every one of the DC ministers and under-secretaries as well as three quarters or more of the members of the National Executive Committee (the party's top policy-making body) have been members of Parliament. Second, decision-making at all levels of the DC party organization is (and has always been) highly factionalized; party policy results from conflict and compromise among the party's well-organized factions (of which there are currently eight or nine), whose top leaders are normally members of Parliament who sit in the National Executive Committee of the party or the Cabinet. The path to career advancement in the DC is largely through factional channels.

The official party rules of the DC (Democrazia Cristiana, 1985), which are rather detailed compared with those of most other parties, provide the general framework within which the faction-based system of the DC works. Candidate selection begins with general, but non-binding, guidelines from the National Executive Committee to the provincial and regional party organizations on what factors to consider in choosing candidates. These may vary somewhat from election to election. In 1983, for example, the local party organizations were told that those with twenty-five or more years of parliamentary service should be renominated only if special justification, based on their national or local work, could be found. Such special justification was eventually found for about two thirds in this category, indicating the difficulty of deselecting incumbents. Local party organizations were also urged not to nominate elected officials from regional, provincial and communal councils serving their first term, or elected officials at these levels serving in administrative positions.

In addition to these guidelines, the National Executive Committee issued a number of binding directives to the local party organizations which were very much like the directives issued in all previous parliamentary elections. First, each provincial party organization is told how many candidates it can choose for the Chamber lists. (Since all but two Chamber constituencies contain two or more provinces, the number of names each provincial party organization in the DC can propose is, as in other parties, based on the proportion of the Chamber constituency's population which resides within that province.) As party rules provide, the National Executive Committee reserves the right (which it generally does not ultimately use) to pick one Chamber candidate in constituencies with twenty seats or less and two in constituencies with more than twenty seats. For the Senate, the National Executive Committee, as set forth in the rules, indicates that it will reserve a certain number of Senate constituencies, safe ones of course, where it will name the candidate itself. In addition to the approximately thirty safe Senate seats which it always reserves for itself, the National Executive Committee in 1983, as discussed below, also reserved twenty-three Senate constituencies in the four largest urban areas.

Based on these guidelines and directives, the provincial party organization puts together its proposed candidate slate for the Chamber and for any Senate district for which it has the right to propose a candidate. Ordinary members are not included in the selection process; their participation is not even mentioned in the party rules governing candidate selection. This list is approved by the provincial party's top organ, the provincial party committee, based on the work of the provincial electoral commission and the initial proposals of the committee itself. It is the result of negotiation among leaders of the various factions, which are represented on both the provincial committee and the provincial electoral commission in proportion to their strength at the most recent provincial party congress. (The strength of different factions, of course, varies from one province to another across the country.) Prominent interests from the Catholic world may also have some positions on the DC ticket. Examples include the Confederation of Small Farmers, which for the entire post-war period has had its candidates placed on the DC lists around the country and currently holds about 10 percent of the DC's seats in Parliament, and a new entrant, the Popular Movement, a political emanation of the dynamic, highly articulated Communion and Liberation religious organization (Borriello, 1985; Magister, 1984; Wertman, 1977).

The regional party organization, whose top officials may also have some informal input into the work of the provincial parties, then receives the lists from the provincial party committees in its region (except for Val d'Aosta, each of Italy's regions contains from two to nine provinces). Virtually all the Chamber constituencies are multi-province (containing from two to five provinces), and it is the job of the regional party to suggest the order of the names in each Chamber constituency by amalgamating the lists of the component provincial party organizations and taking into account the order they have proposed.

The lists arrive at the national level about a week before they must legally be presented, and so the National Executive Committee usually goes through a marathon final six or seven days when it is, in effect, in permanent session. Ultimately it boils down to agreement on the controversial questions among the leaders of eight or nine factions in the National Executive Committee. (Prior to this final week, the 'political office' of the national party, which includes the national party secretary and vice-secretaries as well as representatives of each faction, begins working on the selection of candidates for the reserved Senate seats and on the many other issues to be resolved.) For the Chamber, the National Executive Committee determines the head of the list (*capolista*) in each constituency, sometimes a very difficult task if two or more important national figures come from the same Chamber constituency, and resolves any outstanding problems, such as appeals from incumbents who have not been renominated at the local level (their right to appeal is recognized in the party rules). When there is unanimous or at least very broad agreement on the Chamber lists at the provincial level, which is usually ultimately the case after much negotiation among the factions, the names on the provincial party's lists are only rarely changed at the regional or national level. Much of the National Executive Committee's time is taken up by selecting the candidates for the Senate seats it has reserved for itself. The 1983 initiative to run some independents was a decision taken, and carried out, by the National Executive Committee.

Competition among the factions takes place at two stages: during the selection process itself, and in the electoral battle for preference votes. For the Senate the important phase is clearly choosing the candidates who will run in the safe constituencies. For the Chamber it is very different in that much of the factional conflict is transferred to the election campaign itself, when the individual candidates, factions and interest groups fight for preference votes. Candidate selection for the Chamber is not used to prevent other factions from getting places on the list; this might lead them to take less interest in the campaign, and it might also lead to an appeal to higher party levels to overturn the decisions made at the provincial level. The goal of the majority factions in the inter-factional negotiations is to establish as strong a position (in terms of candidates and list order) as possible in preparation for the battle for preference votes, but without alienating the minority factions to the point of protest.

The result of this central role of factionalism in DC decision-making, coupled with the importance of a parliamentary career for advancement in the party, has been a high rate of renomination of incumbents. In all but two parliamentary elections since 1953, over 90 percent of DC incumbents have been renominated. Largely in consequence, it has had the lowest average turnover among the three main parties; for all post-war elections since 1953 the DC has had an average of 27.7 percent newly elected members in the Chamber of Deputies compared to 36.1 percent for the Socialists and 41.3 percent for the Communists (Guadagnini, 1984: 138). Like the Socialist Party but unlike the Communist Party, about half of its turnover has been due to losses in intraparty electoral battles for preference votes. Furthermore, the DC has by far the largest number of long-serving incumbents among these three parties; 34.2 percent of the DC deputies elected in 1983 had been elected for four terms or more, compared to 12.3 percent of Socialist deputies and 9.7 percent of Communist deputies.

Reflecting its large number of incumbents and its intense factionalism, the DC's Chamber lists are by far the most complex. In particular, its lists are distinctive in having a large middle section (Bardi, 1985: 306–10). The *capolista* is picked by the National Executive Committee and is usually, while being from the local area, either a top national party leader or a Cabinet member. The middle section comprises 40 to 50 percent of the names on the list, in roughly this order: top national party officials, ministers and under-secretaries, top local party officials, and, listed alphabetic-ally, remaining incumbent deputies. The tail contains the rest of the candidates listed in alphabetical order. By contrast, all other parties have at most three or four names in the middle sections of their lists. This construction of lists with top, middle and bottom sections is an invention of the parties; it is not part of the electoral law, and there is no space or indication of any kind on the official ballot which shows this distinction. List order may have some effect on which candidates win in each party in that a high list position may help in attracting more preferences. However, those at the top and, to a large extent, those in the middle section are usually the best-known candidates who would attract most preferences anyway.

The DC's low rate of parliamentary turnover, coupled with the negative image the party had acquired as a result of its permanence in power, led to a two-pronged effort in 1976 and 1983 to change the composition of its parliamentary delegation as part of the overall strategy of projecting the image of a 'new DC'. First, in both 1976 and 1983 the goal of the party, or at least of the party secretary and a majority in the National Executive Committee, was to engineer a greater turnover by denying renomination to a number of long-serving incumbents. This effort had some success on both occasions, with the proportion refused renomination reaching 25.5 percent in 1976 and 17 percent in 1983, compared with 10 percent or less in other post-war elections (Wertman, forthcoming). However, the efforts at creating greater turnover have clearly fallen short of what was intended.

Secondly, in 1983 the DC also decided to try to run some prestigious independent candidates on its ticket to reinforce the image of a party seriously reforming itself. The national leadership aimed to include a number of well-known Catholic intellectuals, leaders of Catholic organizations and, to aid in building credibility among industrialists and managers, some representatives of Italian business. It wanted to nominate these independents in the four largest urban areas – Rome, Milan, Turin and Naples – to help recoup the substantial losses it had suffered there since the mid-1970s. Consequently a number of DC incumbents were moved by the National Executive Committee to safe Senate seats elsewhere in the country, and were replaced in these urban areas by independents. Despite many refusals, the party was able to include a certain number of prominent Catholic and business figures in its lists. However, there is no evidence that this helped the DC either in individual constituencies, with particular demographic groups, or in the country as a whole.

In summary, the DC's candidate selection process is fairly chaotic and disordered, and is primarily a process of negotiation and compromise among the party's factions. The final authority rests with the National Executive Committee, but in practice most Chamber candidates and many Senate candidates are selected at the provincial level with some regional input. The *capolista* in each Chamber district and the candidates in the reserved Senate districts are decided directly by the National Executive Committee, as are any conflicts unresolved at the local level. The result of this time-consuming process is that many of the conflicts are resolved only at the last minute. In 1976 and 1983 efforts were made to change the *content* of DC candidate selection, but the *method* of selection, both in terms of the official rules and real practice, has changed little during the post-war period.

The Italian Communist Party

Candidate selection in the PCI is in several ways unique in Italy. One indication of this is the large number of incumbents not renominated and the resulting high turnover in the PCI parliamentary delegation, which since 1953 has been considerably above that for both the DC and the PSI. In 1983, which was typical of post-war elections, only 57 percent of the PCI's incumbent deputies and senators were renominated. This was well below the other Italian parties, who renominated 80 to 100 percent of incumbents, and is well below most other parties in Western Europe.

The norm in the PCI is that a deputy will serve two terms or possibly three, but rarely more. Candidates know this is the norm, and because of party discipline accept it when chosen initially. Deselection after two or three terms normally means simply returning to another form of party work; it does not, except in rare cases, denote rejection by the party. In 1983, which was typical in this regard, 62.3 percent of the seventy-seven incumbent PCI deputies not renominated had served two terms, and an additional 22.1 percent had served three terms. Of those elected in 1983, only 9.7 percent had been elected four or more times, and half of these were members of the PCI's National Executive Committee, its highest policy-making body. Likewise, very few incumbent PCI deputies – only eight in 1983 – leave Parliament after one term, and then usually only for personal reasons.

This orderly turnover takes place for a number of reasons. First, the PCI's entire decision-making process – of which candidate selection is one aspect – is fairly centralized, and organized factionalism of the type which is at the heart of decision-making in the DC does not exist in the PCI. Secondly, unlike other Italian parties, a parliamentary career is not considered more important than other kinds of work for the party and is not the single most important means through which an individual reaches top power in the party. Thirdly, a local–national interchange and a rotation of elites among party work, parliamentary work and local government work are viewed as valuable for the party (Di Palma, 1984). A large

majority of the PCI's members of Parliament have served previously in local government, and some will return to local
government after their experience in Parliament. Fourth, on a more
practical level and explaining the emphasis on two terms, someone
who serves in Parliament for two terms or more receives a parliamentary pension at sixty years of age; this is not a small consideration for the PCI since many of its candidates are party functionaries
whose pension the party might otherwise have to pay.

PCI party rules give a very brief, inadequate description of the
candidate selection process; what follows is a description of the way
the process takes place in practice. While the preparation for
candidate selection begins well ahead of time, the official opening of
the process comes with the determination of the general, but
binding, guidelines by the PCI's National Executive Committee. In
1983 there were three major guidelines beyond the usual one of a
two- to three-term limit.[7] Two of these were largely continuations of
policies laid down in 1976 and 1979. First, the party wanted to
ensure, as it did in 1976 and 1979, that roughly one fifth of its
Chamber delegation would be women, both for symbolic effect and
to give adequate representation. This goal was ultimately achieved,
with 18.7 percent of the PCI deputies being women. The number
elected in 1983, while much higher than in 1972 and before, was
almost exactly the same as in 1976 and 1979 (Beckwith, 1981).

Secondly, the party wanted to continue, and indeed increase, the
practice of nominating a substantial number of prestigious independents not previously identified with the party. While the Communists had a small number of independents in their lists prior to
1976, it was only in 1976 that this became a central feature of the
party's electoral (and image-building) strategy. In 1976 twenty-five
independents were elected to Parliament on PCI lists. After keeping
the number at about the same level in 1979, the national leadership
decided in 1983 to increase it to thirty-eight, about one eighth of the
parliamentary representation. These independents include some
Catholic figures, several judges, a number of university professors,
cultural figures, some journalists and several ex-Socialists.

Third, the PCI reached an agreement with the Democratic Party
for Proletarian Unity (PDUP), a small party to the left of the PCI
which had won 2.2 percent of the votes and six seats in the 1979
Chamber elections, to include the PDUP candidates in the PCI lists,
which would ensure PDUP seven or eight seats in Parliament.
There was some local resistance to the increased number of
independents and to the addition of PDUP names to the lists,
because this took some seats away from local party activists, but all
the national guidelines on turnover, women, independents and

PDUP were nevertheless implemented by the provincial and regional party organizations.[8]

The PCI candidate selection process is particularly important, because in effect the process determines not only who will be nominated but also who will be elected. When the PCI's Chamber lists are composed, decisions are made on who the winners, marginal candidates and certain losers will be. This is because of the PCI's control over preference voting. Unlike most other parties, the PCI does not allow its Chamber candidates to engage in individual campaigns for preference votes. The names of those candidates to whom preference votes should be given are distributed to party members through the party sections; as one PCI deputy said in a 1983 interview, even the then national party secretary, Enrico Berlinguer, went to his local party section in Rome in 1983 to get the sample ballot showing the party's choices (Padalino, 1983). This control over the casting of preference votes is possible because the PCI is one of the best organized, most deeply rooted parties in Western Europe. PCI voters are among the least likely to cast preference votes (Katz, 1985; Scaramozzino, 1983), and many of those who do are party members who have received the party's guidelines. Nearly all of those designated as winners by the party are indeed elected, and very few incumbents lose. In 1983 only six out of 119 PCI incumbents (5 percent) running for re-election to the Chamber were defeated.

After the general guidelines have been set forth, the national party secretariat, whose six or seven members each maintain direct contact with a certain number of regions, acts as the overall co-ordinator in ensuring that the party's goals are implemented. A number of candidates, all to be winners, are in effect named directly by the national organization; these include top party leaders to head the Chamber lists or be Senate candidates, many of the independents and (in 1983) PDUP candidates. The bulk of the candidates, though, are chosen by the regional and, in particular, the provincial party federations, and are representative of the local reality of the PCI in each area.

In other words, it is the task of the regional and provincial party organizations, who are in continual contact with each other and with the national party secretariat during this period, to implement the national goals, such as finding the requisite number of women. It is also their responsibility to include the national candidates in the local lists, as they do except in very rare cases of strong local resistance, and to find the rest of the candidates from the local area. The regional party secretaries, a number of whom are on the National Executive Committee and all of whom would normally be

Central Committee members, and the provincial party secretaries have an important weight in the party and, therefore, in the selection of parliamentary candidates and winners.

Once the provincial federation has put together its proposed list of candidates, these lists go to 'mass consultations' in which party members, in meetings of their sections, discuss them; 7000 such meetings were held in 1983. These mass consultations are, as Belligni (1980: 192) argues for the same process in local elections, 'primarily symbolic' and held 'with the end of legitimizing the selection procedures'. In only a very few cases, possibly of a locally popular incumbent whom the party had decided to exclude, would there be even small changes in the lists. Once the lists have been prepared at the provincial and regional levels (the latter proposes the order for the lists in the Chamber constituencies in addition to its work in ensuring implementation of national party directives), they are approved by the National Executive Committee in a joint meeting with the regional secretaries. This is usually a one-day meeting to iron out any remaining problems, but these are relatively few since the national party has been in constant touch with the provincial and regional organizations throughout the process.

In summary, the National Executive Committee's initial guidelines play a major role in the PCI's candidate selection process. The National Executive Committee also selects a certain number of candidates to be included in the lists, and these candidates are normally all among the winners. However, the provincial party, in consultation with the regional party, selects the bulk of the candidates. Although these local choices can be vetoed by the National Executive Committee, which has the final and decisive voice, in practice most candidates selected at the provincial level will be accepted by the regional and national levels. The candidate selection process in the PCI remains fairly centralized and has changed relatively little over time, with possibly a gradual trend towards a greater role for provincial and regional organizations. Candidate selection in the PCI is a well-organized, relatively controlled process which largely takes place behind the scenes.

The Italian Socialist Party

The PSI's candidate selection process begins with a letter from the party's top decision-making organ, the National Executive Committee (NEC), to the regional and provincial party organizations, which in turn invite local party sections to propose candidates. Though the party rules provide for ordinary members, through their party sections, to propose candidates to the provincial party organization, this step is largely formal and symbolic. In fact, ordinary members have virtually no effective role in the process. The provincial party organization does most of the work on putting together the list of Chamber candidates from the province and choosing the names for the Senate constituencies within its borders. Since only one in ten of the Chamber candidates will win, and only a limited number are truly competitive in the battle for preference votes, most candidates are there to show the flag and to build their own reputation for future tries at public office. Most incumbents are renominated (87.3 percent in 1976, 76.1 percent in 1979 and 84.6 percent in 1983). Few who want to be renominated are refused; probably half of those not renominated retired voluntarily, or took another job. In the PSI, as in the DC, membership in Parliament is an important factor in achieving national power. PSI Chamber candidates, like those in the DC, must organize personal electoral machines to fight for preference votes, and defeat in this battle is a major source of turnover in the PSI parliamentary delegation.

The provincial party organization sends its proposed lists and preferred order of names up to the regional party organization, which proposes the order for the lists in each Chamber constituency in the region, taking into account the priorities of the provincial party organizations. The regional party will usually also propose the *capolista*, with precedence given, in order, to top national party officials, ministers and under-secretaries, members of the NEC, and incumbent deputies. In the PSI there are usually one to four names at the top of the list, with the remainder in alphabetical order. While most candidates are selected by the provincial party, the regional party's greatest influence is on list order. Once its work is completed, the regional party sends its proposed lists to the NEC.

The PSI's NEC has, in practice, final authority in candidate selection, but it alters only a small proportion of the names on the lists which reach it. It meets in the last few days before the lists must be presented to sort out any problems or to undertake initiatives of its own. Only the NEC can make an exception to the rule that an individual must have been a party member for at least five years in order to be a parliamentary candidate for the PSI.[9] First, all cases of unresolved conflict at the provincial and regional level, usually over the Chamber 'capolista' and list order or over the candidate in a Senate constituency where the PSI has traditionally won a seat, are decided by the NEC. Second, any incumbents not renominated at the local level have a right to appeal to the NEC. Third, under party rules the NEC sometimes intervenes to change local choices, particularly over a Chamber *capolista* or a Senate candidacy, or it reserves several safe Senate seats in which to put its own candidates. The NEC almost always approves the candidates proposed for the

Chamber if there has been general agreement at the provincial level. Furthermore, it is constrained in the same way as the DC national leadership; whoever is nominated for the Chamber must be able to win sufficient preference votes in the local constituency to be elected, or else nominating the person is a futile gesture. For the Senate, however, the NEC intervenes in a number of constituencies, sometimes four or five, sometimes more, either to change a candidate proposed by the local party or to name the candidate directly itself.

As a result of Party Secretary Bettino Craxi's dominance in the PSI since the late 1970s, organized factionalism is less pronounced today. However, significant internal conflict over personal ambitions and the intense battles over preference votes remain much the same. Overall, the PSI candidate selection process has changed relatively little compared to the mid-1970s and before.

The minor parties

Italy's smaller parties look at candidate selection in a way very different from the main three. They know that they will win few seats, that they have few if any safe Senate seats, and that the great bulk of the candidates are there simply to 'show the flag' for the party and to heighten their profile for future contests. Usually it is not very difficult for someone with reasonable qualifications to get his or her name on the lists in these small parties.

The first rule for small parties is that the incumbents are renominated. This is because they usually represent the best prospect of retaining the party's limited number of seats; in addition, they themselves want to stay in Parliament since, as in the DC and the PSI, a parliamentary career is the most important path to top power in these parties. In 1983, typical of post-war elections for these parties, forty out of forty-four Italian Social Movement (MSI) incumbents, all twenty-two Italian Republican Party (PRI) incumbents, twenty-six of twenty-nine Italian Social Democratic Party (PSDI) incumbents, and ten of eleven Italian Liberal Party (PLI) incumbents were renominated; this is a total of ninety-eight out of 106, or 92.5 percent. The few not renominated were mostly long-time members of Parliament who voluntarily retired. Since, in each national election, virtually all the incumbents of these parties – ninety-three out of ninety-eight in 1983 – are re-elected, only a small number of non-incumbents have a chance of being elected even if the party makes gains. In these parties there is often little real competition in individual constituencies for the party's seat(s).[10]

The candidate selection process is very similar in each of these four parties. Final authority rests with the national executive committee, but this top decision-making body intervenes in only a small number of cases. Nearly all parliamentary candidates of the small parties are chosen at the provincial level, where the party organizations are dominated by a small group of notables who frequently also hold important national positions in the party. Central input may be somewhat greater for the Chamber list order and 'capolista', and in the small number of Senate seats traditionally won by the party, than for the names of Chamber candidates; among these four parties, this has been particularly true in the Republican Party, which in 1983 nominated eleven top leaders to be 'capolista' in two or three Chamber constituencies each in order to put its best faces forward around the country.[11] The 'capolista' in each Chamber constituency is the incumbent local deputy or possibly someone with a top party or government job; there is usually also a middle section with one to three names (in some constituencies, these parties may have no middle section), followed by the rest in alphabetical order.

The level at which decisions are taken

In the DC the large bulk of the Chamber candidates and most of the Senate candidates are selected at the provincial level. The National Executive Committee, which has final authority, intervenes in cases in which there is great conflict at lower levels, and names the Chamber 'capolista' in each constituency. It also directly chooses about one sixth of the Senate candidates (who represent about one third of the party's likely Senate winners), but it does not change many of the candidates proposed by the lower levels. The provincial, regional and national leaders of the factions – who are normally members of the top party organs at these levels – play an all-important role in candidate selection; some interest groups have significant influence in the selection of a portion of the candidates.

In the PCI the National Executive Committee issues binding guidelines, which are closely followed by the local levels, and directly chooses a number of candidates (all likely to be winners), including the independents (currently one eighth of the PCI's parliamentary delegation). It also decides on multiple candidacies (of which the PCI had more than thirty in 1983). The national party secretariat then oversees the selection process at the lower levels. The substantial majority of candidates – and the majority of winners – are chosen at the provincial level, with a strong input by the regional party into the work of the provincial party; the regional party's input is probably greater in the PCI than in the other parties.

These candidates are normally then accepted by the national party leadership.

In the PSI a great majority of the candidates are chosen at the provincial level, with the National Executive Committee resolving conflicts, naming the Chamber 'capolista' in some constituencies, and directly choosing the candidate in a number of the party's safe Senate constituencies. The National Executive Committee exercises its power to alter the locally proposed lists in only a small number of cases.

In the four smaller parties (MSI, PRI, PSDI and PLI), the central leadership rarely exercises its power to change locally prepared lists. Most decisions are left to the provincial – and to a much lesser extent the regional – levels, to a far greater degree than in the DC and PCI. If exceptions occur they will concern the Chamber 'capolista' in a small number of constituencies (among the four parties, intervention of this kind is most common in the PRI) and the Senate candidates in a few constituencies traditionally won by the party.

As this discussion shows, while final authority in all Italian parties rests with the national executive committee, in practice most candidates are selected at the provincial level, with the regional party having some influence in some parties. Clearly, however, the degree of central intervention varies among the parties. Central control is greatest in the PCI, achieved by means of the binding guidelines to the local party organizations, the national party secretariat's overseeing of the process, and extensive placement by the national party. Following next in order are the Christian Democrats, particularly for the large number of Senate constituencies the National Executive Committee reserves for itself to name the candidate and for the control over the Chamber 'capolista'; the Socialists; and the Republicans. Central intervention is weakest in the other small parties, the MSI, the PSDI and the PLI.

Candidate selection is confined to the party organizations, and almost exclusively to elites within these organizations. Less than 1 percent of members in the DC, PCI and PSI (somewhat more in the smaller parties with few members) are effectively involved in candidate selection, and almost all of these hold some party or public position. When ordinary members have a role, it is normally only a symbolic one. Even the 'mass consultations' with party members in the PCI only very rarely result in changes in the party's lists. Party voters who are not also members have no direct role at all in candidate selection; one may argue that they have an indirect role through preference voting, but this is only among the candidates already selected by the party organizations.

The candidate selection process is typical of the general decision-making process within the parties. First, rank-and-file members have little influence over policy in Italian parties just as they have little or no influence over candidate selection. Second, ultimate authority on all major questions, including candidate selection, rests with the national leadership in each party. Therefore the national leadership provides the initial guidelines for candidate selection, conducts operations with national significance like the inclusion of independents or increasing the turnover rate among deputies, resolves local level conflicts and gives final ratification to the lists. The local party organizations, which are often important power bases in the parties and which also clearly best know the local situation, pick most of each party's candidates, the bulk of whom, indeed, come from the local area.

The differences between the parties in the candidate selection process reflect the differences in nature among them. Factional conflict plays a major role in decision-making at the local and national levels in the DC and, to a lesser extent, in the PSI and some of the smaller parties. The PCI's more controlled process, including mass consultations and close co-ordination by the central party organization, is characteristic of that party's decision-making process. The local notables who dominate some of the smaller parties do so for candidate selection as they do for many other decisions.

What the selectors seek

Several recent studies (Cotta, 1979, 1980; Guadagnini, 1980, 1984) suggest that there has been little change since 1945 in the characteristics the selectors are seeking in parliamentary candidates, though there has been some standardization, especially in the importance of party work and local government office. Substantial turnover in the 1976, 1979 and 1983 elections has not greatly affected the characteristics of the members of Parliament.

Incumbency is clearly the single most important factor, especially for the small parties, where nearly all incumbents are renominated. It remains very important in the DC, despite the efforts in 1976 and 1983 to refuse renomination to long-serving incumbents. For the PCI incumbency is important for being reselected for a second term and possibly for a third, but after that it is fatal to renomination for all but a very few. A large majority of *top party leaders at the national level*, including the secretary, vice-secretaries and most members of the national executive committee, are members of

Parliament in all parties, and these, of course, are virtually always reselected.

A *good party record* is also an asset, which benefits those who have performed other roles (whether in the party itself or in local government) successfully according to the party's evaluation. Though there are no residency requirements in Italy, most candidates – especially for the Chamber of Deputies – have *local roots*. Local office frequently serves as a 'launching pad' or 'springboard' to a parliamentary career (Pasquino, 1985b: 138–42). It is considered important that most candidates are people from the local area rather than outsiders, so as to try to boost the party's local image, to avoid alienating party members and voters, and to reward local party activists. Of course, the actual selection of the large bulk of the candidates is made by the provincial organization in nearly all parties, and it is not surprising that these local organizations prefer to choose mainly local individuals. Furthermore, in parties such as the DC, PSI or some of the smaller ones, where there is a major battle for preference votes, it is absolutely essential that the Chamber candidates, apart from a very few top national leaders, be well-known local individuals.

In this regard the most standardized career path to candidate selection is in the PCI (Guadagnini, 1980: 78). Nearly all PCI members of Parliament have joined the party early (usually before twenty-five years of age), have held party office early and then have continued on to higher party office at the local or national level and/ or been elected to local government office. Further, studies (Cotta, 1980: 37–8) have shown that over half of the PCI's members of Parliament are party functionaries. Relatively early party membership, holding party offices and having been elected to local government offices are major characteristics of members of Parliament in most Italian parties, but in the other parties there tend to be more people with outside occupations who are not professional politicians, as well as a greater variety of career paths.

There is a specific group – especially in the elections since 1976 – which differs greatly (except in educational and socio-economic status) from the typical pattern for candidates. These are the *independents*, who have not normally been involved in the party or local government prior to their nomination to run for Parliament. The PCI in particular, the DC to a lesser extent and the small parties to a very limited degree have put independents on their lists, and this is always a central party operation. Independents are normally expected to be among the winners, being put in safe Senate seats and, in the case of the PCI, also among the party's preferred Chamber winners.

Interest group affiliation is important for the nomination of a certain sub-group of candidates. In the case of the DC about 10 percent of the party's seats in the post-war period have gone to the Confederation of Small Farmers, whose well-articulated organization ensures that virtually all its Chamber candidates will get enough preferences to win election, while other Catholic organizations, such as the Popular Movement, also provide some candidates. A certain number of union officials – from the CGIL for the PCI, from the CISL (or the Catholic workers' organization ACLI) for the DC, and from the CGIL or UIL for the PSI – are usually nominated as parliamentary candidates; since 1969, by agreement among the unions themselves, election to Parliament means giving up union office during parliamentary membership. In some cases, such as union officials (particularly those nominated by the DC and the PSI), the party selects the candidate, since it is an individual decision to run. In others, such as the Confederation of Small Farmers or the Popular Movement, and possibly also CGIL officials running on the PCI ticket, the names may be co-ordinated with the interest group organization or even directly determined by the organization. Some of these interest group officials may also have been long-time party members, have held party jobs and have been elected to local government office on the party's ticket.

Factional affiliation is extremely important in the DC, and of lesser importance in the PSI and the smaller parties. In the DC candidates from all factions will be nominated on the Chamber lists and will fight for preference votes during the campaign, while for the Senate there will be trade-offs among the factions in picking the candidates for the safe seats.

The one party which most directly takes into consideration *background characteristics* in its candidate selection is the PCI. Though most parties in the past decade have spoken about the need to give women more representation in Parliament, only the Communist Party, whose more controlled candidate selection process makes such an operation possible, has specifically done something to increase female representation. As we have seen, nearly 20 percent of its parliamentary delegation is composed of women, compared to under 5 percent for the other parties. Interestingly, however, the PCI's women candidates do not differ significantly in their other characteristics from its male candidates. As far as social class is concerned, the PCI's lists – both certain winners and certain losers – have the lowest overall status level, with the great bulk of the working-class parliamentary candidates and members of Parliament being on the PCI's lists; this inclusion of some working-class individuals clearly represents a conscious decision by a party with a heavy dependence on its working-class electorate. A little under 10 percent of the PCI's members of Parliament come from working-class occupations, and many of these are union activists. Overall, of course, all Italian parliamentary delegations, as is true in all democratic systems (Ranney, 1981: 101–2), have considerably above-average socio-economic and educational status.

Consequences of the selection process

Among the parties, parliamentary discipline is greatest and absenteeism lowest in the PCI, due to its more centralized candidate selection process, to the fact that many of its parliamentarians come from the ranks of party functionaries, and to the nature of the PCI itself. Furthermore, PCI deputies can devote more time than other deputies to legislative work, since they do not have to spend so much time in the constituency to maintain an electoral machine in preparation for the next battle for preference votes. A major reason for the absenteeism which has on occasion hurt the government in the Chamber is undoubtedly that many deputies of the five government parties (DC, PSI, PRI, PSDI and PLI) spend a significant amount of time in their constituencies building their image and electoral machines.

In all parties, ultimate control by the national executive committee over candidate selection creates an important force for party discipline in parliament, which is normally high for all parties on the very visible and important confidence votes. However, the wide use of the secret vote, which is highly unusual among Western parliaments, makes rebelling against the party's position relatively easy, since the rebels often cannot be identified. As a result of this (most, but not all, rebelling occurs on secret votes), members of Parliament motivated by local interests, philosophical differences and factional and interest group affiliations rebel relatively frequently in parties other than the PCI, especially on amendments to bills, which are normally subject to secret vote. Refusal of renomination on the grounds of breaking party discipline, excessive absenteeism or poor quality of parliamentary work is very uncommon.

If one takes the factors listed by Ranney (1981) – incumbency, local connections, interest group affiliation, factional affiliation, and above-average socio-economic and educational status – as indicative of the characteristics most important for selection as a parliamentary candidate in Western democracies, Italy's candidates are fairly typical in most respects. The Communist Party, with its programmed turnover and its inclusion of a quota of women and a large number of party functionaries, is unusual among Italian parties. The all-important position of factional affiliation in the DC makes it, too, exceptional. The emphasis on independent candidates in the PCI and DC is unusual among Western European parties.

Conclusion

Candidate selection in Italy is important in a number of ways. First, the parties themselves regard it as an important part of their political and electoral strategy, though there is no evidence that any specific tactics have gained the PCI or DC more support. In fact, studies (Penniman, 1977, 1981) suggest that Italian voters look primarily at the image of the party rather than at individual candidates, and neither the efforts made to attract independents nor steps taken to promote greater turnover appear to have changed significantly the images of the PCI or the DC. Secondly, candidate selection plays a crucial role not only in determining the parliamentary membership but also in choosing the pool from which the top party and government leadership will come. Thirdly, the candidate selection process reinforces the dominant role of the parties by making them the main recruiters and promoters of political elites. Fourthly, the nature of the candidate selection process in the Italian parties prevents party members and voters from having a meaningful role.

While some scholars and even some leaders in the parties themselves have proposed at least experimentation with primaries (some suggest among members only, others among voters), there has been relatively little discussion of changing candidate selection as part of the debate over institutional reform. There has been little movement in this direction, apart from a few cases of primaries among members to choose candidates for local elections. Neither the role of candidate selection in the Italian political system, nor the nature of the selection processes used by the parties, is likely to undergo great change at any time in the near future, particularly since the party elites who dominate the process generally have no interest in seeing such changes.[12]

Notes

The views expressed herein are those of the author and do not necessarily represent the views of the United States Information Agency or the United States

Government. I would like to thank Giuseppe Borgioli for his help and advice and would also like to thank the many functionaries and officials from Italy's political parties who discussed candidate selection with me. These discussions, combined with an intensive reading of several daily newspapers from the period of candidate selection during the past three parliamentary elections as well as of the limited academic literature on candidate selection, were the major sources for my views about candidate selection in Italy.

1. For detailed information on Italian elections, parties and political system since the mid-1970s, see Penniman (1977, 1981 and forthcoming) and Pasquino (1985a).

2. Wertman (1977) presents an in-depth discussion of the Chamber and Senate electoral systems.

3. Italy has twenty regions, ninety-five provinces and more than 8000 communes. There are thirty-two Chamber constituencies: thirty of them consist of two or more provinces; one (Trieste) has only one province, but three seats; and one consists of only the tiny region of Val d'Aosta, which has one seat. There are approximately 240 Senate constituencies.

4. Preference voting is by far the most widely researched aspect of the electoral process (Katz, 1985; Scaramozzino, 1983; Bardi, 1985; Wertman, 1977).

5. In most of these regions there are fewer senatorial constituencies than seats to be filled (nationwide there are about 240 Senate constituencies compared to 315 seats). Consequently, two or more senators may be elected from one constituency, and there are also a few Senate constituencies each time where no senator is elected because no single party achieves a high enough proportion of the votes in that constituency.

6. There are a few exceptions, such as Pasquino (1985b), most of whom argue for some kind of primary system involving party members and/or voters.

7. The following discussion of the PCI's candidate selection in 1983 comes from my private discussions as well as from a careful reading of the party newspaper, *L'Unità*, and of the largest circulation Italian daily, *Corriere della Sera*, for the April–May 1983 period.

8. There is also an evaluation of the parliamentary work of each PCI incumbent by the party group in the Chamber and the Senate, with an eye towards which members would be valuable to keep beyond a second term. This is of limited importance.

9. By contrast, neither the DC nor the PCI has a minimum membership period as an eligibility requirement.

10. The only parties not directly considered in the analysis in this chapter are very small ones which altogether won only 3.3 percent of the seats in the 1983 parliamentary elections.

11. Under the electoral law one individual may be nominated in up to three Chamber constituencies in the country as well as in as many as three Senate constituencies, though the latter must all be in the same region. Multiple nominations of the same person are made to a limited degree by most parties for the Senate. For the Chamber they are made only rarely by the DC and, apart from the party secretary, by the PSI, MSI, PSDI and PLI, mainly because of concern over the effect this would have in the battle for preference votes. The PCI, with its more controlled process, uses multiple nominations more extensively to help ensure that its preferred candidates get elected.

12. The selection of candidates for the 1987 parliamentary elections, which was

completed after this book went to press, did not differ in any significant way from the process described in this chapter.

References

Bardi, L. (1985) 'Il Voto di Preferenza in Italia e la Legge Elettorale Europea', *Rivista Italiana di Scienza Politica*, 15 (2): 293–313.

Beckwith, K. (1981) 'Women and Parliamentary Politics in Italy, 1946–1979', pp. 230–53 in H.R. Penniman (ed.), *Italy at the Polls, 1979: A Study of the Parliamentary Elections*. Washington, DC: American Enterprise Institute for Public Policy Research.

Belligni, S. (1980) 'PCI: Il Livello Locale', *Biblioteca della Libertà*, 79 (October–December: 167–200.

Borriello, E. (1985) 'La Coldiretti non è un Partito nel Partito ma è Ancora Potente', *La Repubblica* (12 February): 34.

Cotta, M. (1979) *Classe Politica e Parlamento in Italia*. Bologna: Il Mulino.

Cotta, M. (1980) 'Mutamento e Stabilità,' *Biblioteca della Libertà*, 79 (October–December): 29–45.

Democrazia Cristiana (1985) *Regolamento per la Designazione dei Candidati DC alle Elezioni*. Rome: Centro Stampa DC.

Di Palma, G. (1984) 'Sulla Società Politica in Italia', pp. 117–30 in L. Bonanate (ed.), *Il Sistema Politico Italiano tra Crisi e Innovazione*. Milan: Franco Angeli Editore.

Guadagnini, M. (1980) 'Frammentazione e Omogeneneità', *Biblioteca della Libertà*, 79 (October–December): 47–86.

Guadagnini, M. (1984) 'Il Personale Politico Parlamentare dagli Anni '70 agli Anni '80: Problemi di Ricerca e di Analisi e Alcuni Dati Empirici', pp. 131–52 in L. Bonanate (ed.), *Il Sistema Politico Italiano tra Crisi e Innovazione*. Milan: Franco Angeli Editore.

Katz, R. (1985) 'Preference Voting in Italy: Votes of Opinion, Belonging, or Exchange', *Comparative Political Studies*, 18 (2): 229–49.

Magister, S. (1984) 'A Stelle e Strisce', *L'Espresso* (26 August): 14–15.

Padalino, A. (1983) 'Togli un Rischio dal Futuro', *Panorama* (18 July): 47.

Pasquino, G. (ed.) (1985a) *Il Sistema Politico Italiano*. Bari: Laterza.

Pasquino, G. (1985b) *Restituire lo Scettro al Principe*. Bari: Laterza.

Penniman, H.R. (ed.) (1977) *Italy at the Polls: The Parliamentary Elections of 1976*. Washington, DC: American Enterprise Institute for Public Policy Research.

Penniman, H.R. (ed.) (1981) *Italy at the Polls, 1979: A Study of the Parliamentary Elections*. Washington, DC: American Enterprise Institute for Public Policy Research.

Penniman, H.R. (ed.) (forthcoming) *Italy at the Polls, 1983: A Study of the Parliamentary Elections*. Durham, NC: Duke University Press.

Ranney, A. (1981) 'Candidate Selection', pp. 75-106 in D. Butler, H.R. Penniman and A. Ranney (eds), *Democracy at the Polls: A Comparative Study of Competitive National Elections*. Washington, DC: American Enterprise Institute for Public Policy Research.

Scaramozzino, P. (1983) 'Il Voto di Preferenza nelle Elezioni Politiche ed Europee del 1979 e nelle Elezioni Politiche del 1983', *Il Politico*, 48 (4): 641–75.

168   *Douglas A. Wertman*

Wertman, D. (1977) 'The Italian Electoral Process: The Elections of June 1976', pp. 41–79 in H.R. Penniman (ed.), *Italy at the Polls: The Parliamentary Elections of 1976*. Washington, DC: American Enterprise Institute for Public Policy Research.

Wertman, D. (forthcoming) 'The Christian Democrats: The Big Losers', in H.R. Penniman (ed.), *Italy at the Polls, 1983: A Study of the Parliamentary Elections*. Durham, NC: Duke University Press.

8

Japan: localism, factionalism and personalism

Rei Shiratori

According to the Japanese Constitution, which was promulgated on 3 November 1946 and enacted on 3 May 1947, Japan's National Diet is defined as 'the highest organ of state power, and shall be the sole law-making organ of the state' (article 41). This Diet is bicameral and consists of the House of Representatives (Shuugi In) and the House of Councillors (Sangi In).

The term of office of the members of the House of Representatives is four years, although the term can be terminated before the full term has expired if the House of Representatives is dissolved by the Cabinet through the Emperor. The term of office of members of the House of Councillors is six years, with half the members elected every three years.

Public Office Election Law (Koshoku Senkyo Ho) fixes the number of members of the House of Representatives at present at 511, elected from 130 constituencies, each returning between three and five members according to population, using a single non-transferable vote and simple majority system. The number of members of the House of Councillors is 252, of whom 100 members are elected in one nationwide national constituency under a proportional representation system with lists of candidates ranked by parties. A further 152 members are elected in forty-seven prefectural constituencies, each of which returns between one to four members through a single non-transferable ballot with a simple majority system.

The House of Representatives has a superior position to the House of Councillors in decision-making, for example in passing bills (article 59), passing the budget (article 60), ratifying treaties (article 61) and designating the Prime Minister (article 67).

The electoral system which elects 3–5 members per constituency to the House of Representatives is usually called a middle-sized constituency system (Chu-Senkyoku Sei) in Japan, in contrast with the single-member constituency system and nationwide constituency system. In the case of the election of the members of the House of Representatives, forty-seven constituencies are three-seated, forty-one are four-seated, forty-one are five-seated and there is one single-member constituency.

The selection process

The Liberal Democratic Party
Although some analysts of Japanese politics regard the Liberal Democratic Party (LDP) as more of a coalition of parties than as a single party composed of a number of factions, because the existence of factions and the competition among factions are so apparent, this evaluation exaggerates the reality of the LDP. In spite of the fact that each faction tries hard to increase its own financial resources, the total amount of political funds collected by various factions in the LDP has never exceeded 45 percent of the political funds officially collected by the LDP headquarters. Moreover, the LDP as a party has its own party organization. Two incidents from the 1979–80 period throw light on the fragmented yet unitary nature of the LDP.

In September 1979 Mr Ohira, who became Prime Minister in November 1978, dissolved the House of Representatives in order to consolidate his premiership by re-establishing an absolute majority of LDP seats in the House. However, the number of LDP seats decreased by one from 249 to 248 in the election held on 7 October. Fukuda, Miki and Nakasone blamed Ohira for this and asked him to resign. When the extraordinary session of the Diet to designate the Prime Minister began on 6 November, the LDP put up two candidates, Ohira and Fukuda. In the first vote Ohira acquired 135 votes and Fukuda 125, and neither of them gained an absolute majority due to the opposition parties' votes for their own leaders. In the second vote, when only the top two candidates from the first vote stood for election, Ohira received 138 votes against Fukuda's 121 and was designated Prime Minister. In spite of the fact that the LDP had put up two candidates for Prime Minister, none of the LDP members left the party after the designation of the Prime Minister.

The second incident occurred the following May, when an opposition motion of no confidence in the Ohira government was passed due to the deliberate absence from the vote of sixty-nine LDP Diet members who belonged to the anti-Ohira factions. Even though this brought the government down, Ohira did not exercise his right as party president to expel these Diet members from the LDP, and he ratified their nominations as LDP candidates at the ensuing election, at which the LDP won an overall majority of seats.

These two incidents showed both the strength and the limits of the powers of factions in the LDP. Factions can act independently and overthrow the incumbent, but they cannot split the party in normal circumstances.

Factions play a key role when the LDP selects its President, important party officials and even cabinet ministers. Originally the President of the LDP was elected by the party congress, composed of the members of the National Diet and one representative elected from each of the forty-seven prefectures ('Kens', equivalent to counties in the UK). Even after the introduction of a primary election which selects two candidates for the presidency by direct voting of all the members of the LDP, the members of the two houses of the National Diet vote to decide on the President of the LDP. The factions which support the incumbent President form the main current while the defeated group of factions are called anti-main-current factions.

Beside the President, the LDP has several significant offices which exercise powerful control over party administration; Vice-President, Secretary-General, Director of the Executive Committee and Director of the Policy Research Affairs Council. Because the President of the LDP is inevitably elected as the Prime Minister in the National Diet, the Vice-President is de facto leader of the party. The Secretary-General controls all the administrative staff and party funds. The thirty-member Executive Committee is the most important party organ which takes decisions on daily matters, and the Director of the Executive Committee chairs its meetings. The Policy Affairs Research Council recommends legislative policy decisions and the Director of the Policy Affairs Research Council chairs meetings. All these important offices are usually distributed among the various factions in order to retain the balance inside the party.

The Election Steering Committee, which directly controls the selection of candidates in national elections, consists of the President, the Vice-President and twelve members who are appointed by the President. In the nomination of the twelve members, however, the leadership of the President is limited because here again he must consider the balance among factions. As Prime Minister he is constrained in his nomination of ministers. In the past decade the allocation of twenty ministers of the LDP cabinet has mostly taken place in this way: to the Tanaka faction three or four ministers, to the Ohira–Suzuki faction three, to the Fukuda faction three, to the Nakasone faction two, to the Miki–Komoto faction two, to the Upper House members three, to independent LDP Lower House members three or four. Therefore he can only allocate the number of members to each faction inside the Election Steering Committee after taking into account the balance among factions. The names of the members are usually put forward by each factional leader (in the case of the nomination of ministers, the Prime Minister can select the names from the list of candidates proposed by factional leaders).

The usual process of candidate selection in the LDP starts from the prefectural branch. Each prefectural headquarters proposes the names of candidates to the national headquarters, i.e. to the Election Steering Committee. If there are problems in selection, the prefectural headquarters usually sends all candidates' names to the national headquarters and asks them to decide who should be the official LDP candidates. In general, Japanese parties do not impose any institutionalized official eligibility requirements for candidature, although such parties as Komei or the Japan Communist Party, which have more solid party organizations, prefer to select their candidates from among their registered members.

The Election Steering Committee sends its decision to the Executive Committee which 'decides the important matters related to the management of the party and the activities in the Diet' (article 36 of the LDP Constitution). The Executive Committee consists of thirty members (fifteen members of the House of Representatives, seven members of the House of Councillors and eight members appointed by the President). Here again the balance among factions is considered when the LDP members select the members of the Executive Committee. The candidates are nominated by the President after recognition by the Executive Committee of the proposed list drafted by the Election Steering Committee.

The LDP has invented several devices to solve the problems which often occur in the selection of candidates. First, the LDP issues a certificate of LDP membership (Toseki Shomei) to those candidates who are members of the LDP but who are not selected as official LDP candidates. Secondly, immediately after the election the LDP automatically nominates any LDP member who stood as an independent and wins election. The date of the nomination is retrospective to the beginning of the election. Thirdly, the LDP headquarters carries out sample survey researches into the possible results when it encounters difficulty in selection and tries to increase the appeal of the outcome it favours.

In the end, if they cannot find agreement even at the Executive Committee on the nomination of official candidates among rival factions, the Executive Committee simply adopts a resolution that 'the selection of official candidates in the particular constituency should be done by senior officers (San Yaku) of the party, i.e. the President, the Vice President, and Secretary General, the Director of the Executive Committee and the Director of the Policy Affairs

Research Council'. Because these senior offices are distributed among four factions, the office-holders bargain for the nomination of official candidacies between factions by giving one to faction A in one constituency and by giving one to faction B in another constituency. The LDP does not usually decide the total number of LDP candidates beforehand in an election. Instead, each case is examined separately.

The intraparty competition engendered by the electoral system means that the LDP's factions play a central role in the battles within each constituency. Since the LDP usually wins between 42 and 48 percent of the votes in Lower House general elections, it expects to win more than one seat in most constituencies, and thus runs more than one candidate in nearly all of them. In the 1983 House of Representatives election it nominated 339 candidates in the 130 constituencies, an average of 2.6 per constituency.

The number of LDP supporters, though substantial, is limited, while the multiple candidates have to fight under the same party flag and with the same party programmes. Especially in urban areas, where conservative supporters form a smaller proportion of voters than in rural areas, if one of the multiple LDP candidates acquires a disproportionately large number of votes, the other candidates will inevitably fail to be elected. It might be said, therefore, that the real competition lies not between the LDP candidates and the opposition parties' candidates, but between the LDP candidates themselves.

Table 8.1 *Faction membership in the Liberal Democratic Party (December 1983)*

Faction	House of Representatives	House of Councillors	Total
Nakasone	41	7	48
Tanaka	62	51	113
Suzuki	50	27	77
Fukuda	40	25	65
Komoto	28	8	36
Nakagawa (Ishihara)	6	1	7
Others	31	17	48
Total	258	136	394

In order to get more votes than fellow LDP candidates, every LDP candidate has to distinguish himself from other LDP candidates in some way. He may need the support of some nationally known leader who will make a speech specifically in his support, or he must obtain extra campaign funds over and above the campaign expenses provided by the party. This is the main reason why almost all candidates in the LDP belong to a particular faction (Table 8.1).

There is no constituency where more than one candidate belongs to the same faction. To bolster their strength at national level, LDP faction leaders need at least three kinds of capability. First, they must be able to elicit large donations from the business world to finance the campaign costs of their followers; second, they must attract a wide range of the public by speeches or appearances; third, they must be able to control fellow members of the Diet.

It would be inaccurate to say that the factions inside the LDP are organized only because of the necessity to collect extra political funds. They also adopt distinctive, if rather vaguely defined, political postures or, more precisely, give priority to particular policy positions.

The Ikeda–Suzuki faction has always been more economy-orientated than politically orientated, while the Kono–Nakasone faction has constantly been more politically orientated. The Miki faction has constantly advocated disarmament and an anti-trust economic policy.

Perhaps these rather ambiguous political postures were formed as a result of the history of the establishment of the LDP. When the LDP was established in 1955, it was formed by the amalgamation of the two conservative parties, the Liberal Party and the Japan Democratic Party. Furthermore, the Japan Democratic Party had contained two groups of members who came from the Japan Progressive Party or the Japan Co-operative Party. Those two parties were established in 1945 after the end of the Second World War. It is natural, therefore, even after the amalgamation into one unified conservative LDP, that each group should try to retain its original grouping and its original political posture.

In a short-lived socialist government headed by Tetsu Katayama, the President of the Japan Socialist Party, which survived from May 1947 to March 1948, for example, the Democratic Party provided seven ministers and the Co-operative Party two, while the Liberal Party was the main opposition. The Miki faction inherited the traditions of the Co-operative Party and the Ikeda–Suzuki faction inherited the traditions of the Liberal Party headed by Yoshida.

In spite of the fact that the total number of LDP votes declined constantly during the 1960s and 1970s, each faction leader continued to try to increase the number of candidates of his own faction in order to increase the number of faction members in the Diet and to have a greater chance of becoming President of the LDP. Since the LDP retained an absolute majority in both Houses up to the middle of the 1970s, faction leaders were more concerned about the factional balance inside the LDP than the political balance between the LDP and other parties. Even after the middle of the 1970s, when the LDP's absolute majority in both Houses became endangered, the factional leaders always tried to put up more new candidates to increase their influence inside the LDP.

The LDP faction leaders consider that increased competition between the candidates of various factions will increase the total number of votes cast for the LDP in the longer term, even if the number of elected members of the LDP temporarily decreases. When the faction leaders have enough money and can find a hopeful candidate, therefore, they will openly recommend him to run for election and they will publicly support the candidate even if he is not nominated as an official LDP candidate. The LDP factions in this sense act rather independently in putting up candidates in the elections for the House of Representatives.

Because of this independent activity, the LDP always experiences great difficulty in selecting the official candidates from among these informal LDP candidates in the elections for the House of Representatives. The fact that each candidate, rather than the LDP branch in the constituency, establishes his own organization of supporters ('Koen Kai') exacerbates the disordered way in which the LDP runs elections.

These candidate-based organizations also facilitate the renomination of incumbent members of the Diet because they already have their own campaigning machines. Incumbent Diet members are almost without fail nominated as official LDP candidates. In the 1983 election to the House of Representatives the LDP ran 328 official candidates and issued membership certificates to ten more candidates: 273 were incumbent members (the total number of LDP members at the time of the dissolution of the House was 286), ten were former members of the House and forty-five were fresh candidates. Out of ten certificate-given candidates, one was a former member of the House and nine were fresh candidates.

In the case of the elections to the House of Councillors in 1983, because twenty-six constituencies out of forty-seven prefectural constituencies were one-seat constituencies the LDP could select its official candidates rather easily, as it nominated the incumbent members automatically and won in twenty-four constituencies. In the case of fifteen two-seat constituencies the LDP made every effort to put up two candidates in those constituencies where there was a possibility of two members being elected; in the event the party put up two official candidates in nine constituencies and took two seats in three constituencies. In these two-seat constituencies, too, the selection of the official candidates was not so difficult because incumbent members were automatically selected and because not many prospective candidates appeared in the two-seat constituencies due to the difficulty of electing two LDP members.

The Japan Socialist Party
The selection of candidates does not become a serious problem as frequently for the JSP as for the LDP. The JSP has only 65,000 members in spite of the fact that it gained 11 million votes in both Upper and Lower House elections. At the same time, the main organization which supports the JSP, the General Council of Trade Unions of Japan (Sohyo), had 4,500,000 members and 6800 affiliated trade unions in 1983. Consequently Sohyo plays a decisive role in the selection of JSP candidates.

When the prefectural headquarters select official candidates, therefore, they cannot ignore these two facts. In order to carry on an electoral campaign the JSP must have both the financial and physical support of trade union members because the number of JSP members is so small. The result is usually the selection of left-wing candidates rather than right-wing or moderate candidates and the selection of ex-trade union leaders as official JSP candidates.

In the case of the JSP, the prefectural headquarters first propose the nomination to the national headquarters and the central Executive Committee finally accepts the proposal.

Although the JSP gains a higher proportion of votes in rural areas than in urban ones, the selection of candidates does not become a serious matter because even in rural areas the trade unions of civil servants usually have the initiative in political manoeuvring. The fact that the JSP put up more than one candidate in only twenty out of 130 constituencies in 1983, and was successful in electing more than one candidate in only eight constituencies, as well as its inability to run candidates in all 130 constituencies, also shows why the selection of candidates is not so serious a problem in the JSP. For the JSP, recruiting a greater number of candidates is a much more serious (and difficult) problem.

Nevertheless, the JSP, like the LDP, suffers from internal divisions, including the existence of factions, whose 1984 strengths are shown in Table 8.2.

One problem is that the balance of factions among JSP members of the Diet differs from the balance of factions among the members of the party. First, among the members of the National Diet the number of right-wing members, especially in the House of Representatives, is greater than the number of left-wing members, while at rank-and-file level the left-wing militant members outweigh in number the right-wing moderate members. Second, the Shakaishugi Kyokai (Socialist Association), which advocates an orthodox Marxist-Leninist socialism and insists on socialist revolution by direct action, is the most influential group among ordinary members although it only has two members in the National Diet.

Table 8.2 *Faction membership in the Japan Socialist Party in the House of Representatives (1984)*

Sei Koh Ken (right)	15
Seisaku Kenkyukai (Katsumata) (centre-left)	10
Shakaishugi Kenkyukai (left)	4
Shinsei Kenkyukai (young left)	9
Seisaka Kondankai (left)	2
Shakaishugi Kyokai (left-Leninist)	2
Others (independents)	70
Total	112

As we have seen, the prefectural organization usually first nominates the candidates in both Upper House and Lower House elections. Consequently, since the majority of the party bureaucrats at the prefectural level and at rank-and-file level are left wing, the candidates chosen by the prefectural branch are in many cases ex-trade union leaders and figures of a rather rigid left-wing ideology. It is necessary, however, for the JSP to attract a wider range of the electorate in order to ensure the election of those candidates in their constituencies, but those left-wing ex-trade union leaders are too rigid in ideology, and many left-wing candidates are unsuccessful in their election.

At the same time, it is necessary for the JSP to influence decision-making in the National Diet, where the LDP has an absolute or near majority, by making compromises in day-to-day negotiations with other parties. It might also be appropriate to add here that those ex-trade union leaders have usually lost their energy after being elected as Diet members because they now consider that they have reached the last stage of their lives and feel in a sense that they are now retired.

Candidates of the JSP also have their own supporters' organizations ('Koen Kai') and the incumbent members of the Diet are usually nominated by both local branches and the headquarters. In the election to the House of Representatives in 1983 the JSP nominated 144 candidates. Out of them eighty-eight were incumbent members, fifteen were former members and forty-one were fresh candidates. At the time of the dissolution of the House of Representatives in 1983 the JSP had 101 incumbent members.

The reason why the LDP has constantly kept an absolute majority might also be attributed to the JSP's lack of ambition in running candidates for national elections. The JSP has never run candidates in all 130 constituencies. In the case of the 1983 election to the House of Representatives, for example, the JSP established only 144 candidates altogether, so that even if all the candidates had been elected they would have comprised only one quarter of the total number of members of the House of Representatives, in spite of the fact that the JSP has always claimed to be the major opposition.

The Democratic Socialist Party

In the case of the Democratic Socialist Party (DSP), because the possibility of candidates being elected is less than that of JSP candidates, the support of the trade unions becomes more important. In reality, with a few exceptions, the DSP puts up candidates only in constituencies where there are some big trade unions which belong to the Japanese Confederation of Labour (Domei). In those constituencies candidates are supported both financially and physically not only by the trade unions but also by companies because the trade unions which belong to Domei are usually non-militant, economy-oriented trade unions. It should be observed at this point that almost all Japanese trade unions are vertically organized on the basis of individual companies and not on the basis of industry in a horizontal way.

In short, candidates are first selected by the constituency branches in the DSP and then their names are sent to the head-quarters. Candidates are either leaders of local party organizations or of local trade union organizations. In both cases the decisive factor is the attitude of the trade union of whichever big private enterprise dominates the industry of the particular constituency. In the 1983 election to the House of Representatives the DSP nominated twenty-nine incumbent members and four former members out of fifty-four official candidates.

Komei and the Japan Communist Party

Both Komei and the JCP exhibit solid and centralized organization and tight control by the centre over the members, although the reasons for the solid organization of each party are very different. In Komei it is religion, and in the JCP it is ideology. In both parties the supporters devote themselves wholeheartedly to their party activities. Komei had 176,000 members in December 1982 and the JCP had 480,000 members in May 1984.

Komei had always selected candidates from among the membership of Soka Gakkai, a Buddhist organization, which publicly supports the Komei Party and which claims to have 750,000 devotee households and 16,622,000 believers. However, Komei astounded the public by presenting a list of candidates which consisted entirely of non-members of Soka Gakkai in the 1983 Upper House elections after the introduction of the proportional representation system. Because of the constant nomination of Soka Gakkai members as candidates in elections to the House of Representatives, although Komei has an Election Steering Committee as a party organ, the candidates proposed by the President have always been approved by the Central Executive Committee, and subordinate organs such as the prefectural headquarters, the general branches and the branches were informed of this from the top of the party organization.

The strong devotee attitudes of the members of Soka Gakkai and the tightly controlled and centralized organization of the Komei party enable Komei to assess easily the votes it can obtain in a particular constituency. The proportion of those elected among candidates in national elections is, therefore, always high. It was 98.3 percent in the 1983 Lower House election (see Table 8.3).

Table 8.3   *Number of top unsuccessful candidates by party*
(1983 House of Representatives)

Party	Candidates	Elected	Percentage elected	Number of top unsuccessful candidates
LDP	338	250	74.0	61
JSP	144	112	77.8	19
Komei	59	58	98.3	1
DSP	54	38	70.4	11
JCP	129	26	20.2	24
NLC	17	8	47.1	4
UDS	4	3	75.0	1
Others	103	16	15.5	9
Total	848	511	60.3	130

This strong devotee attitude of the believers of Soka Gakkai can be partly attributed to the nature of Soka Gakkai. Soka Gakkai claims descent from the creed created by Nichiren who lived in the Kamakura period (1192–1339 AD). It was the period when Japan was faced with a critical external threat to its very existence as an independent state because the Mongol Emperor Kublai Khan sent great armadas against Japan in 1274 and in 1281. Nichiren, living in this critical period, appealed to the people to realize the importance of the independence of the nation.

Soka Gakkai, which claims to be an orthodox successor to Nichiren's appeal, is very much politically orientated and nationalistic. When Soka Gakkai established the Komei Party as the Komei Seiji Renmei (Association of Clean Politics) in 1961, Soka Gakkai advocated the principle of 'Ohbutsu Myogo' which means combining political power ('Oh-King') with the creed of Buddhism ('Butsu-Buddha').

The Komei Party, which adopted its present name in 1964 after having been criticized for combining state power with religion which is unconstitutional – according to article 20, 'No religious organization shall receive any privileges from the state, nor exercise any political authority' – publicly abolished this idea of 'Ohbutsu Myogo'. However, it still advocates a Buddhist welfare society, which it calls 'human socialism', and is very nationalistic. Because Komei has organized, as a religious party, the most deprived people in society, handicapped people and unorganized labour, sometimes it adopts a very radical ideological standpoint although as a religious party it is naturally conservative. It has stressed that it represents the materialist interests of the people while at the same time appealing to spiritual values as a religious party. In these matters Komei has received solid support from Soka Gakkai believers although it might be politically opportunistic.

This opportunistic political nature of the Komei Party, however, makes its selection of candidates quite flexible so that it may select members of Soka Gakkai as candidates in the elections to the House of Representatives and non-Soka Gakkai intellectuals as candidates in the elections to the House of Councillors in the future as it did in 1983. By organizing candidate selection in this way, the Komei Party also tries to solve the problem of appealing to a wider section of the ordinary electorate. Although it has a hard core of strong devotees, the Komei Party is the second (after the JCP) most disliked party among the electorate.

The Japan Communist Party advocates the most flexible type of Eurocommunist ideology. It deleted the words 'proletarian dictatorship' from its constitution and changed from cells, as basic organs, to branches. The JCP, however, has never loosened the tight control of the Central Committee over the various organizations inside the party, advocating their control of the party as 'centralized democracy'. Although the delegates to the legislative organs are elected by the subordinate legislative organs, when once the Central

Committee has been established it dominates the whole party and in the case of the selection of candidates it usually nominates the official candidates on its own. However, the JCP makes serious efforts to nominate candidates who have some connection with local affairs. The JCP is, apart from the LDP, the only party which runs candidates in all 130 constituencies in elections to the House of Representatives.

Other parties

The New Liberal Club (NLC) and the United Democratic Socialists (UDS) are new parties. The NLC was established on 25 June 1976 when six members of the LDP (one of them a member of the House of Councillors) left the party after the Lockheed scandal was disclosed in February. Those six ex-LDP members strongly attacked corruption inside the LDP and a 'gerontocracy' which was 'bent on backroom power struggles' (*Statement on the Split of the Party*).

With one exception, all members who left the LDP at that time were younger politicians who had begun their political careers after the end of the Second World War and three were in their thirties. They considered that the post-war democracy, which in their eyes was valuable, was in crisis when they saw that the incumbent Prime Minister Miki, who was considered to be the most active in reforming the LDP, was forced to resign by the old conventional faction leaders. They concluded there was no longer any possibility of reforming the LDP.

Consequently their new party, the New Liberal Club, advocated ethics in politics, the revitalization of democracy by destroying the LDP–JSP two-party system which they considered to be out of date and no longer able to respond to quickly changing public opinion, and disarmament and a non-nuclear policy to prevent the revival of pre-war militarism in Japan.

There is no doubt that the NLC is a conservative party. They publicly advocate a free market economy although they insist on improving the system to bring about a much fairer society. The NLC publicly announced that they had 20,000 members and 40,000 associated sympathizers in June 1984.

In spite of their assertion that 'gerontocracy' should be abolished, there has been no drastic change in NLC party organization and administration. Although it has an Election Steering Committee, because the size of the party is so small (it put up only seventeen candidates in the 1983 Lower House election) almost all party management including the selection of candidates is decided in the Standing Executive Committee, which consists of seventeen members, and is then ratified by the National Executive Committee. In reality, the majority of the NLC's candidates are old LDP candidates who could not get official nomination as LDP candidates.

The UDS was established on 26 March 1977 when the right-wing leader of the JSP left the party and formed a coalition organization with leaders of the citizens' movement. Although the UDS is very interesting in the sense that it is trying to establish a loose organization which is different from that of conventional parties and to bring the citizens' movement, which tries to attain its goals outside the parliamentary system through direct action, into the framework of the parliamentary system, its results have not as yet proved successful. It has not succeeded in recruiting the leaders of the citizens' movements as candidates, with one exception in Tokyo. It might take some time for us to assess correctly any innovations in this party, including the selection processes of the candidates.

The candidates selected

It is generally said in Japan that what is needed for candidates to be successful in elections are three traits: 'Jiban' (a power base in one's local territory), 'Kanban' (advertisement hoarding or well-known name) and 'Kaban' (bag or campaign money). These three traits are also the main criteria when the LDP, JSP, DSP and NLC select their official candidates.

'Jiban' is especially important in Japan because the candidate's connections with the local community are especially appreciated among voters. For example, the proportion of members of the House of Representatives who were brought up in the same prefecture as the one they are elected in has reached 91.8 percent in the LDP, 84.6 percent in the JSP, 80.0 percent in the DSP, 60.0 percent in the Komei Party and 43.6 percent in the JCP (Asahi Shimbun, 1975).

In the LDP (and in the JSP) locality is especially important because these two parties nominate more than one candidate in the same constituency. The local connections of a candidate, and the fact that he has a special area where he can obtain an overwhelming number of votes due to his connections, give him extra strength because he need not worry about that area but can concentrate his campaign outside the area to cultivate new support.

In the LDP and the JSP candidates carry out their campaign on an individual rather than a party basis. The candidate tries to keep his 'Koen Kai' solid by having regular meetings or by organizing sightseeing trips to hot-spring resort areas. In such cases the cost of food and travel of 'Koen Kai' members is subsidized by the candidates.

We can classify the organization of 'Koen Kai' into two types. First, some candidates try to organize the members of the prefectural council and the city mayors or village masters. Because those local politicians have their supporters, national candidates can indirectly recruit the support of the electorate in this hierarchical type of organization. In the case of Mr Matsuno, a member of the House of Representatives, he organizes twelve members out of twenty-one prefectural council members and the majority of city mayors and village masters in Kumamoto I constituency. In the cases of indirect control 'Koen Kais', because prefectural headquarters consist of prefectural council members, the candidate can easily secure nomination as the official candidate of the LDP for national elections.

Secondly, some candidates organize the mass electorate directly. A candidate forms a small group of his supporters in a narrow area, then he combines these groups into some larger organization. In this way he organizes the mass electorate directly. One of the reasons why Mr Tanaka, the ex-Prime Minister who was involved in the Lockheed scandal, still gets an overwhelming majority of votes in his constituency is that he has a solid organization of voters of this type there. He often visits the basic small groups and keeps direct contact with them. He tries to fulfil all the electorate's demands by retaining direct contacts.

It might be said that the LDP (and also partly the JSP) is a kind of coalition of those individual candidates' 'Koen Kais'. In this sense, although the LDP had 2,468,000 members in September 1983, those members are the members of the individual candidates' organizations and not the members of the LDP as a party.

Once the LDP official publication admitted that there was no member of the LDP per se and wrote:

> The organizations which support the parties are ultimately the following three organizations: first the individual Koen Kais which support the LDP members in various levels of the legislative bodies. Secondly, the civil service system which has close relations with the LDP as ruling party in the parliamentary system. Thirdly, in connection with the bureaucratic system, there are many organizations and corporations which exist under governmental control . . . These are not our own party's organizations, but the pseudo-organizations of the LDP. (LDP *Soshiki Koho* [*Organizational Report*], 1 June 1970)

The existence of the individual 'Koen Kais' is one of the reasons why we have 'Nisei' (second generation) members of the Japanese

National Diet. It is safest for the electorate and the party to put up his eldest son when an incumbent member of the Diet dies, because by doing so the electorate can retain the organization which represents their interests in the National Diet. The 'Koen Kai' in this way become a solid organization of the *Gesellschaft* type which articulates members' interests to the outside world while retaining a *Gemeinschaft* character internally. There were ninety-six 'Nisei' members in the House of Representatives out of a total of 250 (38.4 percent) in the case of the LDP and 122 members in total out of 511 members (23.9 percent) in the 1983 election. It is also a fact that around 30 percent of incumbent LDP members of the Diet wish to bequeath their 'Jiban' to their sons or grandsons (see Asahi Shimbun, 1970: 262–3).

The strength of the 'Nisei' implies limited opportunities for ordinary young ambitious people running for election as official party candidates. It is quite natural, therefore, that some very serious antagonistic feeling occurs between the 'Nisei' candidate who succeeds his father's 'Jiban' and the rival candidate who has

Table 8.4   *Career patterns of the candidates in the 1979 election to the House of Representatives*

Total	Career	No. of candidates	Percentage
1.	Local politicians	209	23.5
2.	Senior party members	140	15.7
3.	Trade union leaders	112	12.6
4.	Journalists, lawyers, etc.	101	11.3
5.	Civil servants	93	10.4
5.	Secretaries of National Diet members	93	10.4

LDP		JSP	
1. Local politicians	29%	1. Trade union leaders	52%
2. Civil servants	22	2. Local politicians	26
3. Diet members' secretaries	18		

Komei		JCP	
1. Local politicians	45%	1. Senior party members	53%
2. Senior members of party and		2. Lawyers, journalists	18
Soka Gakkai	39	3. Trade union leaders	15

DSP		NLC	
1. Local politicians	30%	1. Local politicians	23%
2. Trade union leaders	17	1. Diet members' secretaries	23
		1. Journalists, lawyers	23

Source: Shiratori (1980: 117).

been secretary to the same person and wishes to succeed to the same 'Jiban'. Because quite a number of secretaries to members of the Diet have political ambitions and because the proportion of ex-secretary members is large, as shown in Table 8.4, this kind of struggle between the 'Nisei' candidate and the ex-secretary candidate arises quite often.

In the House of Representatives election in December 1983, when Mr Ichiro Nakagawa, the leader of one faction in the LDP, committed suicide, both his eldest son, Mr Shoichi Nakagawa, and his chief secretary, Mr Muneo Suzuki, tried to run for election and wished to succeed to the late Nakagawa's 'Jiban' in Kokkaido fifth constituency. His son insisted that he was the only orthodox successor to the late Nakagawa's political will, as the eldest son, while Mr Suzuki argued that having been his secretary he knew best what the late Nakagawa intended, and as an experienced politician could best represent local interests. Mr Suzuki also added that it was impossible for an inexperienced person who knew nothing about politics to know how to realize local interests in national politics.

In a sense these two candidates advocated two different types of legitimacy in seeking the nomination as the official candidate of the LDP. One insisted on the primacy of blood, like the monarchy, and the other insisted on 'virtù' in the Machiavellian sense as the source of legitimacy in politics. The Hokkaido prefectural headquarters could not decide who should be the official candidate of the LDP and sent a message to the central headquarters which said that the new candidates – including a third – should be treated equally.

The LDP headquarters, however, gave the official candidacy to Mr Shoichi Nakagawa. The Hokkaido LDP prefectural head-quarters designated the other two new candidates, including Mr Suzuki, as 'the candidates officially recommended by the Hokkaido LDP headquarters', after receiving the decision from the central headquarters, and asked every LDP member possible to openly support Mr Suzuki. In the election, due to severe competition between Mr Nakagawa and Mr Suzuki, the total LDP votes among the electorate increased from 31.9 percent in 1980 to 52.7 percent in 1983. But because the LDP's votes were unevenly spread among their five candidates, while the JSP successfully divided their votes equally between their three candidates, the LDP's seats dropped from three to two. Both Mr Nakagawa and Mr Suzuki were elected.

It is well known that a large proportion of members in the National Diet are ex-civil servants, as shown in Table 8.4. This is for several reasons. First, senior civil servants in central government have to resign rather early although the legal retiring age is sixty-five. Second, the extent of central government control over and role in decision-making in Japan is fairly large in comparison with other highly industrialized countries. Third, there is no legal prohibition to stop ex-senior civil servants running for national election. As the LDP has constantly been in power since its formation in 1955, ex-senior civil servants usually run for election as LDP candidates, exploiting the connections which were established while they were in central government.

The interesting fact is that we can classify the factions into two types, 'Kanryo Habatsu' (civil servants' factions) and 'Tojin Habatsu' (politicians' factions) on the basis of the proportion of ex-civil servant members. The Suzuki and Fukuda factions correspond more to the former type, and the Komoto and Nakasone factions to the latter. As ex-civil servant statesmen were rather cautious at the time of the normalization of Sino-Japanese diplomatic relations, 'Kanryo Habatsu' are rather cautious in the initiation of new dimensions in politics, and 'Tojin Habatsu' are more active in the initiation of new policies.

Because senior civil servants have close contacts with party leaders and because they can secretly prepare for their elections by investing public financial resources in their future constituencies, the ratio of ex-senior civil servant candidates being selected as official party candidates and their electoral success is higher than average for new candidates. This second aspect explains why senior civil servants from the Treasury form the largest bloc among ex-civil servant members of the Diet.

Another interesting fact is that many non ex-civil servant Diet members are now considering how they can retain control over the civil servants who are very powerful in policy-formation and political decision-making because they know the techniques of solving societal problems administratively. One response is to try to specialize in a particular sphere by remaining in one particular standing committee. By doing so, they can also acquire the support of various organizations in that sphere.

Another response was the introduction of a proportional representation system into the national constituency in 1983 with party lists of ranked candidates. The politicians tried to control the senior civil servants by threatening them that party leaders would downgrade disobedient senior civil servants in the lists of candidates. Although these efforts by politicians were unsuccessful in the end because PR resulted in an increase in ex-civil servant members of the House of Councillors in the LDP, they illustrate the rise in tension between the ever-increasing number of ex-bureaucrats and University of Tokyo graduate members of the Diet, and non-bureaucrat politicians.

Membership of the National Diet is considered to be a full-time job. Members of the National Diet usually carry out parliamentary activities from Tuesday morning to Friday noon. They are provided with one office suite and one residential flat (if the member is elected from a constituency outside Tokyo). Those who are elected from outside Tokyo return to their country home on Friday afternoons, devote their weekends to constituency activities, and come back to Tokyo on Mondays. Sessions of the Diet and various committees are scheduled from Tuesday through to Friday morning. Junior members spend more time on constituency activities, while senior members spend more time undertaking parliamentary activities.

Conclusion

What are the results of these candidate selections, Japanese-style? How do they influence the future of Japanese politics?

First, the intervention of factions in candidate selection in middle-sized constituencies will cause a gradual but steady disintegration of the two major Japanese parties, the LDP and the JSP. The LDP will suffer more deeply than the JSP. Already the LDP passed a no confidence vote against its own Prime Minister in 1979 in spite of the fact that it had an absolute majority, and put up two candidates for Prime Minister in the Diet. The recent rapid expansion of the Tanaka faction and its policy of nominating its own candidate in any constituency where it is possible in Lower House elections will produce more friction inside the LDP.

Secondly, personal allegiance will become more important in Japanese politics in the future. Professor Robert E. Ward (1978: 69) writes:

There are two major types of political allegiance, programmatic and personal. Programmatic allegiance is based on considerations of policy; personal allegiance on affection for or loyalty to a particular political leader . . . Classifying societies in terms of the degree to which their members' political allegiances are determined by programmatic or personal considerations, Japan would rank toward the personal end of such a scale.

This tendency of Japanese politics to stress increasingly personal allegiance might make Japanese politicians pay less attention to the public good of society. It might also cause them to neglect the necessity of paying attention to the international situation. Those common interests in both domestic and international society will be better served by civil servants in the future. Japanese politics, therefore, is shifting towards a non-political bureaucratic society where the role and influence of civil servants dominate the whole decision-making system.

Finally, the type of candidate selection now taking place in Japan will lead to a greater increase in the localism which has traditionally existed in Japanese politics. People will choose the candidate who gives greater consideration to local problems rather than to the problems of the nation. The increase of localism in politics and the more central organizing of the civil service in Japan will increase the tension between politicians and civil servants in the future and create some kind of political discrepancy in the Japanese political system.

Perhaps the quick adaptability of the Japanese nation and high sensitivity which comes from the traditionally high standard of education in Japan will solve the problems in the rather unstable period of Japanese parliamentary democracy that is approaching.

References

Asahi Shimbun (1970) *Jiminto – Hoshu Kenryoko No Kozu (The LDP – the Structure of Conservative Power)*. Tokyo: Asahi Shimbun Sha.

Asahi Shimbun (1975) *Asahi Nenkan (Asahi Newspaper Yearbook)*. Tokyo: Asahi Shimbun Sha.

Baerwald, Hans H. (1974) *Japan's Parliament: An Introduction*. London: Cambridge University Press.

Campbell, John C. (ed.) (1981) 'Parties, Candidates and Voters in Japan: Six Quantitative Studies', in *Michigan Papers in Japanese Studies*. Ann Arbor, MI: Center for Japanese Studies, University of Michigan.

Curtis, Gerald L. (1971) *Election Campaigning Japanese Style*. New York: Columbia University Press.

Ike, Nobutaka (1972) *Japanese Politics: Patron-Client Democracy*. New York: Knopf.

Ike, Nobutaka (1978) *A Theory of Japanese Democracy*. Boulder, CO: Westview Press.

Langer, Paul Fritz (1972) *Communism in Japan; A Case of Political Naturalization*. Stanford, CA: Hoover Institution.

Palmer, Arvin (1971) *Buddhist Politics: Japan's Clean Government Party*. The Hague: M. Nijhoff.

Pempel, T.J. (1982) *Policy and Politics in Japan: Creative Conservatism*. Philadelphia, PA: Temple University Press.

Richardson, Bradley M. and Scott C. Flanagan (1984) *Politics in Japan*. Boston, MA: Little, Brown & Co.

Shiratori, Rei (ed.) (1980) *Nihon no Seito Chizu, '80–90 (Japanese Party Maps, '80–90)*. Tokyo: Gakuyo Shobo.

Shiratori, Rei (ed.) (1982) *Japan in the 1980s*. Tokyo: Kodansha International.

Shiratori, Rei (1984) 'The Introduction of a Proportional Representation System in Japan', *Electoral Studies*, 3 (2): 151–70.

Shiratori, Rei and Takao Iawami (eds) (1984) *Ran Renritsu no Jidai (The Age of Confused Coalition)*. Tokyo: Ashi Shobo.

Shiratori, Rei, Yasuharu Okino and Nobuo Sakagami (eds) (1983) *Bunkatsu Tochi (Divide and Rule – Upper House Election of 1983)*. Tokyo: Ashi Shobo.

Steiner, Kurt, Ellis S. Krauss and Scott C. Flanagan (eds) (1980) *Political Opposition and Local Politics in Japan*. Princeton, NJ: Princeton University Press.

Stockwin, James A.A. (1982) *Japan: Divided Politics in a Growth Economy*. London: Weidenfeld & Nicolson (first published 1975).

Verba, Sidney, Norman H. Nie and Jae-on Kim (1978) *Participation and Political Equality: A Seven Nation Comparison*. Cambridge and New York: Cambridge University Press.

Ward, Robert E. (1978) *Japan's Political System*. Englewood Cliffs, NJ: Prentice-Hall (first published 1967).

Watanuki, Joji (1977) *Politics in Postwar Japanese Society*. Tokyo: University of Tokyo Press.

9

The Netherlands: the predominance of regionalism

Ruud Koole and Monique Leijenaar

Since its very beginning in 1848 the system of parliamentary democracy in the Netherlands has met with criticism. For some citizens democracy went too far, for others not far enough. Fear of too much democracy was felt by opponents of universal suffrage (introduced for men in 1917 and for women in 1919) and by critics of the allegedly weak, chaotic or even immoral effects of democracy in the interwar period. Demands for more democracy were formulated by, for example, the movements of emancipation of workers around 1900, and by the post-war generation in the 1960s. Notwithstanding all this criticism, parliamentary democracy survived, proving its strength and flexibility.

Recently the discussion has shifted from the call for more participation by and influence of the 'grassroots' towards a call for a better quality of governmental policy. And since it is Parliament that is supposed to control government, it is criticized as well for failing to do this properly. Hence, the quality of the members of Parliament becomes an issue. This evokes an interest in the background of parliamentarians, in their recruitment and more specifically in the changes in selection processes.

During the 1970s the composition of Parliament changed drastically. For example, the average age of members of Parliament decreased and the number of women parliamentarians rapidly increased. In this chapter we describe the selection process, the changes this process has undergone due to recent social and political developments in Dutch society and the impact of these changes on the nature of Parliament. We pay special attention to the role of women in these processes since the rise of the number of women has been one of the most remarkable changes in the composition of parliamentary parties.

The electoral system
Elections for the Second Chamber (Tweede Kamer), the national representative body in the Netherlands, are held at least every four years. The Dutch system is characterized by extreme proportional

representation. There is no threshold as in West Germany; some parliamentary parties consist of only one member, to elect whom 61,147 votes (0.67 percent), possibly scattered all over the country, were sufficient in 1986. The voter casts a single preferential vote for any candidate on one of the lists presented by the parties. The entire country is one constituency, but is divided into nineteen administrative electoral sub-districts in which the parties, if they want, can put forward different candidate lists.[1] The totals in the sub-districts are added up nationally and the number of seats awarded to each party is based on this national sum. If the party uses different lists, as most parties do, a very complex procedure is applied to assign the seats to specific individuals. Of course the parties understand this method and distribute the names of the candidates over the nineteen lists in such a way that, in the end, it is almost always the favoured candidates who get the seats.

Since compulsory attendance at the polls was abolished in 1970, the average turnout for parliamentary elections has been around 83 percent (Schmidt, 1983: 139). The political parties are central to the parliamentary system, even though they are not recognized by Dutch electoral law. A sum of Dfl.1000 (about $400 in 1986) and twenty-five signatures of persons entitled to vote are sufficient to submit a list with a maximum of forty names in one of the nineteen sub-districts. Since 1956 the Electoral Law (article G13) has allowed the name or symbol of the political grouping to be printed on the ballot paper above of the list of candidates. This provision is one of the few concessions to political reality whereby it is political parties rather than twenty-five individuals who nominate candidates.

Although voters may vote for any candidate on the ballot, about 90 percent cast their vote for the first person on a party list and thereby effectively vote for a party rather than for a specific candidate. This behaviour can be explained in two ways. First, preference votes are unlikely to affect the outcome, since a candidate needs a very large number of preference votes (about 50 percent of the votes needed to obtain one seat) to get elected ahead of candidates placed higher on the list. Only three times since 1945 has a candidate placed at a low position on the list been elected to the Second Chamber because of preference votes.[2] Preference votes (i.e. votes not cast for the number one candidate) can be interpreted as signals given by the voters to the parties, to express for instance, a relative preference for women or regional candidates (Koole, 1984a: 21), or disagreement with the order of the list. A second explanation for the large number of votes for the head of the list is that this person is well known to the electorate. The media pay little attention to the other candidates.

It is the party which determines the order of their list and thereby decides the persons to be elected, although the number of seats is of course dependent upon a party's share of the total valid vote. The actual competition for a parliamentary seat takes place within the party, not on election day. The voters decide only on the strength of the respective parties. This means, for example, that, with the exception of the head of the list, electoral appeal is not the most important feature of a candidate. Other criteria count more and such criteria, set by the party, have altered considerably under the influence of social and political changes in the last two decades.

Social changes

We want to focus on three profound developments in Dutch society, which had their impact on selection procedures and selection criteria within the parties: the process of 'depillarization', the democratization wave and the rise of the women's movement. All three are closely interrelated.

Most important of all in this respect seems to be 'depillarization'. Until the mid-sixties the highly fragmented Dutch society was organized on the basis of religious or socio-economic cleavages into four ideological groupings or 'pillars': Catholics, Protestants, Liberals and Socialists. Each pillar included not only political parties, but also other forms of association, from trade unions and employers' organizations to broadcasting systems and soccer clubs. The pillars were isolated from one another. Only at the elite level did co-operation take place and this provided stable government as a rather passive electorate followed its leaders uncomplainingly (Lijphart, 1968; Daalder, 1974). Depillarization refers to a process in which the links within the pillars were loosened, on a psychological level as well as on an institutional level. With the development of the welfare state and the arrival of television, the individual citizen no longer felt obliged to follow traditional paths, and this has led to what some observers have called the 'decolonization of the citizen'.[3] This process occurred first – and with a vengeance – within the religious pillars (deconfessionalization), but it also affected the others.

The democratization wave of the sixties is another important phenomenon that influenced selection processes. The call for more democratic institutions opened the way for other ideas and new political values. On the political level this implied criticism of the old institutions and leaders, a call for a participatory democracy, the introduction of New Left, or post-material, values and the foundation of new parties. It also meant an increase in the floating vote.

Parties could no longer count on their electorate as automatically as before.

The third development, in the seventies, was the demand for more political influence for women. It was made clear to politicians and electors that women, half of the population, were under-represented in political decision-making. Women became more aware of how much politics affected their lives, and therefore how necessary, and indeed acceptable, it was to take part in politics. As a consequence, the interest of women in politics has increased (Van Deth, 1983: 480).

What exactly are the effects of these developments on the selection process within the political parties?

First, the *political climate* has changed. The call for a more participatory democracy implied a politicization of party members and democratization of the internal organization. For some, democratization became an end in itself. Elements of direct democracy were introduced in the structure of parties. As we shall see below, left-wing and centre parties were more affected by these developments than right-wing parties. Democratization also implied new demands on the party leadership and representatives in Parliament. Candidates had to show more respect for the wishes of the rank-and-file, which were not always coherent. The women's liberation movement changed the parties' attitude towards women. Until the mid-1970s parties paid little attention to women's issues and nominated only one or two token women in government and Parliament. This situation has changed dramatically. At least one chapter of the recent party manifestos deals specifically with women's issues and some parties have established positive action programmes to provide women party members with better chances.

Second, the *recruitment reservoirs* have altered and sometimes dried up. Only party members are allowed to participate in the nomination process as selectors or as candidates, but the number of party members decreased rapidly in the 1960s (the small right-wing orthodox parties and the VVD excepted). This has been due partly to psychological depillarization, as described above, but also to unintended results of the call for more participation. Although intended to improve the quality of participation for the ordinary party members, it sometimes led to contrary results, mainly because of a greater load on participants. In 1980, for instance, the combined total membership of all parties participating in the national elections was no higher than the number of members of the Catholic People's Party (KVP) alone in 1955: approximately 430,000 (Koole and Voerman, 1986).

By 1986 only about 5 percent of the electorate were members of a political party. Moreover, it appears that not even 10 percent of these party members can be considered activists, by which we mean those who go to party meetings, discuss party matters, become a member of a (local) party board or participate in the selection of candidates. This implies that only 0.5 percent of the electorate participates in candidate selection.

Table 9.1   *Political parties in the Dutch Second Chamber*

Party	Percentage of votes (1986)	Number of seats (1986)	Percentage of seats for women	Number of members (1985)	Members as % of voters (1985/6)
CDA	34.6	54	14.8	131,267	4.1
PvdA	33.3	52	19.2	99,465	3.3
VVD	17.4	27	14.8	89,120	5.6
D'66	6.1	9	11.1	8,774	1.6
PPR	1.3	2	50.0	7,848	6.8
PSP	1.2	1	100.0	7,767	7.0
SGP	1.8	3	0	21,400	13.4
RPF	0.9	1	0	8,970	10.8
GPV	1.0	1	0	12,909	14.7

CDA: Christian Democratic Appeal
PvdA: Labour Party
VVD: People's Party for Freedom and Democracy (right-wing liberal)
D'66: Democrats '66 (progressive liberal)
PPR: Radical Political Party
PSP: Pacifist Socialist Party
SGP: Political Reformed Party
RPF: Reformed Political Federation (orthodox Calvinist)
GPV: Reformed Political League (orthodox Calvinist)

Source: Documentation Centre on Dutch Political Parties (DNPP),
       University of Groningen

Furthermore, the contribution made by affiliated organizations to the parties' recruitment reservoirs is declining with depillarization. Parties cannot count on candidates coming from labour unions, employer's organizations, etc. At the same time, many of the parties have undergone a rejuvenation and the participation of women in the parties has increased.

Selection processes: theory and practice

In the Netherlands political parties are free to organize the selection of candidates as they consider appropriate. Political parties are treated just like any other association by public law, so no special legal regulations exist regarding nomination procedures. Suggestions have been made for regulating some internal aspects of the life of political parties, such as party democracy, party finance and candidate selections (Elzinga, 1982; Thissen, 1982), but there has never been a majority in Parliament in favour of them. Hence, selection procedures within parties vary considerably. We shall concentrate on the three main parties, the centrist Christian Democratic Appeal (CDA), the right-wing People's Party for Freedom and Democracy (VVD) and the left-wing Labour Party (PvdA). Together, these three parties won more than 85 percent of the popular vote in the 1986 national elections (see Table 9.1).

A study of candidate selection in the Netherlands in 1963, based on party constitutions, concluded that it was highly centralized. Usually a small number of party leaders made the selection (Lipschits, 1963). Contemporary party constitutions, however, show a different picture. Of course, the central bodies still play an important role, but participation in the selection process is now less oligarchic and more decentralized, at least on paper. The realities of the present selection process have not yet been the subject of any systematic empirical research,[4] but a general impression of those processes can be gathered from internal reports of the parties. Therefore we will give a description of the formal procedures within the parties and comment on the reality of the nomination processes based on these reports. We conclude the description of the parties with some details on their attitude towards women aspirants.

In order to clarify the procedural differences between the political parties, we use the terms suggested by Ranney to describe the dimensions of candidate selection (Ranney, 1981). He distinguishes three dimensions: centralization, inclusiveness and direct or indirect participation. We shall consider these three dimensions, first within the CDA, then the PvdA and the VVD.

The Christian Democratic Appeal
The foundation of the CDA in 1980 as a merger of two Protestant parties (ARP and CHU) and one Catholic party (KVP) was a clear reaction to deconfessionalization. A fusion of organizations from two different pillars, once inconceivable, was brought about by electoral losses of the religious parties. In 1963 the three constituent parties still won 49.2 percent of the popular vote, but in 1982 the CDA obtained only 29.3 percent. The speed of their electoral decline, however, was clearly reduced by the amalgamation. In 1986 the party even managed considerable gains (34.6 percent) and became the largest party. This electoral success was attributed to a

large extent to the man who headed their lists, Prime Minister Lubbers, who was able to attract many non-religious voters.

In the first years after the foundation of the new party in 1980 its selection of candidates was governed by a special agreement, the so-called 'fusion protocol', by which each of the four 'blood-groups' (i.e. the former parties plus the group of new direct CDA members) was entitled to a fixed number of eligible candidates on the party list. This procedure was followed for the 1981 and 1982 national elections, but was abolished in 1984. Candidate selection for the 1986 elections followed the stipulations of the party constitution, officially regardless of historical privileges. The foundation of the new CDA also provided an opportunity of adopting a completely new charter. This explains the relatively decentralized character of the selection procedures. Local party branches initiate the process of candidate selection by suggesting names of candidates. These names are put on an alphabetical roster. After consultations with the parliamentary party and advice from the party leadership, a special committee consisting of delegates of the regional party organizations (*Kamercentrales*), corresponding to the nineteen electoral sub-districts, draws up an advisory list. This list is again discussed and voted upon by local party branches and the vote of each branch is then added up by the party executive into *one* final order of eligibility of the candidates.[5] It is a sort of referendum, not of the party members, but of the local party branches.

Thus, formally, local party branches are decisive in the process of candidate selection within the CDA. The party leadership, however, has various opportunities of influencing this process by suggesting the order of the advisory list, although branches do sometimes modify this order. The fact that the local party branches have the final say means that a high degree of direct participation is (formally) possible and all party members are entitled to participate.

The CDA published a report in 1983, drafted by a special commission established by the party executive, in which the internal party structure, still governed by special rules for the transitional period as laid down in the fusion protocol, was heavily criticized because of its rigidity. According to the protocol seats in Parliament as well as other executive posts were to be allocated between the three constituent parties and the group of direct CDA members. The report stated, without giving exact figures, that this agreement prevented recruitment of young and female members and pleaded for a faster turnover of incumbents. In addition, it pointed out that there were too few generalist candidates and too many specialists or representatives of interest groups. The party charter asks for a balanced composition of the parliamentary party in terms of expertise (CDA, 1985: article 6.1) but the report made it clear that such a balance was missing. The report also criticized the priority given by the selectorate to a candidate's regional ties, arguing that this sometimes worked to the disadvantage of the 'best candidate', a term not defined in the report (CDA, 1983: 31).

Certainly, in practice regional ties and activities are valued. On their nomination candidates must promise to attend local party meetings regularly, unless they are party leaders, and incumbents must generally maintain good links with at least one region in order to ensure reselection.

The parliamentary party of the CDA did not greet the report with great enthusiasm. Rejuvenation and feminization, it said, would detract from experience and expertise. Further discussions, however, resulted in the scrapping of the fusion protocol in February 1984 and the party council of May 1984 accepted the propositions made by the commission, but it also decided that faster circulation should not be an end in itself.

Turning to the selection of female candidates, the three predecessors of the CDA have traditionally been more reluctant than the other main parties to positively value women's participation in politics. One of the constituent protestant parties, the ARP (Anti-Revolutionaire Partij) prohibited its women members from being nominated for election until 1953. The religious parties had the lowest percentage of women representatives: from 1945 until 1972 the three confessional parties had an average of 6.2 percent women parliamentarians, compared with 11.2 percent in the PvdA and 16.9 percent in the VVD (Boddendijk, Klein and Nolte, 1980: 155). But now the CDA, like the other main parties, has a women's organization which sends delegates to the party executive and party congress. One of its goals is to increase the number of women representatives; through its delegates it puts pressure on the party executive. Recently the women's organization of the CDA has announced that it will try to make the party adopt a quota of 33 percent women in party boards and representative bodies (*CDA Krant*, 3[1]).

The Labour Party

The Labour Party (PvdA), a moderate left party, introduced a very decentralized selection procedure in 1971. Earlier, the New Left within the party had often criticized the rigid party structure. Discussions about internal party democracy were (and still are) very frequent within the PvdA and consequently procedures often changed. For example, before 1966 *all* party members (and not only party activists, as now) were consulted in the final stage of the selection process. This sort of referendum was abolished in 1966 because less than 25 percent of party members voted and the proposed candidate list was either returned unchanged or not returned at all (Kruijt, 1966: 737). But the call for more participation in the 1970s led to further reform of the system. The aim was to bridge the gap between voter and representative by bringing politics closer to party members' homes. This also corresponded with efforts to democratize the party by fighting the power of the national party oligarchy. Although several observers have warned against unintended results of 'overdemocratization' (Tromp, 1980), the present system of candidate selection is clearly marked by the democratization wave of the 1960s.

Candidate selection within the PvdA is organized by a commission established in 1981, which is independent of the party executive. Six members of the commission are chosen by the party congress (delegates from the local party branches) and the party secretary holds the seventh seat. Without suggesting names, this commission drafts a profile of the future parliamentary party after a consultation with the incumbent parliamentary party. For the election of 1986 this profile mentioned the need for certain expertise, like that of lawyers, economists, experts in the field of social security and environmental experts. Other welcome attributes are a long party career, ties with various interest groups and being a woman. After approval by the party council (delegates from the regional party organizations), this profile is sent to the local branches, which suggest names of candidates to the regional party organizations. These regional organizations (*gewesten*),comprising delegates from the local branches, also receive suggestions from the independent commission as well as from the party executive. The impact of the profile on these suggestions, however, appears to be almost non-existent. In the discussions within the branches and the *gewesten* the profile is hardly mentioned.[6] On the basis of all this information the *gewesten* decide upon the order of the list of candidates in their respective electoral sub-districts. The only exception is that the head of the list is appointed by a special party congress composed of delegates from the local party branches. So, although the PvdA has different candidate lists in all nineteen sub-districts, the head of the list is the same person everywhere.

Thus the degree of centralization is low in the PvdA and the opportunities for the party leadership to influence the process are relatively few. Direct participation by party members, however, is restricted, because there is no referendum and the regional party organizations are decisive. But since party members, except those proposed for election, can participate indirectly in the selection process, the degree of inclusiveness is relatively high.

The PvdA has devoted many publications to the question of its internal democracy (for example, PvdA, 1979, 1980). The lack of good candidates, the exaggerated stress on regional connections and activities, and the lack of balance within the parliamentary party have all caused concern. The candidate reservoir was said to be drying up. According to the PvdA report of 1978, the youth organizations, trade unions and other local organizations no longer contributed candidates (Wiardi Beckman Stichting, 1978). Recruitment was further hampered by strict anti-cumulation laws.

There was also criticism that regional affiliations were too influential, and that this could weaken the parliamentary performance of the party. Regional lobbies sometimes neglected incumbents (and not just backbenchers) who concentrated too much on parliamentary activity and neglected the need to remain visible in their own party region. In consequence, incumbents sometimes have to seek renomination in several regions and may not be successful in any of them – at least, not successful in gaining a high list position. Provincial party cadres are commonly interested in becoming deputies and incumbents who neglect their areas leave themselves open to strong competition from such sources. Proposals by the party executive to overcome this effect of decentralized selection by giving the party council the right to select the same five top candidates for the lists in all electoral sub-districts were defeated by the party congress of October 1981. It was hoped that the independent selection commission would strengthen the position of incumbents but, as yet, it does not appear to have done so.

It was exactly this phenomenon which led to a renewed intraparty debate about the selection procedures after the 1986 national elections, in which the PvdA gained five seats (from forty-seven to fifty-two but remained once more on the opposition benches. The party executive proposed to weaken the autonomy of the *gewesten* in the selection processes. According to this proposal the party executive would gain the right to select the second candidate on every regional list, in order to be able to put more 'national' candidates into eligible places on the lists. The congress in April 1987 decided against this proposal.

The attitude of social democratic parties towards women has historically been more positive than the attitude of religious parties. Already in 1908 the women's organization of the precursor of the PvdA was established and played an important role in the political fight for women's suffrage. As in the CDA, the women's organization in the present PvdA is, like the party itself, organized nationally as well as regionally and locally, giving it its own network to lobby for women candidates. Under such pressure, the PvdA resolved in 1977 that women should comprise at least 25 percent of party committees and representative bodies. This quota has not been met (Leijenaar and Niemoller, 1986: 189). In April 1987, the party congress decided that the 25 percent quota must be considered the absolute minimum and that a 50 percent quota should be the target.

The People's Party for Freedom and Democracy
The selection processes within this party (the VVD), a conservative-liberal party, are more centralized than those of the CDA and the PvdA. An explanation for this phenomenon might be the fact that the VVD seems to have been less affected by demands for democratization in the 1960s and 1970s than the other parties, despite the fact that it developed from a medium-sized loosely organized party of well-to-do voters in the 1960s into a large party with many blue- and white-collar workers among its voters.

Local party branches may suggest names of candidates, but do not have any control over selection. The selection process is an interplay between regional party organizations (*Kamerkringen*) and the party leadership. After some consultative rounds a special election council, consisting of delegates from the regional party organizations but presided over by the chairperson of the party, meets to determine the final order of the various lists of candidates in the nineteen electoral sub-districts. It does so on the basis of a proposed order of candidates drafted by the party executive. Hence the party leadership (including the chairperson of the parliamentary party) possesses an important lever to influence the process.

For the 1986 national elections the party executive decided to have the same three candidates heading the lists in all electoral sub-districts. The next twenty candidates (who were regarded as certain of election), were distributed over various sub-districts, but the order of the following seventeen candidates (the 'dangerous zone') were to be the same everywhere in order to provide a balanced parliamentary party. The tail of the list, comprising hopeless candidates, could be decided freely by the sub-districts (VVD, 1982, 1985).

This rather strict proposal was a clear effort by the party executive to fight the problem of regionalism, which was already severe in 1982, when various regional party organizations disregarded the qualities of incumbents in favour of candidates living in their own region. A report of a Commission on Candidate Selection, established by the party executive to assess the procedures, recommended the above-mentioned strict scheme. The complaints of some other regional party organizations that the old procedures promoted narrow regionalism by agreements among several regional party organizations ('If your delegates support our (regional) candidate, we'll support yours') were taken seriously by the commission. The party executive admitted that, because non-incumbent aspirants are unknown to most party bodies, 'promoters' and 'cliques' affect the listing in an arbitrary fashion (VVD, 1982). But, as mentioned before, the new procedures did not lead to less regionalism in 1986. On the contrary, regionalism was even more pronounced in the nominations for those elections (*Nieuwsblad van hed Noorden*, 12 December 1985, and *NRC*, 3 February 1986).

Formally the degree of centralization is fairly high in the VVD. There is no direct participation by party members but all party members, except those proposed for election, have the right to be included in the process.

The VVD and its precursors always took a positive stance towards women's participation in politics. They were in favour of women's suffrage and until the seventies the VVD had more women in its parliamentary party than the CDA or PvdA. Although a women's organization is active in the VVD, no special measures have been taken to increase the number of women representatives.

The selection processes in CDA, PvdA and
VVD compared
Of the three main parties the CDA provides for the most extensive participation, giving all members a direct voice in the final decision on the candidate list although the advice of the centre in this issue is very influential. The VVD is the most centralized of the major parties. These variations reflect the differing impact of the demo-cratization wave of the 1960s, which left the VVD relatively unaffected.

There is little difference in rules for eligibility. Candidates in all parties must be members and accept the party platform (although some dissent is permitted in exceptional circumstances). Candidates are also required to make various promises regarding their behaviour, although these would be enforceable only through the threat of deselection at the next election.[7] Particularly in the CDA and the PvdA aspirants are drawn from the ranks of long-serving party activists. A long party career, preferably starting from the lowest ranks, counts positively in the eyes of selectors and increases the chances of nomination. The party activists of the present become the political representatives of the future.

In spite of important procedural differences between the three major parties, all struggle with regionalism. In all three parties a large part of the selectorate tends to value the regional background of a candidate more highly than other qualities. Only national figures (party leaders, ministers) do not need special support from one or more regions to get reselected. Promotion of a regional candidate, however, is often justified by stressing qualities other than his or her regional background. Features like parliamentary ability and professional experience do of course play a role in the selection processes, but usually a secondary one. Observations at local and regional party meetings make it clear that these features are often used as a façade behind which the real game of regional interests is played. Defending regional interests overtly is still considered by the public as an undesirable practice that detracts from the ideal of a professionally balanced and experienced parliamentary party.

This ideal corresponds with the traditional feature of Dutch politics, by which recruitment of political personnel or civil servants, given the proportional representation of ideological groupings, is based mainly on technocratic abilities rather than on other qualities of the candidate. Criticism of the functioning of the parliamentary party is very often prompted by a perceived divergence from this traditional idea. But during the last two decades this ideal has been accompanied by another: that of a more representative parliament containing more young members and more women. These two approaches, technocratic and representative, may not always be compatible, but are generally regarded favourably.

Neither ideal justifies the regionalism which is predominant in the selection processes. Within the regional and local party echelons regionalism is evident; at the national party level, however, it is hidden or criticized. This partisan schizophrenia explains why in the reports of all three parties (drafted by national committees) regionalism is severely condemned, while in reality regionalism is paramount.

According to its 1983 report the CDA is also concerned about stagnation at the top, with too few young deputies, women and direct members. In contrast, the PvdA perceives the professional and educational imbalance on its party committees and parliamentary party as a problem, something not considered by the CDA and the VVD in their reports. Owing to its enormous electoral growth in the 1970s the VVD has succeeded – in a simple way – in combining continuity with rejuvenation, something that was difficult in the CDA and the PvdA. Yet the drop in its parliamentary strength at the last election may result in stagnation in the VVD too.

Considering the call for more women aspirants there seems to be a climate in which the party leadership takes into account the fact that women candidates must have some safe places, and in which it is unacceptable to replace an incumbent woman with a man.[8] Yet the 1986 results show no imminent feminization or rejuventation of the parliamentary parties.

The outcome of selection procedures

In determining the effect of selection procedures and criteria, we will try to answer two questions:

1. Do selection procedures have a direct impact on the composition of the parliamentary party? In other words, do parliamentarians of parties with different selection procedures differ much in terms of background?

2. Do selection procedures have an effect on the behaviour of parliamentarians?

The composition of the parliamentary party

In the previous section we described the changes that have taken place within the party structures, the reasons for change, and the reaction of sections of the political parties to the present state of the selection process. The way a party selects its candidates seems under eternal scrutiny. Demands for procedural changes sometimes arise from the bottom, from the local party activists, sometimes from the top. A demand for more centralization generally means that the leadership is not content with the candidates from previous selections. Others, as we have seen, define the need for balance in terms of representativeness.

In the absence of any results from systematic research it is difficult to assess the impact of selection procedures on parliamentary composition. However, the following remarks indicate some of the complexities of the relationship. First of all, the extent of decentralization and, more specifically, the degree of decisiveness of the local or regional party organizations matters. For example, it is possible that due to regionalism within the PvdA, well-qualified aspirants will not be nominated because too many of them live in the same sub-district, whereas in other districts no qualified aspirants can be found.[9]

One might expect that in parties with a higher degree of centralization the final candidate list will be more balanced in terms of expertise (professional background), party ideology, sex, age and ties with non-political organizations. But observations of the selection process in 1985–6 indicate that a high degree of formal centralization does not necessarily mean that the influence of the party executive is always predominant. For example, within the VVD, where the degree of formal centralization is rather high, wheeling and dealing at the regional level detracted much from the power of the party executive.

Party leaderships are more concerned about the male–female balance than are the local or regional branches. It is clear that decentralized procedures induce tougher competition, possibly resulting in less chances for women to obtain a safe place. Yet the support and activities of local branches of the women's organization within the party can help women where the selection process is decentralized. And central direction may not always be helpful. Quota setting may have an eye-opening effect, making selectors more aware than before of women as possible representatives. However, many women politicians in the PvdA have pointed out that quotas can also be used as a maximum, instead of a minimum, percentage, which then affects the nomination of women negatively (Leijenaar et al., 1983: 140).

In this context an interesting question is whether certain selection procedures offer better chances for the nomination of women than others. For example the Democratic Party '66 (D'66) – a small progressive liberal party – operates a kind of referendum. Every party member is contacted by mail and asked to rank the proposed candidates for the list of the party. Until the 1986 elections D'66 has always had relatively more women participating in party boards and elective offices than other main parties. But many other factors have probably influenced the degree of participation of women in D'66, such as its time of emergence (1966) and its appeal to young, well-educated and progressive people. In 1986, this referendum was accompanied by an 'advice' from the party executive, giving a recommended list order. Hence the result of the 1986 elections, when D'66 won nine seats, of which only one is occupied by a woman, stresses once more the need to be prudent in drawing conclusions.

So, in general, the question whether selection procedures have an impact on the composition of the parliamentary party cannot be answered positively. If rules play a role, it seems that it is only a minor one. Changes in the composition of Parliament which have occurred must therefore be explained by factors outside the parties, such as developments in society. Changes in procedures may themselves reflect these developments. The VVD, for example, profited enormously in the 1970s from the depillarization of Dutch society, following which religious voters did not vote as solidly as before for religious parties. In a growing party it is easier to combine the interests of incumbents with the call for more young people and more women than it is in parties in electoral decline.

Another important phenomenon is the growing isolation of the political sphere, also induced to a large extent by depillarization (Van den Berg, 1982, 1983). Where parties are limited more and more to their own ranks for recruitment of the political elite, the outcome of selection processes will change, whatever the formal procedures.

Against the background of these developments differences between selection procedures have only a limited impact. In a more centralized party the executive is in a better position to ensure a balanced parliamentary party, but the selection process of the VVD show that regionalism is still rife. In a less centralized party like the PvdA, the executive has few means to secure a parliamentary party of high quality.

The behaviour of parliamentarians
How do selection procedures affect the behaviour of parliamentarians?

The positive role played in all parties by central agencies might be expected to reinforce parliamentary discipline. Certainly discipline is high, with voting across party lines relatively unusual. Its occurrence may have consequences for later selection. Six CDA parliamentarians who voted against the installation of Cruise missiles on Dutch soil in 1986 paid the penalty by being relegated to much lower positions on the advisory list at the next election, although their supporters in the branches did manage to get them moved up a little on the final list.

Incumbents must also maintain good relations with regional selectorates. This is done by visiting local and regional party meetings but also by ensuring publicity for parliamentary work. Especially before and during selection processes deputies try to attract media attention by, for example, addressing questions to a minister or publishing a report. This apparent 'political publicity complex' is common to most political parties but in those with less centralized procedures it is particularly necessary for those who are not established leaders. Whilst it is rare for deputies who seek renomination to be denied it completely, many are given places low on the list, which effectively denies them re-election. This de facto deselection is difficult to quantify but perhaps as much as a quarter of deputies are treated in this manner. Such 'deselection' may be a result of indiscipline – as illustrated above – or may result simply from the lack of any power base within the party which makes it easier for ambitious regional party activists to supplant them. Even so, there is little link between local voters and deputies, and very few voters contact parliamentarians in order to articulate grievances. In addition, deputies do not see themselves as mediators, bridging special interests with policy-makers in the manner of British deputies (Gladdish, 1985: 141). Yet regional affairs are carrying greater weight with the parties and regional specialists are playing a greater role in party policy-making and this may reflect the realities of power within the parties (Gladdish, 1985: 145).

Conclusion

The recruitment of members of the Dutch Second Chamber changed considerably over the last two decades. Party control over representatives grew, while the social composition of political parties and Parliament became less representative. Both psychological and institutional depillarization have isolated the political sphere. Efforts to increase participation in parties very often led to contrary results; only professionals or special categories of party members were able to meet the high demands of democratized decision-making procedures within parties. Only women seem to have profited from the democratization wave, though not without difficulties, and their number in politics is still relatively low.

Whereas before the mid-sixties pillarization compensated somewhat for the absence of personal links between the voters and the elected, institutional desegregation cut those fragile ties. In order to bridge this gap between the electorate and their representatives there was some decentralization, particularly in the left-wing PvdA. Yet, rather than raising levels of participation in political parties, this only strengthened the position of the local and even more the regional party oligarchies. To diminish the distance between Parliament and voter, D'66 has often argued for the reintroduction of an electoral system with more than one district, but has failed to win a majority for this idea.

Although the electoral system has not changed, stricter party regulations have increased the parties' grip over their representatives. These regulations are the results of a changed political climate, promoted by an active party cadre that forms less than 0.5 percent of the total electorate. Notwithstanding the rigidity of the party structure, a new generation of active party members emerged in the 1960s and changed the procedures by promoting its participatory ideas. However, these new procedures can reinforce new rigidities. For example, looking at the outcome of the selection process for the elections of 1986, the strong influence of regional lobbies is clearly present in all three parties. Their influence has been responsible partly for the fact that the number of women in parliament has not increased.[10]

Recent changes in candidate selection processes, therefore, are the result of developments in society and intraparty dynamics and illustrate the evolution towards a more autonomous political sphere. Notwithstanding these changes, the selection of political personnel remains the most important function that political parties fulfil in Dutch society. Whereas other functions of parties are being eroded because of technological and societal developments, the recruitment of politicians is still a monopoly of the parties. In consequence the nomination process forms the key arena of intraparty conflict. As long as this monopoly is not challenged, politics in the Netherlands will continue to be dominated by partisan interests.

Notes

1. There are two reasons why parties use different lists instead of the same list in all electoral sub-districts. First, the use of different lists makes it possible to put regional candidates higher on the list of the electoral district where they live. This may enhance the electoral attractiveness of the party there. Second, electoral law allows the parties to put only forty names on a list, whereas the big parties are entitled to have more representatives in Parliament. The use of different lists makes it possible to have more than forty candidates elected. For more information on the electoral system of the Netherlands, see Seip (1979).

2. In the last parliamentary election (1986) many of the voters of the VVD expressed their disagreement with the list order by casting their votes for a badly placed incumbent candidate, Joekes. Due to these preference votes he was elected.

3. An expression introduced by the journalist H.J.A. Hofland.

4. Recently, a special project on the subject of intraparty decision-making processes (including candidate selection) has been started at the initiative of the Political Science Department of the University of Leiden. The authors participate in this project.

5. Only under special circumstances can the party leadership advise the party council (the delegates of the regional party organizations) to alter the list. This alteration has to be approved by a two-thirds majority of the national party congress, which consists of delegations from the local party branches.

6. Our own observation of the selection process in three regions.

7. These promises are most extreme in the CDA and PvdA where candidates place their seats at the disposal of the party leadership, if they leave the parliamentary party. CDA deputies promise to attend local party meetings whilst PvdA deputies undertake to be responsible to party bodies and, if necessary, move their home to the appropriate regional sub-district. They promise to pay a percentage of their income to party funds and abide by the PvdA's anti-cumulation rules regarding other representative offices. Yet few of these promises are of any consequence and most are either unenforceable or ignored. What is important, however, is that the deputy maintains a visible presence in his or her own region.

8. In the study by Leijenaar et al. (1983) a large majority of the interviewed women (65.0 percent) mentioned that the fact that they were women had a significant (mostly positive) effect on their chances for nomination (p. 53).

9. This has been the case for the Amsterdam sub-district which was allocated four seats in Parliament and had seven well-qualified candidates. But in the sub-district of Maastricht no qualified candidates could be found (J.J. Lindner in *De Volkskrant*, 18 January 1986).

10. Our own observation of the selection process in three regions.

References

Boddendijk, F., M. Klein and E. Nolte (1980) *Mijnheer de Voorzitter ...!* Mededelingen no. 8. Amsterdam: VU Uitgeverij.

CDA (1983) *Appel en Weerklank: rapport over overtuiging en organisatie van het CDA.* Den Haag: CDA.

CDA (1985) *Statuten.* Den Haag: CDA.

Daalder, H. (1974) *Politisering en Lijdelijkheid in de Nederlandse Politiek.* Assen: Van Gorcum.

Elzinga, D.J. (1982) *De Politieke Partij en het Constitutionele Recht.* Nijmegen: Ars Aequi.

Gladdish, K. (1985) 'The Netherlands', pp. 135–48 in V. Bogdanor (ed.), *Representatives of the People.* Aldershot: Gower.

Hessing, R. (1984) *Bij Voorkeur: Een Onderzoek naar het Gebruik van Voorkeurstemmen*, master's thesis, University of Leiden.

Heyne den Bak, G. (1982) *Democratie in Problemen. Participatie en Besluitvorming in de PvdA.* Amsterdam: Wiardi Beckman Stichting.

Koole, R.A. (1984a) 'Voorkeursstemmen en Politieke Praktijk', *Intermediair*, 17 August 1984: 19–21.

Koole, R.A. (1984b) 'Recrutering en Leiderschap binnen Partijen', *Beleid en Maatschappij*, July/August: 214–22.

Koole, R.A. and G. Voerman (1986) 'Het Lidmaatschap van Politieke Partijen, na 1945', pp. 115–76 in R.A. Koole (ed.), *Jaarboek DNPP 1985.* Groningen: University of Groningen.

Koopman, M. and M.H. Leijenaar (1983) 'Het Vergeten Electoraat: Vrouwen en Verkiezingen', pp. 246–61 in C. v. d. Eyk and B. Niemöller (eds), *In het Spoor van de Kiezer.* Meppel: Boom.

Kruijt, J.P. (1966) 'Interne Partijdemocratie', *Socialisme en Democratie*, 23: 131–9.

Leijenaar, M.H. and B. Niemöller (1986) 'Vrouwen in Politieke Partijen', *Verslag van een Onderzoek naar Vrouwen in Politieke Functies.* Den Haag: VNG Uitgeverij.

Leijenaar, M.H. and B. Niemoller (1986) 'Vrouwen in Politieke Partijen', p. 177–94 in R.A. Koole (ed.), *Jaarboek DNPP 1985.* Groningen: University of Groningen.

Lijphart, A. (1968) *The Politics of Accommodation: Pluralism and Democracy in The Netherlands.* Los Angeles, CA: University of California Press.

Lipschits, I. (1963) 'De Politieke Partij en de Selectie van Kandidaten', *Sociologische Gids*, 10: 273–81.

PvdA (1979) *Eindrapportage van de Commissie Meerjarenramingen en Partijsorganisatie.* Amsterdam: PvdA.

PvdA (1980) *Rapport van de Commissie Interne Partijdemocratie*. Amsterdam: PvdA.

Ranney, A. (1981) 'Candidate Selection', pp. 75–106 in D. Butler, H.R. Penniman and A. Ranney (eds) *Democracy at the Polls: A Comparative Study of Competitive National Elections*. Washington, DC: American Enterprise Institute.

Schmidt, O. (1983) 'Kiezersopkomst van 1971 tot 1982', pp. 242–62 in C. v. d. Eyk and B. Niemöller (eds), *In het Spoor van de Kiezer*. Meppel: Boom.

Seip, D. (1979) 'The Netherlands', pp. 193–216 in G. Hand, J. Georgel and C. Sasse (eds), *European Electoral Systems Handbook*. London: Butterworths.

Thissen, G.G.J. (1982) 'Politieke partijen en Recht: Discussie zonder Einde?', pp. 203–25 in R.A. Koole (ed.), *Jaarboek DNPP 1982*. Groningen: University of Groningen.

Tromp, B. (1980) 'Participatie-Democratie en Participatie: Vermeende Oplossingen en echte Problemen', *Socialisme en Democratie*, 37: 159–65.

Van den Berg, J. Th. J. (1982) 'Geisoleerd op het Binnenhof', *Socialisme en Democratie*, 39: 3–16.

Van den Berg, J. Th. J. (1983) *De Toegang tot het Binnenhof: De Maatschappelijke Herkomst van Tweede Kamerleden*. Weesp: v. Holkema's Warendorf.

Van Deth, J. (1983) 'Leeftijd en Emancipatie de Ontwikkeling van Politieke Interesse', *Acta Politica*, 83 (4): 469–87.

VVD (1982) 'Advies van de Commissie Kandidaatstelling en Technisch Advies', *Vrijheid en Democratie*, 30 November 1982: 24–8.

VVD (1985) *Vrijheid en Democratie*, 19 February 1985: 5.

Wiardi Beckman Stichting (1978) *Partij, Parlement, Activisme*. Deventer: Kluwer/WBS.

10
Norway: decentralization and group representation

Henry Valen

Some years ago a passionate discussion occurred in a political science seminar at the University of Oslo concerning nominations at parliamentary (Storting) elections. One of the students presented a well-documented paper on the electoral system, but on nominations he only said that electoral lists are determined by the national leaders of the respective parties. I had attended a nomination convention a few weeks earlier, and I found this statement inconsistent with my experience. My impression was that decisions were made at the constituency level. I did not obtain much support, however, because everybody in the seminar took it for granted that the central leaders of political parties do select the candidates. The young political scientists were acquainted – superficially at least – with Robert Michels' Iron Law of Oligarchy, and they perceived the strong party discipline in the Storting as an indication of the oligarchic character of Norwegian parties. The overwhelming majority of the participants contended that national party leaders simply had to control nominations in order to keep a grip on party policies.

This incident triggered my curiosity about the nomination process, and particularly about the role of national leaders in it. The discussion revealed misconceptions and lack of knowledge concerning internal processes in political parties, a phenomenon which is not peculiar to Norwegian political scientists. Strangely enough, nobody in the seminar was aware that a separate Act of Nominations, dating back to 1921, prescribes the procedures for nominations, and that Norway is one of the very few nations in which candidate selection is regulated by law.

In 1920 the Norwegian electoral system was changed from majority elections to proportional representation. The legislators included in the reform rules for nominations because they expected that the introduction of proportional representation would affect the choice of electoral candidates. Inside the parties the conditions for selection would change, since the new system entailed multi-member constituencies. Each constituency in this sparsely populated country would cover a relatively large area, involving in almost every instance a number of small communities geographically separated by fjords and mountains. The new system was also bound to affect the electorate in the sense that voters would be faced with lists of candidates rather than single candidates as hitherto.

The parliamentary commission which created the new electoral system was also asked to frame nomination procedures.[1] The latter task was not an easy one because of the dearth of information about nominations in other nations. The notable exception was the United States, concerning which the commission found both relevant literature and a substantial body of legislation on nominations. The result was that the Norwegian Act of Nominations set up a system which resembled the American convention model.

The following examination of this system attempts to explain nominations from a political as well as an institutional perspective. I will start by describing briefly the party system and a few aspects of the electoral system which form the essential institutional context of the nominations.

The Norwegian system consists of seven parties, which are, from left to right: the Socialist Left Party (Socialistisk Ventreparti), the Labour Party (Arbeiderpartiet), the Liberals (Venstre), the Christian People's Party (Kristelig Folkeparti), the Centre Party (Senterpartiet), the Conservative Party (Høyre) and the Progress Party (Fremskrittspartiet). The two oldest parties are the Liberals and the Conservatives, which were both formed in 1884. Next came the Labour Party (1887), while all other parties emerged in the present century. It is a polarized system with the two major parties, Labour and the Conservatives, obtaining (in recent years) electoral support of some 40 and 30 percent of the votes respectively. All other parties are small (Valen and Katz, 1964; Svaasand, 1985).

The electoral law requires that the parties present lists of candidates, and the candidates on each list are ranked in the order in which the party wishes to see them elected. The voters are permitted to change the list by crossing out the name of one or more of the nominated candidates. In practice, such deletions by individual voters have no impact on the final result, since an overwhelming percentage of the voters must make the same change in order to overrule the ranking on the lists.[2] In fact the voters have never successfully changed the parties' rank ordering at Storting elections.

There are nineteen constituencies, one for each of the eighteen provinces (*fylker*) and one for the city of Oslo. The number of seats varies with size of population from four to fifteen.[3] The number of candidates on a given list must equal the prescribed number of seats for that constituency. In addition, the parties may nominate six 'reserve' candidates; thus if a constituency has ten seats, each party may nominate up to sixteen candidates. The parties tend to nominate the maximum number permitted. Obviously, only some of the top candidates can expect certain election. A few others have some chance of being elected, either as representatives or as alternate representatives, but the vast majority have no electoral chance at all.[4] As will be discussed later, list position is very important in the selection of candidates.

The Act of Nominations is not mandatory upon the parties. They may ignore it as long as they observe the rules of the main election law in presenting their electoral lists. However, the parties must abide by this law if they wish to obtain public funds for nomination conventions. In practice the parties apply the Act of Nominations, with the notable exception of Oslo, where distances are so small that expenses for nomination meetings are negligible. However, public funding is probably not a strong incentive for abiding by the law, since expenses are not very high even in large constituencies. According to party secretaries the procedures are generally observed even where the law is not formally applied. This would suggest that the principles of the law are generally accepted.

Organizational procedures

The Act of Nominations states that electoral lists are decided by party conventions in each constituency. The decisions are final and can be overruled neither by public authority nor by national party bodies. However, the law permits the convention to submit the list to a referendum among party members, and in that case the result of the referendum is the final decision. But such a referendum has never been arranged. The convention is an elected assembly composed of 20–150 delegates from local party organizations in all communes within the constituency. In each locality the delegates are elected at local meetings in which all dues-paying members of voting age are permitted to participate. The delegates are elected by a majority vote. The number of delegates from each commune varies according to the number of votes obtained by the respective parties at the proceeding Storting election, although small communes are somewhat overrepresented.[5]

Before the meetings, which are normally six to nine months before the election, the constituency nomination committee asks local party organizations to discuss potential nominees. The nomination committee consists of between five and fifteen members.

It is appointed by the constituency branch of the party about one year before the election and normally reflects the interests of major sub-groups within the constituency, e.g. representatives of various geographical areas, of different occupational groups and of the party's youth and women's organizations. No fixed rules exist as to the role of the executive board of the constituency party. In some cases the nomination committee is identical with the board, but more often the executive seems to be represented in the committee by one or more members.

In all parties it is common that nomination committees start by asking whether the candidates from the party's lists at the preceding election are available for renomination. Responses to this question are then circulated to the local organizations. When local units have had time to discuss the nominations, the committee drafts a list on the basis of local proposals. Normally this draft is sent out for a further round of discussion. After receiving local reactions, the committee submits a revised draft to the nominating convention. In some cases, mainly in minor parties, the procedure seems to include only one stage: candidate proposals are sent from the local organizations to the nomination committee, which then drafts a list proposal and presents it directly to the convention.[6] Practice varies regarding the number of candidates proposed by each commune party. Normally local organizations discuss the rank ordering of the top candidates, and try to promote local aspirants.

All parties report that local organizations carry heavy weight when the committees draw up their list. Frequently, the proposed rank ordering of candidates is determined by the number of votes cast in favour of the competing persons at local meetings. The wishes of the local party organizations are also expressed in the vote of the delegates, although delegates are not mandated to vote in accordance with local decisions.

Obviously, the nomination committee's list structures debate at the convention. Yet all parties report that committee proposals are rarely accepted in their entirety. On the other hand the proposal is never rejected completely. In the convention the decision on each candidate is reached by a majority vote. Voting procedures in the conventions are determined by the individual parties. The pattern seems to be that if several aspirants compete for a specific place on the list, e.g. number 1, and if none of them obtains a majority in the first vote, there is a new vote between the two leading aspirants to get a majority.

This organizational framework applies to all parties. However, formal procedures do not cover the whole process of candidate recruitment. The Act of Nominations only legislates the rules for selection. Normally the convention has to choose between many prospective candidates. Hence, the most important questions are: Which criteria are applied in selection? How do political considerations affect the choice? How do candidate selections reflect group conflicts inside the various parties? These questions will be discussed in later sections. First it is necessary to comment upon two structural aspects: the confinement of nominations to the party organizations, and the decentralized nature of the process.

Selectorate
Only dues-paying party members are permitted to participate in candidate selection meetings. The parties observe this rule strictly. Conceivably the parties might turn informally to the electorate for advice, but so far such attempts have been unsuccessful.[7] Nevertheless, the convention may open the proceedings to the public and in recent years public interest in candidate selection has been increasing.

Table 10.1   *Selectorate and number of delegates at nominating conventions, 1985, by party*

Party	Party members: % of voters[a]	Participated in nomination process: % of voters[a]	Number of delegates in nominating conventions[b]	Delegates as % of voters	Delegates as % of members
Socialist Left	11	9	1,433	1.1	9.2
Labour	15	4	2,806	0.3	1.8
Liberal	21	7	710	0.7	4.2
Christian	29	8	1,260	0.6	2.0
Centre	26	5	988	0.6	2.2
Conservative	16	3	2,787	0.4	2.2
Progress	8	8	703	0.6	9.2
Total	15	5	10,687	0.6	4.5

[a] Figures from 1985 election survey.
[b] Estimated on the basis of 1981 election statistics (cf. note 5). Figures for Oslo were obtained directly from the parties.

Candidates are recruited from among active party members. About 15 percent of the electorate are dues-paying party members, according to reports from party headquarters, and this figure has been rather stable over the last three decades (Svaasand, 1985: 49–53). The proportion of party members has been confirmed in nationwide voter surveys, the last time at the Storting election of 1985.[8] In the same study those surveyed were asked if they had participated in meetings dealing with nominations (i.e. conventions and/or local meetings discussing candidates or electing delegates to conventions) at the 1985 election. Nearly 5 percent responded affirmatively, all of whom also indicated party membership. Although all party members are permitted to participate in the nomination process, only one out of three indicates having done so. By computing the number of delegates permitted under the Act of Nominations I have estimated the proportion of party members attending nominating conventions in 1985 at some 4.5 percent (see Table 10.1).

A decentralized system

The nomination system is basically a decentralized one. The law does not permit national party leaders to interfere directly in nomination proceedings in individual constituencies, and they have no veto over the decisions of the conventions. The constituencies of Oslo and Akershus (the province surrounding Oslo) are exceptions. Since the parties have their national headquarters in the capital, the top leaders tend to be involved in the party branches of those provinces, and many of them are nominated for election there. Party branches in other constituencies, however, seem to be zealous defenders of their autonomy (Valen, 1956).

A rather illuminating incident occurred at the 1985 Labour Party nominations. The previous year the party's national convention introduced a gender quota for nominations in order to improve the representation of women in Parliament.[9] At the 1985 election this rule was generally accepted by the party branches, except in the constituency of Sogn og Fjordane on the west coast. In this constituency, in which Labour could hope to obtain two seats at most, the two top candidates from the preceding election, both men, were renominated and ranked first and second. This led to an outcry in the Labour women's movement, which appealed to the national leaders to support its demand that one candidate should be replaced by a woman. Both the executive committee and the national committee recommended that the party in Sogn og Fjordane reconsider the nomination.[10] But the constituency party refused to obey, referring to the rule in the Act of Nominations saying that decisions of a nominating convention are final. The central leaders had no choice but to accept the situation. A direct confrontation between national and constituency leaders was unthinkable, partly because it implied violation of the electoral law, partly because politically it might ruin the party's electoral chances in the constituency.[11] At a few recent elections the Labour Party had suffered from internal splits over issues related to territorial divisions in Sogn og Fjordane. The balancing of district interests was a major concern when the constituency convention composed its 1985 electoral list.

National party leaders who might wish to influence nominations are politically unable to do so through direct interference – except perhaps in Oslo and Akershus. The question is, however, whether they can do so indirectly. For one thing, leaders can appoint prospective candidates to positions of high prestige and visibility. This method is particularly applicable to parties holding power. By appointing somebody as a member of the government, or as chair of some important committee, they can bring him to public attention and thus strengthen his chances for nomination – provided he is otherwise acceptable to his home constituency.[12]

Furthermore, national leaders can conceivably influence the constituency level by working through informal networks inside their respective parties. As indicated above, the nomination committee holds a key position in the proceedings of the convention. This committee would therefore be the best arena for leaders to influence decisions, although (officially at least) national party headquarters are not informed about the composition of nomination committees in the various constituencies.[13] How do national leaders fit into the internal channels of communication as reported by members of nomination committees?

Table 10.2   *Groups reported to have contacted members of nomination committees, by party*

Party	Aspirants	Members of the Storting	National party leaders	Mayors, local politicians	Provincial and local party	Groups outside the party	Number of respondents
Socialist Left	17	4	15	16	83	17	76
Labour	28	22	1	53	84	33	109
Liberal	15	2	15	35	83	19	52
Christian	17	16	10	34	77	18	95
Centre (Agr.)	10	7	4	41	74	10	68
Conservative	43	38	10	55	90	22	103
Progress	64	11	20	24	93	0	45
All parties	27	17	9	39	83	20	548

Note: Entries indicate percentage responding affirmatively.

A study of the 1985 nomination process confirms that there is little contact between national party leaders and committee members.[14] The respondents were asked: 'Which of the following groups contacted you about the selection of candidates?' (The names of the groups are indicated in Table 10.2.) Only one of ten respondents reported that they had been contacted by national leaders. A somewhat higher proportion indicated contact with members of the Storting. Nearly three out of ten were contacted by potential candidates. The main message conveyed by Table 10.2 is that most of the discussion was with local politicians as well as leaders of local party organizations. Finally, 20 percent of the respondents reported having been contacted by leaders of organizations outside the parties. This figure is not surprising, considering the strong corporatist tendencies in modern Norwegian society (Olsen, 1983).

Some striking differences between parties emerge from Table 10.2. Without entering into a detailed analysis, a few tendencies deserve mention. Although contacts with local and provincial leaders appear to be equally important in all parties, local politicians were mentioned least frequently in the Socialist Left and the Progress parties. The explanation is that these small parties have relatively few representatives in local office. A similar explanation may probably be applied when small parties report relatively low contact with members of the Storting. The possibility of contact is limited by the low number of party representatives. However, the relatively large number of Conservatives mentioning this kind of contact suggests that it is not only the size of representation that counts. After all, the Labour Party has a larger parliamentary group than the Conservatives (Valen and Aardal, 1983: 16). According to long tradition, the parliamentary group constitutes the most important centre of power in the Conservative Party (Sejersted, 1984: 198–200). The fact that Conservative respondents were most inclined to mention contacts with parliamentarians may well reflect the power structure of the party. In the Labour Party, by comparison, the party organization tends to wield relatively more power (Valen and Katz, 1964: 63–95).

Respondents of the three smallest parties – Socialist Left, Liberal and Progress – were more inclined to mention contact with national party leaders. This may simply mean that parties with only a handful of representatives in parliament feel more need than larger parties to choose candidates who can perform certain roles in parliamentary work.

It is not surprising that few respondents report having been contacted by aspirants. In Norwegian political culture it is not considered good manners to advocate one's own political career, with a notable exception for persons who have already been representatives to the Storting. Table 10.2 indicates a striking difference between on the one hand the two parties to the right, Conservatives and Progress, and on the other hand all other parties, with respondents of the former parties reporting greater contact by aspirants. Liberalistic values are most prevalent in the parties to the right (Valen and Aardal, 1983: 146). Finally, contacts with groups outside the parties were most frequently mentioned by Labour respondents. This probably reflects the close ties between Labour and the trade union movement. Outside contacts were reported also in other parties, in particular the Conservative Party, which has close links to business.

The respondents were also asked to what extent they had made contacts with the groups listed in Table 10.2. The response patterns were practically identical with those referred to in the table.

In summary, the data support the notion of a highly decentralized nomination process. Reported communications with leaders and groups within the constituency by far outnumber contacts with national leaders. However, this does not exclude the possibility that national leaders might exert influence. Conceivably they may do so by contacting local or constituency leaders and asking them to promote the aspirant concerned. Although organizational procedures at nominations are similar for all parties, some striking party differences are evident regarding communication patterns. The question of party differences will be dealt with in more detail in subsequent sections.

Selection criteria

Normally the nominating convention is faced with many aspirants, only a few of whom can be nominated. Which criteria are used? When party activists are asked this question, they usually argue that candidates are selected according to 'political competence'. This answer is unconvincing, however, since no common standards exist for evaluating political competence. Terms such as 'skill' and 'competence' are frequently used in the debate, but a person whose competence may be highly regarded by one section of a party may be seen as rather ordinary by others.

A close look at the reasons given for the nomination of individual candidates reveals that the most important device for selection is a system of group representation or ticket-balancing which is applied with varying rigidity from one party to another. Three sets of basic groups seem to occur in all parties: territorial groups, representation of women and representation of youth. A number of other occupational, cultural and issue-specific groups compete more or less regularly varying from one party to another depending upon ideology and electoral base, and varying inside a party between different constituencies. Group representation will be spelt out in more detail in the subsequent section. At this point we may look at the rationale behind it.

Why is ticket-balancing important? For one thing, through ticket-balancing parties are able to appeal directly to the voters. Arguments for or against specific candidates almost invariably refer to the expectations and likely reactions of the electorate. Hence it may be argued that considerations of voters' preferences serve as the ultimate legitimacy in the selection of candidates. A pertinent question is: To what extent do voters really know about candidates? In a nationwide representative voter survey of the 1985 election (p. 214) the respondents were asked to identify candidates in their constituency by name. The data revealed a rather low level of information: a third of respondents were unable to name a single candidate, while only 39 percent could identify three or more. As might be expected, there was a substantial difference between organized party members, i.e. the selectorate, and ordinary voters. In the latter group 37 percent were unable to name correctly a single candidate, while the corresponding figure for members was 16 percent. Despite low information about the candidates, ticket-balancing implies that a variety of voters' demands have to be recognized.

Secondly, ticket-balancing constitutes a link between parties and organizations in the community. One of the major functions of political parties is to aggregate a variety of social interests (Almond and Coleman, 1960: 16–17; Epstein, 1980: 13–16). This can easily be achieved through a selection of candidates (Valen and Katz, 1964: 318–23). By nominating candidates who belong to several different organizations, parties present an image of concern with a variety of social interests without being narrowly committed to some specific group.

Thirdly, ticket-balancing fulfils important functions inside the party. It provides the convention with a mechanism for choosing among a number of eligible aspirants and serves to reduce intraparty conflicts in the selection process. At the same time ticket-balancing implies competition between internal sub-groups. By being represented on the list groups are given a visible access to party leadership, and are thus encouraged to render the party their active and loyal support. Indeed, it may be argued that ticket-balancing unifies the party.

Although ticket-balancing constitutes a major guideline for the selection of candidates, the convention is still faced with a choice among a number of aspirants. For one thing, there may be disagreement as to the evaluation of competing group demands. Second, several aspirants may fit the requirements of specific groups. Thus the convention will also have to evaluate the personality characteristics of competing aspirants. How do parties decide which individuals to pick?

Norwegians do not 'run for office'. Candidacies are expected to emerge from active participation in party work. Political ambitions do not occur less frequently in Norway than in other nations, but expression of ambitions is restrained by national political culture. Personal modesty is seen as a virtue, and it is dangerous for a politician to be stigmatized as 'pushy'. A person cannot propose himself or herself for nomination; somebody else has to do it.

During the early stages of the nomination process a number of persons are suggested as possible candidates. Quite a few of these disappear because they are not considered eligible. Norms for eligibility are rarely explicit in party statutes (although the Christian People's Party requirement that office-holders must be personal Christians is a notable exception). They cannot be identified easily, but a clue may be found in evaluations by political activists of the personal characteristics required of a candidate. This question was examined in a community study in the Stavanger area of south-western Norway at the Storting election of 1957. Local political leaders emphasized political and professional competence (Valen, 1966: 124). Next came moral qualities like honesty, reliability and fairmindedness. In the third and fourth place came party loyalty and platform abilities respectively. Cross-party evaluations resembled each other, with one notable exception: Labour leaders were far more inclined than leaders of other parties to emphasize party loyalty and firmness of conviction. This trend was interpreted as an expression of differences in party structure and party philosophy (Valen, 1966). Labour was seen as closer to the Party Democracy type of party, and the bourgeois parties more as examples of Rational-Efficient parties (see Chapter 1 for a discussion of these paradigms).

The question of candidate evaluation was also included in the 1985 nomination study (p. 216). Once again political and professional competence was strongly emphasized as a requirement for nomination, while moral qualities, as well as party loyalty, were mentioned less frequently than in 1957. A strong increase in the number of respondents mentioning platform abilities (including charisma, eloquence, ability to perform in the mass media, being a communicator) is the most striking difference. Since different samples were applied in the two studies, one should be cautious in making direct comparisons.[15] Nevertheless, the increasing significance of platform abilities is likely to reflect a current trend in modern politics, the trend towards the greater visibility of political leaders (Ranney, 1983: 88–122).

Another interesting trend is that the parties seem to have become more similar in terms of desired qualities. In the 1985 study the response patterns of various parties were practically identical. Emphasis on party loyalty was no stronger in Labour than in other parties. This may mean that bourgeois parties have developed in the direction of the Party Democracy type, or alternatively that Labour has lost some of its original character. Whatever the reason, the data suggest that requirements for nomination do not differ much between parties.

In a previous section a distinction was made between top candidates, i.e. candidates who might have at least some chance of being elected, and those lower down the list. The 1985 study included a question designed to see if requirements for nomination differ for the two groups.[16] The data presented in Table 10.3 reveal that requirements are surprisingly similar for top and lower candidates. For both groups confidence in own party is mentioned most frequently, while platform abilities are mentioned more often for top than for lower candidates, and so is experience in public office. On the other hand, representation of group interests, involvement in organizations outside the parties, and active participation in party work are mentioned most frequently for lower candidates. In general the data suggest that abilities as a professional politician are most strongly required for top candidates, while the less important places on the list can be used to make a symbolic appeal to groups of voters and to maintain party cohesion. The mention of party activity suggests that nominations are also being used as a reward for party work.

Table 10.3   *Characteristics considered most important in being selected*[a] *(percentages)*

	Platform abilities	Enjoys confidence in own party	Experience of public office	Enjoys support in important organizations	Active in party work	Represents some group interest	Independent in relation to group	No answer	Total	(n)
Top candidates[b]	31	50	9	2	4	1	3	0	100	(584)
Lower candidates	27	36	5	6	10	14	1	1	100	(584)

[a] Respondents were asked to mention the three most important characteristics for each group. The table only includes the first characteristic mentioned. The pattern is identical when the second and the third characteristics are also considered.

[b] The number of top candidates is not fixed. It varies with the size of the party, or rather with electoral support in the respective constituencies.

An attempt to compare responses from the various parties did not show any systematic differences. This may simply mean that the abilities required for nomination are generally rooted in national political culture. However, some of the categories applied in the study are so broad and general that they might well conceal important partisan differences. 'Confidence in party' is a good case in point, since confidence may result from widely different sources. Thus solidarity with the working class and loyal support for the party's ideas and policies have traditionally been a major requirement for office-holders in the Labour Party. Conceivably other values, like professional achievements or status in the community, are more likely to inspire confidence in the bourgeois parties. Similarly, 'platform abilities' may be evaluated in different ways from party to party. For example, personality characteristics seen as appealing may vary since parties differ substantially in social composition (Valen, 1981). Likewise ability to communicate with the public is likely to be evaluated in relation to campaign strategies. Our data do not render information on candidate evaluation regarding the suggested categories.

Group representation

In the Stavanger study of 1957, local leaders were asked why each one of the five first candidates on their party's list had been nominated (Valen and Katz, 1964: 126–7). A similar approach was applied in 1985 when the chairmen of the nomination committees in four constituencies (Oslo, Akershus, Hedmark and Oppland) were interviewed, but this time the enquiry covered the composition of the entire list. In general, the information obtained confirms the conclusions in Table 10.3 about differences between top and lower candidates. Most of the discussion in the nominating convention concerns competition for the 'promising' places on the list, i.e. places where the candidates will have some chance of being elected. It is easier to fill the lower places, but even these selections are important because lower candidates help shape the political and social profile of the list.

Apparently parties have no difficulty finding people willing to be nominated even for lower list positions. It adds to the prestige of a person – in the party and in the community – to be a candidate for Storting elections. Irrespective of electoral chances the nomination may be a stepping stone to a career in national politics or in the commune or provincial level of government.

As to criteria for candidate selection, two general tendencies should be observed. First, there is the significance of incumbency. That candidates from the preceding election are asked whether they are interested in renomination önstitutes a constraint upon the nominating convention, although nobody can claim an automatic right to be renominated. In Norway, as elsewhere, many parliamentary representatives are reselected. Similarly, candidates lower on the lists regularly reappear, albeit to a lesser extent than top candidates.

The other set of criteria for selection is group representation, but more information is needed about the character of the groups. Each candidate on the list may be identified not only by Christian name, but also by sex (since Norwegian names are sex-specific), by occupation and by commune of residence, information highly relevant for group representation.

We shall now discuss the main aspects of group representation.

1. *Territorial groups* or district representation within the respective constituencies. Territorial sub-groups are not always topographically well defined.[17] The geographical balancing does not concern only the number of candidates; it also affects the rank ordering on the lists. Except for some of the largest cities, two candidates ranked next to each other rarely come from the same commune or even from neighbouring communes.

District representation is linked to the local political interests of various parts of the provinces, for example, construction of roads and other facilities for public transport, location of schools and hospitals, development of new industries. Frequently, competition occurs between different districts of a given province concerning these kinds of goods. Mayors and other local politicians also play an important role in nominations (Valen, 1966). Oslo, containing a single commune, is an exception to district representation.

2. *Representation of women*, largely promoted through the women's organizations of the various parties. Traditionally, having perceived women as one of several sub-groups, the parties nominated only a few women candidates in each constituency, mostly among the lower candidates. Recent years, however, have witnessed a change owing to women's demand for representation equal to men's. The election of 1985 constituted a major breakthrough. A quota system introduced by the parties of the left assured a high proportion of women not only among the total number of candidates nominated, but also among the top candidates (Valen, 1986). These parties tended to nominate men and women alternately from top to bottom of the list. But, as demonstrated in the Sogn og Fjordane case, even a quota system is not absolutely certain of creating equality of representation between the sexes.

3. *Representation of youth*, which is promoted by the parties' youth organizations. Besides creating a political platform for organized youth, youth's representation seeks a renewal of leadership within the respective parties. However, unlike candidates from

women's and territorial groups, youth candidates cannot be directly identified from the lists.

Other types of groups occur less regularly, and they are not identifiable from the list, except for occupation. The city of Oslo is a case in point. In the absence of territorial conflicts other group considerations develop correspondingly more importance. All parties represent youth and women, but individual parties comprise a number of specific interests. In the Labour Party a variety of trade union interests dominate. In the Christian People's Party several religious organizations and the temperance movement are important. The Conservative party emphasizes the involvement of candidates in current issues.

District representation or the attachment of candidates to local interests apparently constitutes the most important criterion. It is consistent with the notion of a decentralized nomination process. It is also reflected in the fact that lists, with few exceptions, consist of residents of the respective constituencies. Originally the Constitution stated that only people living in a given province could be nominated on the list for that constituency. A constitutional reform of 1952 abolished this residential requirement, but did not result in any great change in candidate selection. Thus in 1985 only twenty-three out of some 1900 candidates did not live in the constituency in which they were nominated. Even these 'alien' candidates tended to belong to their constituencies through work or kinship and were temporarily absent, with the notable exception of a handful of real 'aliens' in Oslo and Akershus. The representation of women, youth and other groups tends to cut across territorial sub-divisions and has to be fitted in with district requirements.

The notion of group representation, however, should not be interpreted too narrowly. Expectations regarding the ability of prospective candidates to represent the party will presumably be a major concern of the nominating convention. And as suggested above, this consideration seems to be stronger for top candidates than for lower ones. But in order to be promoted a candidate needs the support of some specific section of the selectorate. Everybody will, of course, argue in terms of the general abilities of their favourite candidates, but the convention is concerned with how candidates will attract voters. Indeed, evaluations of leadership abilities tend to be group-related, and aspirants' chances of selection depend upon the support given them from specific sub-groups. If it can be argued that a particular candidate will appeal to several important groups in the constituency, his or her chances of selection are normally very high. Ticket-balancing is observed even for the top candidates. Thus if a party gains several seats the

representatives always come from different parts of the constituency.

The group perspective is also essential in studying the impact of
incumbency upon candidate selection and a related question, the
promotion of candidates from lower to higher list positions. Group
affiliations of the candidates are probably major determinants in
explaining these phenomena. After entering office a representative
may broaden his or her base. This is likely to strengthen his chances
of renomination, even if he loses support in groups that he belonged
to when originally nominated. On the other hand, renomination
may be in danger if the representative has lost the confidence of his
original groups and has not been able to extend his political base to
other sections of the party. A typical example is a candidate
representing youth. Since the youth organizations will support his
candidature only at one or at most two elections, he will have to
extend his base in order to survive.

A similar reasoning applies for list promotions. As indicated
above, group representation is seen as particularly important for
candidates in lower list positions, but these candidates tend to have
rather narrow group support compared with candidates in higher
positions. By broadening their political support lower candidates
are likely to improve their chances for a higher list position at
subsequent elections.

Background of candidates

Finally, we look at the outcome of nominations. What kind of
candidates, in terms of social and demographic background, does
the system produce? By comparing the background of candidates
with the composition of the electorate some basic trends have been
established (Valen, 1966; Hellevik, 1969). People in middle-class
occupations are strongly overrepresented on the lists, and so are
farmers, while manual workers are the most underrepresented
group. The middle-class bias in candidate selection is also evident if
variables like income and education are considered. Women have
traditionally been strongly underrepresented compared to men.
Similarly the proportion of young people as well as older ones is
much lower among the candidates than in the electorate. The
'typical' candidate has been characterized as 'a middle-aged male of
middle-class background' (Valen, 1966: 161).

The described tendencies are stronger for candidates in top
positions on the lists than for lower ones (Valen, 1966). Similar
trends are evident if we consider the career patterns of elected
representatives in parliamentary work: representatives of high

social status are most likely to arrive at positions of distinction, such as the presidency of the Storting, membership in committees of high prestige and chairmanship of standing committees (Hellevik, 1969).

The middle-class bias of Norwegian parliamentarians is consistent with a cross-national trend observed in a great variety of countries (Putnam, 1976). One may wonder if this trend is equally strong in all kinds of parties. The notion of group representation in candidate recruitment implies some relationship between the background of candidates and the social composition of the electorate of various parties. Hence it should be expected that socialist parties, which enjoy their greatest electoral support in the working-class population, are more inclined than bourgeois parties to nominate candidates of low social status. A recent study of the recruitment to the Storting from 1945 to 1985 provides a test of this hypothesis (Eliassen, 1985). The study presents the background of representatives with regard to sex, occupation, education and involvement in local politics.

Table 10.4 *Percentage of women in the Storting, 1945–85, by party*

Party	1945–61	1961–73	1973–85	1985
Communist	1	—[a]	—[a]	—[a]
Socialist Left	—[a]	0	22	50
Labour	9	15	29	42
Liberal	3	7	0	—[a]
Christian	0	4	14	25
Centre (Agr.)	0	3	21	17
Conservative	5	4	24	30
Progress	—[a]	—[a]	0	0
All parties	6	10	23	34

[a] Party was not established or not represented in the Storting.
Source: Eliassen (1985: 120)

Gender

As long as women had to compete with other groups their representation was very low, and they tended to be listed among the lower candidates. Thus in 1957 women constituted 18 percent of all candidates but only 7 percent of the elected representatives (Valen, 1966). The growing demand for parity of representation between men and women has decisively affected the criteria for selection and consequently the proportion of women nominated. Table 10.4 indicates that the main growth has occurred during the 1970s and the 1980s. The proportion of women among elected representatives rose from 23 percent in 1981 to 34 percent in 1985, which is probably the highest proportion of seats ever obtained by women in any national parliament. Table 10.4 also indicates differences between the parties. The propensity to nominate women has always been greatest in the parties of the left.

Occupation

The data on occupation confirm the tendencies reported above, with strong middle-class dominance and a relatively high proportion of farmers and fishermen, while very few manual workers have been elected. As expected, the middle-class bias is stronger in bourgeois than in socialist parties, but the difference is not big. The proportion of parliamentarians belonging to some middle-class occupation is 68 percent for the bourgeois parties and 55 percent for the socialists. The bourgeois parties also have the highest proportion of farmers and fishermen, of which farmers constitute an overwhelming majority. There are very few manual workers in the bourgeois parties (1 percent) but even amongst the socialist bloc the proportion is only 12 percent.

Lawyers are a rather insignificant group in the Storting, unlike the case in many other parliaments. Only 3 percent of representatives during the period 1945–85 belong to this category. The low number of lawyers in politics is a distinguishing feature of all Scandinavian countries (Pedersen, 1972).

Education

The greater middle-class character of bourgeois parties is more evident when we consider the educational background of candidates. The proportion of representatives with a university degree is 52 percent in bourgeois parties but only 25 percent in socialist parties, and the proportion with elementary education only is 37 percent for socialists but 16 percent for the bourgeois parties. Compared to most other parliaments, the educational level in the Storting is rather low (Sartori, 1967), probably because of the system of group representation in Norway. Although people in middle-class positions tend to be preferred for nomination, high education is not a favoured criterion for selection, particularly in socialist parties.

Local office

An overwhelming majority of elected representatives have experience in communal and/or provincial office. Three out of ten have been a mayor, and nearly nine out of ten have served in a communal council. Membership in provincial councils (*fylkesting*) is less common, since the total number of council members is much lower for the provincial than for the communal level. Experience in local office is about equal for socialist and bourgeois parties. The data are consistent with the notion that constituency interests are dominant in the selection of candidates for Storting elections.

That differences between parties in socio-demographic composition are moderate is not surprising, considering the great similarities in candidate evaluations. Group representation, which follows roughly the same pattern in all parties, has a similar effect. Functional groups based on, for example, occupation, age and sex, may obtain a skewed representation because locality is the dominant selection criterion. It should be observed, however, that the increased representation of women in recent years has also contributed to the class bias, since most new female representatives have middle-class background and university education.

A system evaluation

In the previous discussion the Norwegian nomination system has been described as decentralized, with decisions being made by elected conventions at the constituency level. The fact that the Act of Nominations is applied almost without exceptions, although it is not mandatory, suggests that the political parties agree with the principles laid down in the Act. In general this system is well adjusted to the requirements of other political institutions, particularly the electoral system. The nominations for multi-member constituencies covering relatively large geographical areas would seem to require some kind of representative bodies. Furthermore, ticket-balancing, which is the dominant pattern of candidate selection, appears to be an adequate method for intraparty conflict resolution.

The system does not conform with the notion of an oligarchic selection process directed from the top of the political parties. The possibility that central leaders have some influence on the selection cannot be excluded, but in that case they have to operate through informal channels.

Since recruitment of candidates for public office is one of the most important functions of political parties, one may wonder if the parties are satisfied with the present system. Does it produce the kind of representative they want? Unfortunately there has been no public debate on the nomination system, and parties have not expressed any opinions on it with the exception of a report in 1966 by a centrally appointed committee of the Labour Party.[18] The committee focused upon three major aspects: the role of local organizations in the nomination process, the demographic and social background of candidates, and the ability of selected candidates to perform specific functions at parliamentary level. Until the 1960s the procedure had been that local party organizations were only invited to propose candidates. In order to increase their influence, the committee proposed that local organizations should also be given the opportunity to take a stand on the rank ordering of candidates, although it has required that the proposed list should be accepted beforehand by a centrally appointed committee.

The committee was concerned with the overrepresentation of farmers and people in middle-class occupations and a corresponding underrepresentation of manual workers. The committee found it unacceptable that a socialist party could nominate so few candidates coming from the manual working class. Furthermore, the report regretted the underrepresentation of women and youth. The committee favoured a list composition that would be more in accordance with the social composition of the party's electorate. The group competition at nominations was seen as the major cause of the skewed list composition. The committee argued that district representation particularly tended to prevent other groups from obtaining a fair share of the candidates.

The committee, referring exclusively to Norwegian data, seemed to be unaware that the described tendencies are rather universal in character (Sartori, 1967; Putnam, 1976). In fact, it may be argued that middle-class dominance in parliamentary recruitment is less pronounced in Norway than in most other nations (Eliassen, 1985). Nevertheless, the committee was justified in drawing attention to the impact of the nomination system upon recruitment patterns.

The third weakness reported by the Labour Party committee referred to the role of elected representatives in parliamentary work. It was argued that candidates were selected on the basis of constituency interests without regard for the needs of the parliamentary party. In order to match competing parties in a variety of committees as well as in parliamentary debate the party needed representatives skilled in areas like economics, education, foreign policy and defence policy.

The committee was not in favour of a total change of the nomination system, but it did recommend that the national party leadership through a centrally appointed committee should be permitted to express its opinion on candidate selection before the nominating conventions made their final decisions.[19] The proposal was supported by the 1967 national convention but the debate signalled great caution concerning the role of national leaders in nominations. The decision did not prompt any change on this point in existing procedures. A special committee was appointed at each subsequent election, but by and large its activities boiled down to a circular letter at nomination times to the party's constituency organizations reminding them about the need for a more equitable representation for specific groups like workers, women and youth. After 1980 the committee disappeared entirely.

Interestingly enough, the committee report did call for some central influence on nominations, but not for the purpose of selecting candidates according to their loyalty towards national party leaders. Perhaps the committee did not see any need for more conformity, since party discipline in parliamentary work was already very high. It is possible, however, that the committee shied away from a touchy problem by not discussing political and ideological requirements for nomination. Irrespective of motivation, the fate of the reform indicated that attempts to introduce central control of candidate selection were unwanted.

The arguments developed in this Labour Party report are relevant for all parties. They indicate the costs of a decentralized nomination system. National demands or requirements for the composition of the parliamentary party cannot be achieved when candidates are selected on the basis of constituency interests alone. The only exceptions are found in Oslo and Akershus, where national leaders – particularly in the two large parties – tend to promote the nomination of some prominent candidates who are highly appreciated in parliamentary work.

The decentralized nomination process is consistent with the main character of Norwegian politics. Although Norway is a unitary state the political system is rather decentralized (Eckstein, 1966; Valen and Katz, 1964; Olsen, 1983), with a strong tradition of local self-government dating back to 1837. Furthermore, a longstanding controversy between central and peripheral parts of the country has been one of the dominating cleavages in the political system (Rokkan, 1970; Valen and Rokkan, 1974). The representation of the periphery in national politics is directly affected by the recruitment of nominees at Storting elections. Local control of the selection process might be expected to produce representatives oriented towards their locality, perhaps at the expense of a national role. Norwegian representatives are expected to spend a lot of time in their constituencies and generally live up to that expectation, but not to an extent that has provoked any adverse public debate.

The decentralization of nominations has important consequences for the role of individual representatives in relation to national party leaders. If a representative opposes the leaders regarding some important matter, the leaders are not in a position to enforce their will by threatening to have the representative removed at the next nomination – provided the representative maintains his or her support at home. Hence the overwhelming party discipline in parliamentary work may seem like a paradox. Why are representatives so strongly inclined to follow the party line? Three possible explanations may be suggested. Socialization through party work is likely to create party loyalty and affect the behaviour of individual representatives. All parties tend to require substantial experience of local party activity as well as of public office in order to be nominated. Another possibility, related to the first, is that the constituency party may perceive deviant behaviour in parliamentary work as a violation of party loyalty. Representatives may simply follow the party line because they are afraid of being deselected by the constituency if they are rebellious in the Storting. On the other hand, opposition to national leaders may strengthen a candidate's chances for renomination if he or she defends positions popular with dominant groups in the constituency. Third, sanctions available to party leaders are not insignificant. It is likely that representatives have to be acceptable to the national leaders in order to make a career in parliamentary work, for example through becoming the chairperson of an important committee or member of the government.

Does it matter who the candidates are? This question has become fashionable in the study of political leadership. The high degree of party cohesion in parliamentary behaviour may suggest that it is the party rather than individual representatives that matters in political decision-making. It should be taken into account, however, that within the framework of the electoral platform a great number of decisions are made collectively by the parliamentary party, in which each representative has a vote and the opportunity to affect the outcome.

The strength of the Norwegian nomination system is its ability to produce candidates closely affiliated with demands and conflicting interests of domestic politics. Most members of the Storting have arrived at their current position through experience of local or provincial government and through involvement in groups inside and outside their respective parties. By funnelling a variety of group demands into the decision-making bodies of national politics, the present method of candidate selection contributes to the legitimacy of the representation system. Thus, the symbolic significance of this method may easily be recognized. It is more difficult to assess its impact on policy-making processes. How and to what extent do representatives pursue the interests of groups which supported them for nomination? To what extent are these groups included in their network of communication? How important is the group base for individual representatives? In general, how does the role of the representative fit with perceptions and expectations generated in the selectorate during the nomination process? These questions call for a study of attitudes and behaviour of representatives after they have taken their seat in Parliament. A study along these lines would provide new insight into the question of who are the candidates and what is their impact on the decision-making process.

Notes

This article was written when the author was a Fellow at the West European Program at the Woodrow Wilson International Center for Scholars in Washington, DC. He is also indebted to Hanne Marthe Narum and Kjeld Drevvatne for research assistance in Oslo, and to Donald R. Matthews, Prosser Gifford, Martin Klein, Austin Ranney and Derek Urwin who have read an earlier draft of the manuscript and made valuable suggestions. But the author takes full responsibility for the contents.

1. Valgordningskommisjonen av 1917. *Innstilling II.* See also *Stortingsforhand-linger 1920* 3a. Ot. prop. nr. 1–50.
2. The Electoral Law, paragraph 44, states: 'When the number of seats for each list has been decided by electoral results, a new count is undertaken for candidates on the list. The candidate who has obtained the most votes as number one is elected. If there are two seats to be filled, the candidate with the highest number of votes as number two is elected, etc.' If some party's voters prefer candidate 2 to candidate 1, the name of the latter would have to be crossed out by at least half the voters or, more exactly, by at least one voter more than 50 percent. If candidate 3 is the favourite, the situation becomes even more complicated because both candidates 1 and 2 must be omitted by a majority of voters.
3. The number of seats is not directly proportional to population size, since sparsely populated provinces are overrepresented compared to the more densely populated areas. This principle was introduced in the Constitution of 1814 and has been maintained ever since. Thus at present one vote in the northernmost province of Finnmark weighs about twice as much as one vote in Oslo and surrounding provinces.
4. By-elections are unknown in Norway. If an elected representative leaves office owing to death, illness, travel abroad, etc., he or she is succeeded by the next candidate on the list, who becomes the 'alternate representative'.
5. According to paragraph 3 in the Act of Nominations the number of delegates is defined as follows: 20–150 votes at the preceding Storting election: 1 delegate. For a greater number of votes up to 1900: 1 delegate for every 400 or fraction thereof. And when the vote exceeds even this figure: 1 delegate for every 700 or fraction thereof.
6. The role of local organizations has been strengthened in recent years. Until the 1960s the normal pattern was that local organizations could propose candidates, but they did not take a stand on the rank ordering of aspirants (see Valen, 1956).
7. The most notable attempt to involve the voters in the nomination process was made by the Liberal Party (Venstre) in the 1950s and 1960s. Liberal voters were invited to send proposals for candidates to the party's organization in their respective

constituencies. But, almost without exception, proposals received came from active Liberal Party members.

8. Unpublished figures. The study is part of a programme of electoral studies at the Institute for Social Research in Oslo. On this programme, see Valen (1981). The 1985 study has been directed by Bernt O. Aardal.

9. It was decided that neither of the sexes should have less than 40 percent of the candidates on the lists. The Socialist Left Party and the Liberal Party have decided that 50 percent of their candidates shall be women.

10. The national committee, which includes members from all provinces, is the governing body of the party between national conventions. The executive committee constitutes the executive branch of the national committee. Both committees are appointed by the national convention (see Valen and Katz, 1964: 50–3).

11. If the provincial party of Sogn og Fjordane had given in to pressures from the national party, it would have been obliged to convene a new nominating convention, which would not have been funded by public means.

12. It is not necessary to be a member of the Storting in order to be appointed to a cabinet position, and one is not permitted to hold simultaneously a seat in the Storting and in the cabinet. If a member of the Storting is appointed to the cabinet, he must temporarily resign from his seat in the Storting, where he is replaced by his alternate (see note 4). Normally about half of the cabinet ministers are members of the Storting. Thus in the bourgeoise coalition government from 1983–6 ten out of eighteen ministers were members of the Storting, exactly the same figure as in the current Labour government. The prime minister, however, is always the parliamentary leader of one of the parties.

13. Apparently they are intentionally uninformed because the constituencies want to avoid interference from party headquarters. When the author turned to party headquarters for help in identifying committee members for the 1985 study (see note 14), he was informed that lists of names were not available at national level, and national leaders would not take the risk of infuriating the provincial organizations of their parties by asking about the composition of the nomination committees. Thus the questionnaire had to be distributed through the provincial secretaries of the respective parties.

14. The study was conducted at the Institute for Social Research by the author in collaboration with Professor Donald R. Matthews immediately after the nominations had been completed in 1985. A mail questionnaire was sent to all members of nomination committees in the seven parties represented in the Storting during the period 1981–5. Some 550 members returned the questionnaire, a response rate of 60 percent.

15. The Stavanger study was limited to a local area (Valen and Katz, 1964: 236–349), while the 1985 study was nationwide (cf. note 14). However, nearly all respondents in the Stavanger study had been involved in nominations at the 1957 election. In this respect there is considerable similarity between the two studies.

16. The respondents were asked: 'Here is a list of characteristics attributed to candidates for Storting election. Concerning top candidates, i.e. those who have some chance of being elected, which one of these characteristics do you consider most important, and which one is most important for lower candidates?' (The list is given in Table 10.3).

17. Some of the provinces are clearly divided into a few major districts by fjords and mountains as well as by historic traditions. A good example is the province of More og Romsdal on the western coast, which consists of three distinct districts,

234   *Henry Valen*

Sunnmore, Romsdal and Nordmore. But in some provinces natural borderlines do not exist.

18. The committee, which was appointed after the Storting election of 1965 to evaluate the nomination system, consisted of eight centrally located leaders of the party and its sub-organizations for youth and women. Two of the members held positions in the trade union movement as well as in the Labour Party. The report of 1966, *Nominasjonsordningen ved Stortingsvalg*, was subsequently sent out for discussions in the local organizations of the party, and finally debated in the party's national convention.

19. It was proposed that a nine-member committee, representing the central leadership of the party, the party's women's and youth organizations, and the trade unions should be appointed to co-ordinate candidate selection (*Proceedings of the 1967 Labour Party National Convention*, pp. 141–54).

References

Almond, G.A. and J. Coleman (1960) *The Politics of Developing Areas*. Princeton, NJ: Princeton University Press.

Bjurulf, B. and Glans, I. (1976) 'Fran Tvablocksystem till Faktionalisering' (From Two-Bloc System to Factionalization'), *Statsvetenskapeleg Tidsskrift*, 3: 231–52.

Eckstein, H. (1966) *Division and Cohesion in Democracy: A Study of Norway*. Princeton, NJ: Princeton University Press.

Eliassen, K. (1985) 'Rekrutteringen til Stortinget og Regjeringen 1945–1985' ('Recruitment to the Storting and the Government, 1945–1985'), pp. 109–30 in T. Nordby (ed.), *Storting og Regjering*. Oslo: Kunnskapsforlaget.

Epstein, L.D. (1980) *Political Parties in Western Democracies*. New Brunswick, NJ: Transaction Books.

Hellevik, O. (1969) *Stortinget – en Sosial Elite* (*The Storting – a Social Elite*). Oslo: Pax Forlag.

Olsen, J.P. (1983) *Organized Democracy*. Bergen: Universitetsforlaget.

Pedersen, M. (1972) 'Lawyers in Politics: The Danish Folketing and American Legislatures', pp. 25–64 in S. Patterson and J. Wahlke (eds), *Comparative Legislature Behavior Research*, New York: Wiley.

Putnam, R.D. (1976) The Comparative Study of Political Elites. Englewood Cliffs, NJ: Prentice Hall.

Ranney, A. (1983) *Channels of Power: The Impact of Television on American Politics*. New York: Basic Books.

Rokkan, S. (1970) *Citizens, Elections, Parties*. Bergen: Universitetsforlaget.

Sartori, G. (1967) 'Members of Parliament', in *Decisions and Decision-Makers in the Modern State*. Paris: Unesco.

Sejersted, F. (1984) *Høyres Historie*, Volume III. Oslo: Capellen.

Svaasand, L. (1985) *Politiske Partier* (*Political Parties*). Oslo: Tiden Norsk Forlag.

Valen, H. (1956) 'Nominasjon ved Stortingsvalg' ('Nominations at Storting Elections'), *Statsokonomisk Tidsskrift*, 70 (2): 115–42.

Valen, H. (1966) 'The Recruitment of Parliamentary Nominees in Norway', *Scandinavian Political Studies*, 1: 121–66.

Valen H. (1981) 'Electoral Research in Norway', in *Research in Norway 1981*. Oslo: Universitetsforlaget.

Valen, H. (1986) 'The Storting Election of September 1985: The Welfare State Under Pressure', *Scandinavian Political Studies*, 9 (2): 177–88.

Valen, H. and B.O. Aardal (1983) *Et Valg i Perspektiv. En Studie av Stortingsvalget i 1981* (*An Election in Perspective: The Storting Election of 1981*). Oslo: Central Bureau of Statistics.

Valen, H. and D. Katz (1964) *Political Parties in Norway*. Oslo: Universitetsforlaget.

Valen, H. and S. Rokkan (1974) 'Norway: Conflict Structure and Mass Politics in a European Periphery,' pp. 315–70 in R. Rose (ed.) *Electoral Behaviour*. New York: Free Press.

11

Conclusion

Michael Gallagher

In this concluding chapter we shall attempt to identify patterns in the large amount of information we now possess on the subject of candidate selection. First, we shall examine, on a comparative basis, the extent to which candidate selection is centralized, and the degree of member and voter involvement in the process. Second, we shall review the evidence as to the qualities for which the selectors seem to be looking. Third, we shall evaluate explanations for the wide variations that exist between parties, concentrating on the factors discussed in the introductory chapter. Fourth, we shall ask whether and under what circumstances the selection process has a discernible effect on parliamentarians' backgrounds and behaviour. Finally, we shall return to the question: How important is candidate selection?

The selection process: centralization and participation

In this section we shall review the evidence relating to the degree of centralization of candidate selection, and to the extent of members' and voters' involvement in the process.

Attempting to identify the precise place in the party where the key decisions are made is not always easy since, as was observed in Chapter 1, many actors, individual or collective, at different levels of the party may play a role. Also, in some federal countries, such as the USA and Australia, the parties nationally do not prescribe a method of selecting candidates, so that practice varies from state to state. Nonetheless, it is possible, for most parties, to single out one actor as the decisive one. The parties in the countries covered in earlier chapters are categorized in Table 11.1.

Party voters

Only a few parties widen the process to the maximum extent, allowing all voters to participate in choosing the candidate. The most prominent cases in this category, of course, are the American parties, where selection processes are governed by state law.

Table 11.1 *Who picks candidates: the pattern in nine countries*

Locus of greatest influence over candidate selection

	Party voters	Party primaries	Subset of constituency party members	National executive	Interest groups	National faction leaders	Party leader
Belgium		CVPᵃ SPᵃ PS PRLᵃ	CVPᵃ SPᵃ PVV PRLᵃ PSC		CVPᵃ		
Britain		Liberal SDP	Conservative Labour				
France			PS PC	RPR UDF			
West Germany			All parties[b]				
Ireland			FFᵃ FGᵃ PDᵃ Labour WP	FFᵃ FGᵃ PDᵃ			
Italy			DCᵃ PCIᵃ PSIᵃ Small parties	DCᵃ PCIᵃ PSIᵃ	DCᵃ	DCᵃ	
Japan			JSPᵃ DSPᵃ	JCP	JSPᵃ DSPᵃ	LDP	Komei
Netherlands		D'66	CDAᶜ PvdAᶜ	VVD			
Norway			All parties				

[a] Denotes that more than one actor is significant.

[b] The West German parties select candidates for single-member constituencies and for multi-member (Land) constituencies. Each selection is made at the level of the relevant constituency.

[c] On the categorization of the Dutch CDA and PvdA as having constituency-level selection, see note 2.

Procedures vary across the country, but most states prescribe the use of 'direct primaries', allowing any elector to participate in the selection of the nominee of any one party. Variations between states are, for the most part, relatively minor, and concern details like whether the elector must register in advance as a 'member' of a party in order to qualify for a vote in its primary, and whether the elector must declare publicly which party's primary he or she wishes to vote in (for details see Ranney, 1981: 85–6; Scott and Hrebenar, 1979: 124–7). One important distinction is between states where anyone can run in a primary (subject to payment of a small fee or collection of a certain number of signatures), and those few states where the party organization has a screening role. In Colorado, for example, only aspirants who receive 20 percent of the votes at the state party congress are allowed onto the primary ballot (Ware, 1979: 82).

State party organizations, such as they are, have little influence on the outcome of the primaries, and national organizations none. Attempts by presidents to try to 'purge' maverick congressmen of their own party, by supporting their rivals at the nomination stage, have been seen as 'interference in purely local affairs' and have failed completely (Ranney, 1975: 178–9). Contrasts with European practice are obvious: party 'members' need not pay a membership fee or attend branch meetings, and the selection process is opened up not only to party voters, in itself an unthinkable prospect for most European parties, but even to electors who may support another party.

Very few parties elsewhere have made use of primaries. The CDU in Rhineland–Pfalz experimented briefly with them in the early 1970s.[1] They, or their equivalent, have been used in Canada (Williams, 1981: 104–5). They were also employed by the Austrian People's Party (OeVP) in 1969–70 and in 1975, when all electors, regardless of affiliation, were able to vote (Mommsen-Reindl, 1980: 291; Sully, 1981: 81). But, according to Sully, the voters did not have the final word; the party's constituency organizations were only 'bound to take note of these decisions' when drawing up their lists. The experiment was regarded as not entirely successful, and was not repeated in 1979.

Some eastern European states use 'voters' meetings' to receive nominations. In the USSR, Poland and East Germany these have, even in theory, only 'nebulous' power, but in Yugoslavia and Hungary, even though the ruling party is naturally unwilling to allow them to throw up 'opposition' candidates, their formal power is significant (Pravda, 1978: 177–9, 184–6). In Hungary aspirants need to obtain a third of the votes in at least two meetings. At the 1985 elections dissidents used them to highlight their platform, and one came close to being nominated at one meeting (*Keesing's Contemporary Archives*, 1985: 33812–13). In Yugoslavia, where Pasic (1966: 27) has commented on the 'insufficient interest' taken by the voters in these meetings, some candidates unwelcome to the ruling party have been nominated (Carter, 1982: 132–54).

Although there do not appear to be any other parties which allow voters a voice in the formal selection process, it should be noted that in several countries the electoral system gives the voters a de facto input. In countries using preferential PR systems the party nominates a certain number of candidates and its voters then decide, by their use of preference votes, which will be elected. This applies to list systems with effective preference voting (Italy, Denmark, Finland, Switzerland, Luxembourg), to STV (Ireland, Malta), and to the single non-transferable vote in multi-member constituencies (Japan). It is also true under the alternative vote (STV in single-member constituencies) when a party chooses to run more than one candidate, which is occasionally done by the Australian National (formerly Country) Party (Cribb, 1977: 151). Mention should also be made of the practice of the two French blocs, under the two-round electoral system, of using the first round to allow the voters to decide which party's candidate should represent the bloc in the second round. The same applies to single-party or hegemonic-party states which allow voters a choice between candidates, such as Hungary, Yugoslavia, Kenya, Tanzania, Côte d'Ivoire and Sierra Leone. Of course, in all of these cases the voters can choose only among names put forward by the party organization, but one could argue that their role in the selection process is not significantly different from that of American voters, and is especially comparable to that of voters in states where pre-primary assemblies of paid-up members determine who can run.

Party primaries
If almost all parties are reluctant to open the process to ordinary voters, a substantial number are willing to allow all paid-up party members to vote in the selection of candidates. In some cases the members may choose only among names already vetted by some organ of the party. The 'party primary' method is used widely in Belgium (especially by the CVP, PS, SP and PRL), occasionally in West Germany, by D'66 in the Netherlands, and by the Liberals and SDP in Britain. Party primaries have been compulsory under law in Finland since 1978, and were used by the SDP before then (Thomas, 1985: 202; Elder, Thomas and Arter, 1982: 146; Arter, 1980: 371–2). They are regularly used by Social Credit in New Zealand, sometimes employed by the Canadian parties, and have been used, though less so in recent times, by the Australian Labor Party (Jackson, 1980: 102; Williams, 1981: 106–7; Epstein, 1977: 26). In Denmark the Social Democrats' candidates, once selected, 'must be reselected annually by a meeting at which all party members may attend and vote' (Fitzmaurice, 1981: 107). The Swedish bourgeois parties have used 'consultative' party primaries (Andren, 1961: 33).

In Turkey the 1965 Political Parties Law prescribed the selection of at least 95 percent of candidates by party primaries, as part of an unusual attempt to use the law to make parties more internally democratic. This marked, at least in theory, quite a departure from previous practice, under which central agencies were dominant (Dodd, 1969: 133), but the powerful position of notables in the local organization, and the 'vague' notion of party membership in the Turkish parties (Sayari, 1980), raise questions about how much significance should be attached to this apparent case of intraparty democracy. They are also used by Bermuda's ruling United Bermuda Party, where they approach American-style primaries because of the high proportion of voters who are full party members. A particularly interesting case, which we shall refer to again in view of its outcome, was that of the Democratic Movement for Change (DMC), an Israeli party founded in 1976 with internal party democracy among its principles. The DMC held a nationwide party primary (Israel's electoral system involves only one, national, constituency) in which each of its 35,000 members could both run and vote (Torgovnik, 1979: 153; Hoffman, 1980: 292).

Subset of constituency party members
Rather more common is selection by a subset of constituency party members, either a constituency convention containing delegates from party branches or a smaller group such as a constituency committee. In all of the countries covered in this book some parties at least pick their candidates at this level. In the Belgian PSC a constituency committee draws up the list, which may need ratification by party members, and the same procedure is usually followed in the PVV. In the British Labour and Conservative parties the selection is made by a convention-like body representing local members, though from a shortlist drawn up by a committee. However, the important role of the centre should not be overlooked. In the Conservative Party the centre screens most aspirants and allows only a minority through. In both major parties the 'clearing house' role of the centre, informing all approved aspirants of all forthcoming selections, constitutes a greater involvement than the centre has in many countries.

In the French Socialist Party in 1986 the list was drawn up by a constituency committee, and was then merely put to a vote of members, but under the two-round electoral system a constituency convention had made the effective decision. The PCF, too, gives members a chance to vote on the proposals of the constituency organization. All parties in West Germany select most of their candidates for the single-member constituencies at constituency conventions; list candidates are also chosen at constituency conventions, though these conventions comprise a smaller proportion of members since the 'constituency' for list seats covers a much larger area. In Ireland, too, constituency conventions pick all the minor parties' candidates and most of the major parties'. Constituency committees are important in Italy, playing a decisive role in the small parties, and selecting most of the candidates in the DC, PCI and PSI. In Japan the prefectural headquarters is the main selector of Socialist Party candidates. In the Netherlands the most powerful actors in the PvdA selection process are the party committees in the nineteen regional 'sub-constituencies', and these bodies are also important in the CDA.[2] In Norway, under law, all the parties select their candidates at constituency conventions.

Elsewhere, selection by a subset of constituency members is practised in New Zealand by the National Party, which uses conventions, while the Labour Party uses selection by a committee, three of whose six members are from the constituency organization (Jackson, 1980: 101–2). The Canadian parties sometimes use constituency conventions, as, it seems, do the Australian Liberals (Williams, 1981: 105–6; Epstein, 1977: 26–7). Australian Labor's methods vary from state to state: branch members' views are decisive in New South Wales, a state-wide party conference makes the selections in Tasmania, and the state organization has a voice in Victoria (Weller, 1983: 62). In Scandinavia the process 'is firmly set at constituency or district level'; in Sweden national authorities 'have neither the opportunity to propose nor the power to veto candidates' (Elder, Thomas and Arter, 1982: 147). The OeVP, despite its flirtation with primaries, usually selects candidates at constituency (Land) executive level, though the national executive can name 5 percent of the places on the list (Sully, 1981: 81). In Switzerland selection is controlled at the level of the canton or even lower, with the federal party often lacking even nominal power in the process (Steiner, 1974: 99). In 1982 candidates of Sierra Leone's only party, the All Peoples' Congress (APC), were chosen at the level of the constituency executive (about thirty people), the national executive vetoing only two (Luke, 1985: 30–1), though a different system was used in 1986 (see below). In parties which are little more than alliances of local notables, each notable is likely to be the effective selector in his or her own fiefdom. An example comes from pre-civil war Lebanon, where aspirants had to curry favour with the notable whose list they wished to be on, and in some cases 'declare their total and unrelenting obedience to him' (Khalaf, 1980: 260–1).

The practices of two of the parties in Israel's Likud could also be included in the category of selection by a subset of constituency members, with the qualification that since under the electoral system the entire country is one large constituency, one might also consider them to be examples of national-level selection (Goldberg and Hoffman, 1983). In 1981 the Herut party's candidates were selected, over several days, by a 900-member 'Center', whose members had been appointed by the party convention, itself directly elected by the branches. The Center first met to pick the head of the list and another thirty-five candidates from seventy-four aspirants, and some days later it convened again to rank the candidates selected (an important task since Israel's list system is non-preferential). The Liberals selected and ranked in one round. In the National Religious Party a 300-member body picked the candidates. Proof that in Herut, at least, these conventions were not merely ratifying decisions already made elsewhere comes from the fact that 'Center members were taking bets on the results while the computer tabulating the ballots was still running' (Goldberg and Hoffman, 1983: 73).

Deciding where to categorize Communist parties is especially difficult because of the general pattern of formal decentralization coexisting with strict ('democratic' or undemocratic) centralism. In sizeable non-ruling parties, such as those of France and Italy, and the ruling parties of eastern Europe, the centre allows lower units to select most of the candidates, and these parties could thus be regarded as examples of selection by a subset of constituency members. However, the centre usually closely scrutinizes the whole selection process and ensures that only candidates acceptable to itself are selected. In the Soviet Union the CPSU employs the system of 'nomenklatura', under which only those who have already been vetted will be promoted to any important position, including that of deputy (for candidate selection in eastern Europe see Pravda, 1978: 177–9, 184–6; Hill, 1976; 592-6; Pelczynski, 1959: 142–8).

National executive

Selection by the national executive of the party is rather less common than selection at lower levels. Even though this body has ultimate formal power, in most parties, to veto locally selected candidates and/or to select candidates itself, the effective decisions are usually made elsewhere. Exceptions include France's two right-wing parties, the RPR and UDF, where an active and decisive role is played by small 'commissions' answerable to the national executive, though they often have to confront the power of local notables. In the three largest Irish parties, Fianna Fáil, Fine Gael and the Progressive Democrats, the national executive picks a number of candidates itself and adds them to the names selected at constituency level. In Italy the national executive in the DC, PCI and PSI picks a substantial proportion of the candidates, and its selections feature strongly among the elected deputies. A national party council selects the candidates in the Dutch VVD.

In the Austrian Socialist Party (SPOe) the national executive seems to be the decisive actor, although its choices are influenced by the recommendations of the Land executives, and may also be altered by a national mini-conference (Sully, 1981: 55; Mommsen-Reindl, 1980: 291–2), a body which also plays a role in the French Socialist Party. In Israel selection in all the parties before 1977 was by a small central body (the 'vaadat minuim') equivalent or answerable to the national executive or the leadership, but in 1977 and 1981 only the Alignment parties (Labor and Mapam) and (in 1981) La'am, one of the Likud parties, continued with this method (Aksin, 1979: 107–10; Aronoff, 1979: 125–6, 140–1; Arian, 1979: 300; Goldberg and Hoffman, 1983). It is the national executive in the two main parties in Venezuela, AD and COPEI, which makes the final decisions on names and list order (Wells, 1980: 43–4). In Colombia the national executives tend to pick the candidates because lower units in the organization are unable to reach agreement among themselves (Duff, 1971: 383). In the New Zealand Labour Party, already mentioned, the centre has three of the six members of the committee which picks candidates in each constituency.

In several African one-party states, too, the national executive is decisive. In Kenya, where the KANU party scarcely exists as an organization, candidates are self-starting local notables who need only to be 'certified' by its executive committee to run (Barkan and Okumu, 1978: 100–1). In Sierra Leone, another country where candidates of the one party (the APC) compete against each other at elections, selection in 1986 was more centralized than in 1982: aspirants at the 1986 election had to be screened by a national committee chaired by former president Siaka Stevens. The commission withheld the party symbol, and thus the right to stand in the election, from 163 of the 513 aspirants (*West Africa*, 11 November 1985, and 12 May 1986, p. 981). In Tanzania the final decision is made by the national executive of the CCM (formerly TANU), although it is only the last voice in the process, the first belonging to constituency conferences which hear all the aspirants and rank them in order of preference (Martin, 1978: 109).

Party leader

Centralization reaches its limit in parties where candidates are selected by just one person: the party leader. This practice is rare in the developed world. The only European country where it appears to happen is Greece. In New Democracy party members at a 1977 congress approved giving the leader this power, while in the socialist PASOK 'Papandreou personally chooses the party's candidates' (Loulis, 1981: 71; Kohler, 1982: 121; Elephantis, 1981: 124). In Japan the president of the religiously based Komei party is the effective selector. The other examples of selection by leader come from Latin America, Africa and elsewhere in Asia. In Costa Rica, where a national congress has the formal power to select candidates, each party's presidential candidate plays 'a crucial role', and in Guatemala 'the selection of candidates is limited to a few party leaders' (Baker, 1971: 57–8, 102; Verner, 1971: 302). In Zambia at the 1968 election, although the constitution of the ruling party (UNIP) declared that candidates were to be selected by the central committee, Kenneth Kaunda actually made the selections (Molteno and Scott, 1974: 168–9). In India candidate selection in the Congress Party was controlled by the national executive until the split in the party in 1971, after which Indira Gandhi effectively selected candidates herself, as a result of which thousands of aspirants from all over the country descended on her Delhi home to press their case (Palmer, 1975: 115–25). At the 1980 election Indira and Sanjay Gandhi 'personally played an active role in the selection of Congress (I) parliamentary candidates', and Sanjay ensured that many of his associates in the Youth Congress received nominations in safe seats, creating resentment among local party leaders (Weiner, 1983: 43). The other Indian parties, though, lack a strong national organization.

A slightly different case comes from the Middle East. In one of Israel's religious parties, Agudat Israel, final authority lies with the Council of Sages, the party's 'most august Rabbis' (Goldberg and Hoffmann, 1983: 69–70). As the extreme case there is Iran under Pahlavi, when aspirants had to be 'thoroughly investigated and approved by the Secret Police', who are 'very active in the recommendation and disqualification of candidates', and then faced the final hurdle of the Shah himself, who allowed 'only proved and loyal personages to pass' (Bill, 1971: 363–4). Candidate selection under the Khomeini regime does not seem, so far, to have received its due share of attention.

Interest groups and factions

Finally, it is necessary to mention a few cases where the important decisions are taken outside the formal structure of the party, either by interest groups or by factions. In the Belgian CVP, where candidates are selected either by a poll of all members or by a constituency committee, most candidacies are in fact arranged by negotiations between interest groups representing farmers, employers and workers. In the Italian DC, agreement reached within constituency or national bodies of the party actually signals agreement among the factions within the party and the interest groups affiliated to it; the party bodies are merely the arenas within which factions and interest groups compete and bargain, rather than the effective decision-makers. Much the same applies to Japan's highly factionalized Liberal Democratic Party, while in the Democratic Socialist Party affiliated trade unions play an important role. Factions are also important in Uruguay, where the faction ('sub-lema') leader's popularity is crucial to the appeal of the list, and so it is this individual 'whose word sets the rank-order on the sub-lema election list' (McDonald, 1971: 117). Candidates of Liberia's True Whig Party, which ruled the country from 1877 to 1980, were allegedly selected at Masonic Lodge meetings.

Centralization: a summary
On the subject of centralization, then, the evidence described above suggests that in a slight majority of countries the centre, i.e. the national executive or a small group of party leaders, has little if any power in the candidate selection process. Leaving aside those countries for which our information is very partial or may be outdated, we find that the centre plays an insignificant part in Belgium, Britain, West Germany, Norway, the USA, Australia, Canada, Finland and Austria. In several of these countries (Britain, West Germany and Norway) it is said that to be perceived locally as a favourite of head office can amount to a kiss of death. In Ireland, Italy, the Netherlands, Israel, New Zealand and India the centre plays a significant part in some parties, but is decisive in the selection of only a minority of candidates. Only in France, Greece, Japan, Venezuela and Sierra Leone can it be regarded as the main selector of candidates.

Participation in candidate selection
Rates of participation vary considerably between parties, both within and between countries. An attempt is made in Table 11.2 to summarize the power of the centre, and participation rates, for the nine countries covered in this book. The figures for participation should be treated with some caution, for the reasons explained in

the first note to the table. Subject to this qualification, they show that the involvement of members reaches about a third in France and Ireland, but is below 1 percent in Britain, Italy and Japan. The involvement of voters depends, clearly, on how many voters are enrolled as party members. In none of our nine countries are as many as 3 percent involved in candidate selection, and in some the proportion is minuscule.

Table 11.2   *Centralization and participation rates in candidate selection in nine countries*[a]

	Effective power of centre	% involvement of Members	Voters
Belgium	Very limited	12	2.1
Britain	Very limited	<1	—[b]
France	Varies; quite significant in all parties	35	0.1
West Germany	Very limited	1.3	0.1
Ireland	Limited but increasingly significant	30	1.5
Italy	Varies; significant in main parties	<1	—[b]
Japan	Significant in all parties	<1	—[b]
Netherlands	Varies; some significance in all parties	10	0.5
Norway	Very limited	4.5	0.6

[a] All figures are estimates, and in some cases are rough averages of figures for individual parties. For details, see specific chapters.
[b] Figure is negligible.

Information from other countries is extremely fragmentary. In the New Zealand National Party selection conferences are attended by up to 150 delegates, representing about 5 percent of the membership (Jackson, 1980: 102). Membership involvement is, naturally, highest when party primaries are used. In the Finnish SDP about 50 percent of members voted in the primaries of the 1970s, while turnout reached 80 percent in the Israeli DMC's primary in 1977 (Arter, 1980: 371–2; Hoffman, 1980: 292). Those voting in the OeVP's 1975 primaries represented about 63 percent of its members (Sully, 1981: 81). Data on the involvement of voters is impossible to obtain for all but a few countries, since we do not have figures for the total number of people involved in candidate selection. In Israel the 28,000 members who voted in the DMC's 1977 primary represented about 15 percent of those who voted for the party at the ensuing election, but those taking part in candidate selection in the Likud parties in 1981 amounted to only about 0.2 percent of Likud voters. Because of the exceptionally high members to voters ratio in Austria, those voting in the OeVP's 1975 primary represented about 41 percent of its voters. Finally, in the USA turnout in the 1976 presidential primaries came to 43 percent of registered voters, or 28 percent of the voting-age population (Ranney, 1977: 20).

The selection process: what the selectors are looking for

Turning to the question of what qualities the selectors seek in aspirants, we can distinguish between formal eligibility require-ments and informal criteria. Many parties do not have any formal requirements which an aspirant must fulfil to be eligible for selection as a candidate; many others merely stipulate a minimum period, commonly about a year, for which aspirants must have belonged to the party. The general pattern is that left-wing parties, especially Communist parties, are more likely to have such a requirement in their rules than right-wing ones; the longest period stipulated seems to be the five years of the Italian and Belgian Socialists. It must be said, though, that whatever the party rules say, many parties succumb to the temptation to waive them on occasions when this is expedient, for example if a non-member of the party with a strong local following declares an interest in a candidacy at a late stage.

Another common stipulation is that candidates must be under a certain age (usually sixty-five); this too may be more marked among parties of the left, though the tendency is not very pronounced. Some parties have 'anti-cumulation' laws preventing holders of other elected positions (such as local government office, member of the European Parliament or perhaps a party post) from seeking a candidacy, or at least requiring them to vacate such positions if they are elected to the national parliament. Kenya's KANU debars aspirants who are not literate in English, while Sekou Touré's PRG in Guinea excluded aspirants who had been engaged in 'private industrial or commercial activities' (Barkan and Okumu, 1978: 100–1; Lawson, 1976; 128). The Belgian Socialist parties, too, rule out directors of private companies, and have a plethora of unusually demanding requirements, but, as De Winter points out in Chapter 2, many of these are now unenforceable because they assume the existence of a subculture which has in fact passed away. A few parties, to ensure 'rotation' of the position of deputy among the membership, do not permit the candidacy of persons who have been deputies for more than a certain period. In the Yugoslav League of Communists deputies can serve only two consecutive terms (Cohen,

1982: 15), and the German Greens do not allow MdBs to serve more than four consecutive years.

In virtually all cases, then, the selectors are left with a good deal of discretion as to whom to choose, and a wide range of criteria they might wish to employ. In Chapter 1 it was suggested that the qualities they seek can be classified as either subjective or objective personal characteristics, and we shall now examine them under these headings.

Subjective personal characteristics

The most widely valued are aspirants' track records in the party organization and in the constituency. One or both of these is mentioned in virtually all of the earlier chapters. In most other countries, too, a solid background in the party and/or in local government are assets. A party record is usually measured temporally, but in 1986 the Sierra Leonean APC used a novel way of testing aspirants' fidelity: some of those appearing before its national screening committee found themselves asked to prove that they could sing the party song (*West Africa*, 12 May 1986, p. 981).

Occasionally, though, parties actively seek non-members, if they are trying to broaden their appeal and feel that the membership is unduly narrow in its outlook. The Belgian Liberals and Socialists have both by-passed their routine procedures in this way, and the Italian DC and PC, from the mid-1970s onwards, have selected high-profile independents on their lists. The Canadian Liberals, too, do not always welcome a party record. Whereas the socialist New Democratic Party 'has always been suspicious of recent converts and values loyalty and involvement with the party over a reasonably long period of time', the Liberals are glad to select newcomers, there being a view that long-time members may be positively undesirable as they often 'have blinkers on' (Williams, 1981: 101–2). This probably illustrates a pattern: as with formal requirements, it seems that parties on the left are especially keen to see proof of loyalty over time.

The best type of record, of course, is to be an incumbent deputy.[3] In virtually every country for which we have evidence, incumbents stand a far better chance of being selected than any other group of aspirants. Even in the USA, a deviant case in almost every other respect, incumbents rarely suffer defeat in primaries (Keefe and Ogul, 1981: 97–8). In quite a few countries the deselection of an incumbent is a newsworthy event. Incumbents usually have an organizational base within the party, and may thus be able to ensure their reselection. Even where they depend entirely on the decisions of others, it is not surprising that they are usually successful. An incumbent has a higher profile than most non-incumbents, and a certain degree of electoral appeal. Moreover, in countries where the electoral system requires or allows voters to vote for candidates as well as for parties, an incumbent might seem to have acquired a personal mandate to be a parliamentarian, so that it would violate democratic norms for a relatively small number of party members to prevent him, without due cause, from at least 'taking his chance' at the voters' hands. Although few parties appear to have rules specifically protecting incumbents from the full uncertainties of the selection process, the great majority survive nonetheless. The introduction of 'mandatory reselection' of MPs in the British Labour Party in the early 1980s led to very few casualties.

Nevertheless, incumbency may sometimes be a handicap. Apart from those parties whose rules limit the time anyone can serve in parliament, there are others, such as the PCI, which make a point of rotating their deputies after two or three terms. Ruling Communist parties, such as the CPSU, also 'deselect' many incumbents, often after only one term (Hill, 1972: 49). There are other parties which make a half-hearted attempt to do this, by imposing hurdles which incumbents of a certain duration must overcome. The Israeli Labor and Liberal parties have rules that all two-term MKs (Members of the Knesset) need the support of 60 percent of Center voters to be eligible for reselection, a provision which caused the deselection of seven Labor MKs in 1977, though none failed to attain the mark in 1981 (Arian, 1979: 300; Goldberg and Hoffmann, 1983: 63–6). The Italian DC in 1983 urged local organizations to think carefully about reselecting veteran incumbents, but left a loophole which resulted in the reselection of most of them. In West Germany, too, there are reservations, which do not necessarily lead to deselections, about picking 'sitting tenants' of more than eight years' standing. In the Netherlands up to a quarter of deputies may be dropped completely, or effectively deselected by being placed in a hopeless position on the list. Besides, any assessment of incumbents' success in avoiding deselection must take account of the unknown proportion of deputies who retire from politics because they face or fear deselection. Incumbents are not necessarily as impregnable as figures on deselections might suggest.

The other subjective characteristics sought are mainly those which the selectors assume are related to electoral appeal. These include being articulate (especially from a platform), 'presentable' in appearance, and having an ability to get on with people. Aspirants' potential as government ministers is mentioned for very few countries, and commentators on the Labour parties of Britain

(Bochel and Denver, 1983: 50) and Australia explicitly describe it as relatively unimportant. When the Australian trade union congress president and future prime minister Bob Hawke, 'whose popularity rating was always higher than that of any other public figure', first sought a nomination in 1980 he was vehemently opposed by a left-wing faction within the local organization, and was selected by only thirty-eight votes to twenty-nine over an 'unknown' opponent (Weller, 1983: 62–3).

In most countries it is hard to tell whether the selectors pick the most electorally appealing aspirants or not, but the preferential electoral system of Finland enabled Pertti Timonen to test this by correlating the votes received by Social Democrat aspirants in their party's primary and the preferences they received in the actual election (reported in Pesonen, 1972: 216–19). He found a high degree of correspondence, with a Pearson coefficient of 0.72, and concluded that 'the popularity of the certified and selected persons among party members is a rather good predictor of their electoral success as well'. A similar analysis for the 1975 election came to much the same conclusions (Arter, 1980: 371–2). In Italy there is a strong tendency for the candidates whom the selectors place highest on the ticket to receive most preferences from the voters, which might be interpreted as a sign of selectors being responsive to the voters' desires, although of course a high list place does of itself also attract preference votes. In several countries it is suggested that the selectors anticipate voters' attitudes when structuring their lists (Marsh, 1985: 373, 377), but the evidence, as Marsh observes, is only impressionistic. The relative unimportance of the individual candidate in winning votes in countries where party identification is reasonably strong, and indeed the complete 'invisibility' as far as the voters are concerned of many candidates on party lists, might lead activists to treat aspirants' appeal as a minor consideration. In Britain, though, Bochel and Denver (1983: 48–50) observe that despite most political scientists' conclusion that the 'candidate effect' is minimal, most Labour selectors believe the candidate is 'very important' electorally. It would be surprising if they were the only group of selectors to believe this.

The political views of aspirants are inevitably a factor, especially in parties with internal divisions such as the British Labour Party, but it is hard to find cases where selectors allow this consideration to outweigh the prospect of genuine electoral advantage, i.e. the possibility of gaining or losing a seat. The only sizeable party in which it is suggested that this occurs is the Japan Socialist Party, where the relatively ideological membership picks candidates whose left-wing views are unpopular with voters. The selectors of small purist parties, or of other parties in areas where they have no chance of representation, may feel free to indulge themselves, but most selectors do not. An exception occurs where parties cluster together on a common ticket; the components may then be under no pressure to aim at a broad appeal. Mapam is in such a position: it is the minor party in Israel's Alignment, and the overall popularity of the Alignment list depends mainly on the Labor Party's appeal. Consequently Mapam 'does not have to worry much about its appeal to the electorate', and 'its main focus of concentration is its own ideological purity' (Goldberg and Hoffmann, 1983: 78).

Objective personal characteristics
When it comes to objective personal characteristics, one almost invariably sought is the possession of local roots. This, of course, is often bound up with having a track record in the party or constituency, but is distinguishable from it; in particular, in not a few countries a non-member from the locality may be looked on more favourably than a party member whose record was established in another part of the country. Ranney (1981: 100) notes that pejorative terms like 'carpetbagger' or 'parachutist' are often given to aspirants who seek a nomination in a part of the country with which they have no connections. One reason for aversion to outsiders is that selectors are likely to feel that it reflects poorly on an aspirant if he chooses not to seek selection in the part of the country where he is best known. In addition, local candidates may be more appealing electorally, especially in countries where deputies are expected to involve themselves deeply in casework on behalf of constituents. Also, confining nominations to local people increases the incentives a party can offer to local members.

Since the demand for local candidates is practically universal, there is no point in mentioning more than a few noteworthy cases. In France *parachutage* has declined greatly since its peak in the early years of the Fifth Republic. Although it still exists, outsiders now find it more prudent to spend some time establishing themselves locally before seeking a candidacy. In Israel, where there are no sub-national electoral units, it appears that selectors back aspirants from their own part of the country (Goldberg and Hoffman, 1983: 72, 77–8). In Zambia in 1968 even UNIP's powerful leader, Kenneth Kaunda, found the demand for local roots too strong to resist. He initially decided that candidates should stand outside their province of origin so as to foster national unity, but local activists persuaded him to change his mind, and in the event nearly 80 percent of UNIP candidates stood in their birth province, most of the rest standing in city constituencies (Molteno and Scott, 1974: 172). In Japan and Ireland it helps to be not just local but also in possession of a local political pedigree; in each of these countries' parliaments about a quarter of deputies are related to former deputies.

The only exception to this pattern seems to be Britain, where many, perhaps most, major party candidates are 'outsiders' when first selected. This is not a feature only of recent British politics: in 1807 the young Palmerston was 'given' a seat on condition that he would 'never, even for the purpose of an election, set foot in the place' (Kavanagh, 1970: 2). Charles Dickens, in *Our Mutual Friend*, caricatured Victorian candidate selection through the parvenu Veneering, who issues his first election address before he has even discovered where his constituency is, let alone visited it. Even in Britain, though, local roots are regarded as an advantage for an aspirant, and being a certain type of outsider – an Englishman seeking a candidacy in a Scottish constituency – is as damaging to an aspirant's prospects as in any other country. But in general, by being only an advantage rather than a virtual sine qua non, local roots count for less in Britain than in any other country.

Other than local roots, no one factor emerges as being universally sought by selectors. There is little evidence of any group of selectors consciously looking for candidates of above-average socio-economic status. Nor is there any clear evidence of selectors deliberately seeking high educational achievements. Similarly, most selectors do not explicitly seek wealthy aspirants; indeed, ostentatious wealth may damage an aspirant's prospects in left-wing or populist parties. Few parties nowadays expect aspirants to pay money in furtherance of their cause. This has been mentioned for Sierra Leone in 1982, Iran, Guatemala and Lebanon (Luke, 1985: 30–1; Bill, 1971: 363; Verner, 1971: 302; Khalaf, 1980: 260–1), but would be regarded as unethical in most countries – which is not, of course, to say that it does not happen.[4] Having said that there is little evidence of selectors actively seeking candidates with high socio-economic status, high education and wealth, though, it must be emphasized that this is not to deny that these qualities are usually assets for aspirants, or that the dominance of people with such characteristics in the political elite may be among the *consequences* of the selection process (see below).

In societies divided along communal lines, candidates' backgrounds are all-important. In some countries (India, New Zealand) certain seats are reserved for candidates from a particular racial or religious community. In the Lebanon all seats are reserved in this way (Baaklini, 1977: 246; Khalaf, 1980: 260). But though the law thus dictates to the selectors part of what they must seek, candidates for reserved seats may, as in the Lebanon, need the electoral support of voters from other communities to be elected. In Northern Ireland there are no reserved seats, but practically all nationalist candidates are Catholics, while the Unionist parties have only ever had one Catholic MP (Farrell, 1980: 90). In Sri Lanka, with few exceptions, 'the first consideration in candidate selection is that the nominee be of the same ethnic community, caste and religion as the majority of the constituency residents' (Kearny, quoted in Jewell, 1977: 44). In the Indian Congress Party, Nehru's initial hope that the 'integrity' of aspirants would be the main criterion employed by selectors was soon disappointed, as factors like locality, community and caste came to the fore (Palmer, 1975: 119–21). Candidates' communal background, in terms of linguistic ability, is also important in Quebec, Belgium and Switzerland. European Christian Democrat parties expect their candidates to be practising Christians, ideally in good standing with the church, so that divorced people, for example, are at a strong disadvantage. Candidates of Japan's Komei Party at House of Representatives elections are drawn from members of Soka Gakkai, the Buddhist organization on which it is based.

Under PR electoral systems the selectors' usual concern is not to maximize any one objective characteristic but to 'balance' a number of them on the ticket. Ticket-balancing is an obviously rational strategy; it ensures commitment to the list from all groups or factions within the party, and might broaden the list's appeal in the voters' eyes. An unbalanced ticket will cause internal discontent and, even though voters in most countries may have little knowledge of the composition of parties' lists, any gross underrepresentation of some group is likely to be brought to their attention, by other parties and/or by the underrepresented group.

One of the most commonly balanced factors is location: parties almost everywhere try to ensure that their ticket covers the whole constituency, for much the same reasons as they pick local candidates in the first place. Parties which have interest groups affiliated to them or among their financial backers, such as the Belgian CVP, the three long-established West German parties, the Italian DC and all Labour parties, will take care to include their representatives on the ticket. In highly factionalized parties – the French PS, the Italian DC, the Japanese LDP, Israeli Labor, the Dutch CDA in its first few years – each faction will expect a proportionate share of the candidacies. A special case of this concerns 'cluster parties' – party blocs composed of several autonomous parties, such as the French UDF and the Israeli Alignment and Likud (Mendilow, 1982). In addition, under non-PR electoral systems allied parties need (the Liberals and SDP in Britain) or often choose (the RPR and UDF in France, the Liberals and National Party in Australià) to divide the candidacies up between themselves.

Parties will try to balance demographic characteristics, too; which ones they balance depends mainly on whom they hope to draw electoral support from. The Belgian parties used to balance French- and Flemish-speaking candidates on their Brussels lists before they broke up into separate French and Flemish parties. Since all parties hope to appeal to all age groups, they usually include young candidates on the ticket, though, as we have seen, they do not feel the same about the over-sixty-fives. Ticket-balancing is taken very seriously in single- or hegemonic-party systems like the Soviet Union, Romania and Poland, where the objective characteristics of politically acceptable aspirants are perhaps as important as their subjective ones (Hill, 1973: 207–12; Nelson, 1982: 89; Pelczynski, 1959: 147–8).

All parties also seek votes from both sexes, and thus may think it wise to include both on the ticket. It is noticeable that in fairly recent times, from about the mid-1970s, parties have been much more concerned than before to increase the number of women candidates. Some (usually minor parties such as the German Greens and some Communist parties) adopt rules which ensure that around half of their elected deputies will be women. Others (usually parties of the left such as the French Socialists, the PCI and three left-wing Norwegian parties) set target quotas for women (20 percent in the PS and PCI). In 1986 Sierra Leone's ruling APC said it would select all female aspirants 'to increase the chances of having more women in Parliament', though in the event two of the sixteen female aspirants were not selected (*West Africa*, 7 April 1986, p. 748, and 12 May 1986, p. 981). A third group of parties contents itself with pious but non-binding declarations of intent to select more women.

When list PR systems are used, parties often find the lower, electorally hopeless places on the list especially useful for producing a balanced ticket. In Norway data on selectors' values show that they regard an aspirant's ability to 'represent' a group as more important when selecting candidates for hopeless list positions than for top ones. In Belgium the selectors take care to construct a balanced ticket, even though in most constituencies outside Brussels many parties will win only one seat, so apart from the top name all the other candidates are purely honorary. In Poland in 1957 the 'united front' used the bottom places on the list for balancing purposes (Pelczynski, 1959: 147–8). It seems that in many countries there has been a tendency to assign lower, often hopeless, places to candidates with characteristics usually underrepresented in parliaments, such as women, people of lower socio-economic status and members of minority ethnic groups. This is analogous to British constituency parties' greater willingness to pick women for hopeless seats than for safe ones. Parties, then, find hopeless slots valuable for giving symbolic or pseudo-representation to groups who are underrepresented among the 'genuine' or realistic candidates.

An outstanding example of the tokenism often involved in such gestures occurred in the Finnish general election of 1966, when the Social Democrat leadership altered the lists initially selected, usually adding more representatives of groups like women and youth in order to provide a better 'balance' and, they hoped, make the list more electorally appealing. This moved displeased the youth and women's groups within the party, though, because, under Finland's preferential system, it was likely to split the vote for candidates in these categories and thus actually reduce the number of women and young people who would be elected to parliament (Pesonen, 1972: 224). In general, although one might think that voters would react with cynicism to empty gestures of this nature, parties appear to believe that any electoral impact it has is positive. More probably, the use of hopeless slots to provide some kind of overall balance is done to prevent internal party disunity, as a face-saving consolation for minority groups or as a way of rewarding loyal members with a nominal candidacy which may enhance their esteem.

Of course, the attraction even of ticket-balancing has its limits. If a party's appeal is defined exclusively in terms of defence of, or opposition to, a particular community, its candidates' backgrounds will reflect this. France's Front National does not include representatives of ethnic minorities among its candidates, and the Nazï party (NSDAP) did not select any Jewish candidates, even in hopeless positions. Nor (*pace* Jewell, 1977: 35) have the main parties in Northern Ireland attempted to broaden their support across the sectarian divide at PR elections by 'slating' candidates of the opposite religious persuasion to the vast majority of their supporters; since the Unionist parties, in particular, define themselves in terms of preserving Protestant unity, such a move would be pointless and electorally damaging to the party which did it. Northern Ireland's Alliance Party, on the other hand, which aims to bring the two communities together, does make a point of picking both Protestant and Catholic candidates.[5] It may be that a party has ideological reasons for refusing to pick candidates of a certain background, even when it wins support from voters of that background. An example is the Nazi Party, which won strong support from women but never had a woman member in the Reichstag because of its views on women's proper place in society (Kohn, 1980: 148–9).

Thus, even without there being a great deal of first-hand information as to exactly what the selectors are looking for, and without making the methodological mistake of assuming that the selectors 'must have been' looking for every characteristic which parliamentarians possess to a greater extent than the adult population at large, it is still possible to reach fairly reliable general conclusions as to what considerations influence selectors when making their choices. Nevertheless, inference of this nature is a poor substitute for the type of knowledge which can be gleaned from surveys of selectors or from some kind of participant observation approach. Some early results from a Norwegian survey are reported in Chapter 10 of this book, but at the moment the only systematic account of 'what the selectors seek' to adopt such an approach is Bochel and Denver's (1983) study of British Labour Party selectors. The insight this article provides into Labour's selection process is itself a recommendation of the method of actually asking selectors what they are up to rather than merely drawing inferences from the outside.

Their study is valuable for the questions it raises as well as the answers it provides. Bochel (1985: 9) reports that 57.5 percent of the selectors they surveyed were attending their first selection conference; this lack of experience, admittedly, may be due to the unusual practice in the British parties until recently of not holding selection conferences unless an incumbent retired. He also says (1985: 22) that many indicated that they had not thought system-atically about some of the factors involved until interviewed by the researchers. Perhaps there is a danger of academics attributing to the selection process a degree of care and rational calculation it does not always possess, in the way that the sophistication involved in voters' decisions as to which way to vote was once overestimated. The approach of Bochel and Denver is time-consuming and not always possible, but it points to perhaps the most useful direction in which future research into candidate selection could go.

Influences on the selection process

In the introduction to this book we outlined five factors which may commonly be thought to influence the candidate selection process: legal provisions, governmental organization, the electoral system, political culture, and the nature of the party. We shall now examine the impact of each of these in the light of the information available.

Legal provisions
Legal provisions play no part in most countries. Of coure, there are usually laws preventing certain categories of people (such as foreigners, those certified insane, or people under a certain age) from being valid candidates, or at least from becoming members of Parliament, while countries in which some parliamentary seats are 'reserved' have laws confining certain candidacies to citizens with particular characteristics. But within these broad limits the law usually keeps out of candidate selection. Only in Finland, West Germany, Norway and the USA are there laws governing it, and even in Norway these are not binding. In each of these four countries the selection process is highly decentralized, and the relevant laws are clearly designed to keep it that way. It might be argued that the law cannot be a decisive and independent influence on parties' behaviour, given that they could change it if they wished. However, legal provisions affect political culture as well as being affected by it. Once a law exists, the process it prescribes may come to acquire a certain legitimacy, and the parties in each of these countries would court unpopularity if they attempted to change the law to permit a more centralized, apparently less 'democratic' form of candidate selection.

Structure of government
The structure of government undoubtedly has an impact on the distribution of power within parties, including candidate selection. In general, selection is less centralized in federal states than in unitary ones. West Germany, the USA, Canada, Australia and Switzerland are federal states where candidate selection is highly decentralized, to the extent that the national party organs in most cases do not even make the rules on the subject – this is left to the state party organs except in the USA, where it is the state legislature – let alone have a decisive role in the process. Norway could be added to the list since local government is strong and candidate selection is locally controlled. On the other side of the coin there are certain unitary states – France, Ireland, Italy, Japan, the Netherlands, Israel and New Zealand – where the centre does play a significant part, in some parties at least. The greater role of the centre in the New Zealand Labour Party than in the rather similar Australian Labor Party seems clearly related to the different structure of government in these two countries.

The relationship is not clear cut, because counter-examples can be found. In federal India, candidate selection in the Congress Party has always been highly centralized, and in federal Austria the SPOe is relatively centralized. In unitary Britain the centre has very little influence on the selection process, and in Belgium it is as weak as in any federal country, unable even to make the rules let alone make the nominations. But even so, it is apparent that there is a relationship between the structure of government and the locus of greatest influence over candidate selection.[6]

Electoral system

Turning to the impact of the electoral system, it is clear that most of the more simplistic and deterministic relationships hypothesized do not hold true. There is no support whatever for Hermens's proposition that PR list systems result in the party leader eventually gaining conrol over the selection process. Nor is it the case that list systems 'go with' central party dominance over candidate selection. Of course, given that PR systems employ larger constituencies than single-member systems would within a given country, it is obvious that the unit of decision *can* (though will not necessarily) be lower under the latter. If a single-member constituency system is used, the organization covering each constituency can decide autonomously on its own candidate, but if the country then changes to PR with ten-member constituencies, the same organizational unit will merely have a voice, along with the other nine corresponding units, in the selection; there will be a need for some decision-making mechanism at the level of the new large constituency to combine and arbitrate between the choices of the ten smaller units. But this does not necessarily mean that membership participation is reduced, or that central party agencies have become more powerful.

The point can be illustrated by looking at candidate selection in Israel, which uses a non-preferential list system with one nationwide constituency. For many years candidates were picked by the parties' national executives or similar small bodies, and so Israel appeared to be the extreme case bearing out theories linking PR with centralized selection (Epstein, 1980: 226, seems to treat it in this way). But, as we have seen, most of the Israeli parties have recently altered their selection mechanisms, and in 1977 the DMC picked its candidates by means of a nationwide poll of its 35,000 members. Selection in the DMC could, of course, be seen in one sense as highly centralized, in that all of its candidates were picked via just one 'decision'. But, at the same time, central party agencies such as the leadership or the national executive had no formal power, and opportunities for membership participation could not have been greater. The reason why a small group in the party elites seemed to control the process in Israel before 1977 (though Hoffman, 1980: 287–92, argues that even before 1977 the selection process was less restricted than often suggested) has been attributed not to the electoral system but, partly at least, to the deference commanded by the 'founding fathers' of the state. Their final fading away in the 1970s, together with growing public disillusionment with the parties, produced pressure on all parties to broaden their selection processes (Arian, 1979: 300; Hoffman, 1980: 299–300).

Wider empirical evidence, too, does not lend any support to the view that PR, in whatever format, gives more power to central party agencies than single-member systems. It is true that the centre is weak in certain countries using a single-member constituency system (Britain, Canada, Australia, the USA) and more influential in some countries using some form of PR, either list systems (France in 1986, Italy, the Netherlands, Israel, Greece, Venezuela) or STV (Ireland). But, as against this, the centre has more power in India and New Zealand (which both employ the British single-member plurality system) and in Japan (SNTV in relatively small constituencies) than in Belgium, West Germany, Norway, Finland and Austria, which all use PR list systems. In short, the available evidence does not substantiate any hypothesis positing a deterministic link betwen electoral system and the degree of centralization in candidate selection.[7] If it is true that in Anglo-Saxon countries there is a belief that PR list systems engender central control over candidate selection, then this belief should be dispelled. It is ironic that some non-British writers (for instance, Weller, 1983: 61) sometimes see Britain as an example of a powerful central influence on the selection process.

This is not to say that the electoral system can never affect the degree of centralization. It was shown earlier (in Chapter 4) that the change from a two-ballot system to a non-preferential list system in France in 1986 led to the locus of control in the RPR, UDF and PS drifting slightly higher up the party hierarchy, which was attributed to the more partisan character of the vote and the reduced importance of the individual candidate under the 1986 system. Thus it could be argued on the basis of this case that the electoral system does have an impact once all other factors are controlled for, although only a fairly marginal one. West Germany does not, unfortunately, provide a test of the impact of the electoral system, because even though there are, formally speaking, two different types of MdB and two distinct selection processes, it was made clear in Chapter 5 that the parties think in terms of only one unified process, and so there is considerable overlap of personnel between the two sets of candidates.

There is no sign of a relationship betwen centralization and the degree of voter choice permitted by the electoral system. In some countries where voters are able to express a preference for a particular candidate among their party's selection (such as Ireland, Italy, and arguably France under the two-ballot system) the centre has some influence, but in Finland it does not. Among countries where voters have no such power, the centre is weak in some (Belgium, Britain, West Germany, Norway, the USA, Canada and Austria) but influential in others (the Netherlands, Israel, New Zealand, India).[8]

The fact that certain deterministic hypotheses about the impact of the electoral system upon the degree of centralization do not stand up does not mean that it has no impact on the selection process. The electoral system strongly affects the *mechanics* of the selection process in every country. Candidate selection under a single-member system tends to be a much simpler affair than under PR. In France the adoption of PR in 1986 increased the complexity of the selectors' task.

The electoral system may have more of an impact on what the selectors seek than on the degree of centralization. PR systems carry with them a need for a balanced ticket with, perhaps, a greater emphasis on aspirants' objective personal characteristics such as gender, age and group affiliation. Qualities which selectors might feel, accurately or otherwise, could be electoral liabilities in a party's sole candidate, like being a woman or a member of an ethnic minority, are needed for purposes of balance when several are being picked. When it comes to the question of whether preferential systems induce selectors to pay more attention to voters' wishes than non-preferential systems, it must be said that we do not have enough information to answer this, mainly because of the already noted lack of data on what the selectors seek. We have already mentioned some evidence that the candidates most favoured by selectors under the preferential systems of Finland and Italy are those with most appeal to the voters, but the relationship has received little systematic attention within countries, let alone cross-nationally.

Under non-preferential list systems it would be easier for the selectors, if they wished, to 'slip through' an unappealing candidate under cover of the list, knowing that his presence will arouse little attention, especially if he is in a fairly low (albeit safe) position. We do not, though, have any specific examples of parties using non-preferential lists to secure the election of people who would be unable to gain it if they needed the direct personal endorsement of the voters. The only case which might come into this category is Israel's Mapam, which, as we have seen, is to some extent sheltered from the judgement of the voters by being the junior partner in the Labor Alignment, and places a high value on ideological orthodoxy when selecting its candidates. It may thus be able to pay less attention to the voters' wishes than if it operated under a preferential system, but even this is not certain.

Political culture
Political culture should be treated with caution as an explanatory factor; it provides in effect a residual explanation, a way of saying that the phenomenon happens because people expect it to or believe it should, and that we are unable to explain it further. Thus to attribute the dominance of local roots among the qualities sought by selectors in France, Ireland and Norway to a strongly localistic political culture, and the lower importance they are given by British selectors to a less localistic political culture, is perhaps only a superficially impressive way of saying that we do not really know why it happens.

Nevertheless, there is no doubt that the values of voters and selectors, even if we cannot really explain why they hold them, do have a major impact on the selection process. American voters would regard as undemocratic any move to deprive them of the right to select their candidates via primaries, whose widespread use in the USA has been attributed to 'ambivalence about political parties' (Ranney, 1975: 22–57, 131). Yet European voters have shown no desire for this degree of power and seem to see nothing wrong in the parties' control of the nomination process.[9] In the Netherlands changes in national political culture brought about by the 'democratization wave' and 'depillarization' of the 1960s and 1970s led to attempts to broaden participation in the parties' selection processes. In seeking to explain why new parties in any country (such as the PDs in Ireland or, with qualifications, the SDP in Britain) adopt selection procedures very similar to those of the existing parties, some sort of explanation in terms of a belief in the legitimacy of accepted practices seems justified. In Canada one explanation given for the very limited role of the centre in all parties is that 'a successful modern party could not openly deny the local party membership a role while its major competitors operated with some form of open candidate selection' (Williams, 1981: 98). If one party adopts a more open selection process, others may feel obliged to follow. In Israel the DMC's 1977 primary was 'highly instrumental in creating pressures for reform in other parties' (Goldberg and Hoffmann, 1983: 71).

The nature of the party
In the introduction we outlined the views of several writers that parties tending towards a certain type (sometimes termed Party

Democracy) of party would have a more centralized selection process and/or would place a higher emphasis on aspirants' ideological commitment, whereas parties approximating the Rational-Efficient paradigm would subordinate all other considerations to electoral expediency. Some suggest a difference between parties of the left and of the right, and others believe that the heterogeneity of the party's support will make a difference to the degree of centralization of candidate selection. The most obvious way of testing this is to explore interparty variation within each country. If there is little variation between different parties within countries, then it seems reasonable to conclude that the nature of the party is not a strong influence on candidate selection.

We have already seen that there is indeed a strong tendency for left-wing parties, both socialists and Communist, to require longer party membership than right-wing parties. When it comes to centralization, though, the picture is not so clear cut. In Belgium all parties' processes are highly decentralized, though the role of interest groups in the CVP sets it somewhat apart from the others. In Britain there is not a great deal of variation between the parties; what little there is distinguishes Labour and the Conservatives, on the one hand, from the Liberals and SDP on the other, as the latter allow wider participation by members. In France there is more variation, but contrary to some theories it is the less ideological, more election-oriented RPR and UDF which have a more centralized procedure than the Socialists. In West Germany and Norway the law ensures that there is no difference between the parties when it comes to centralization of the selection process. In Ireland the centre plays a slightly higher role in the large, pragmatic centre-right parties, Fianna Fáil and Fine Gael, than in Labour. In Italy the minor parties are the most decentralized, while the unusual nature of the DC, not so much a party as a conglomeration of factions and interest groups, clearly has a strong impact on its selection process. In Japan, too, the very factionalized nature of the LDP, and the religious basis of Komei, help to explain why candidate selection is more centralized than in the socialist parties. In the Netherlands it is the centrist VVD which has the most centralized procedure; the more right-wing CDA and more left-wing PvdA come next, and the centre-left D'66 is the most decentralized.

There does not seem to emerge from this any kind of relationship between centralization and a party's position on the left–right spectrum. It is true that Communist parties all seem to select their candidates in much the same way, with nominal local selection under close central scrutiny, and that this is clearly related to the broad nature of these parties, but there seems to be no general tendency for socialist parties to be either more centralized or less centralized than bourgeois parties. If there are general patterns, one seems to concern size rather than political position: in smaller parties selection is usually more decentralized, if only because the appeal of the party per se is so limited that it has to rely on the drawing power of local notables, who consequently acquire a degree of autonomy within their own bailiwicks. A more obvious pattern is that members play a greater role in parties (often relatively new ones) whose ethos involves intraparty democracy, such as the Dutch D'66, Israel's short-lived DMC, and perhaps the Liberals and SDP in Britain. The role of the permanent organization is, not surprisingly, minor in parties whose organization is weak, but this does not of itself fix the locus of selection. In the American parties the power of selection devolves to the voters, but in the equally weak Indira Congress of India it ascends to the party leader.

With regard to the heterogeneity of a party's support, the hypothesis outlined in Chapter 1 – that centralization is inversely related to the diversity of support – is if anything disconfirmed by the evidence. Archetypal catch-all parties like the Belgian CVP, Ireland's Fianna Fáil and the Italian DC have slightly more centralized procedures than other parties in their respective countries whose support comes to a greater extent from voters of one social class. Perhaps this should not be particularly surprising, as the original hypothesis rested on the assumption that local selectors would be more sensitive to local circumstances than national selectors, so that if circumstances varied across the country the national organs would feel it wise to give the local organs autonomy in candidate selection. In reality it cannot be assumed that local members, left to their own devices, will necessarily pick the most locally appealing candidate or set of candidates. It is noticeable that in Ireland, and to some extent in Italy, the effect of central intervention is not to impose 'outsiders' on the local organization but, very often, to promote local aspirants overlooked by the selectors, with the aim of producing a better balanced and more attractive ticket. The same reason is cited for the changes made to the lists selected in party primaries by Finnish Social Democrat members in 1966 (Pesonen, 1972: 224).

Looking at other countries outside the nine covered in this book, we find no sign of significant interparty variation on the dimension of centralization in several, such as Australia, Canada, Finland, Greece, the USA and Venezuela. In three, though, such variation does exist. In India the practice of candidate selection by leader in the Indira Congress clearly results from the leader-dominated nature of that party, and contrasts with the decentralized processes in the other parties. In New Zealand the centre plays a greater role in Labour than in the National Party.

The third case, and not for the first time the most illuminating one, is Israel. In 1981 two of the Likud parties (Herut and the Liberals), the smaller Alignment party (Mapam) and one of the religious parties (the NRP) used a relatively decentralized form of selection, allowing a body roughly similar to a national convention of members to make the decisions, while the other three main parties (La'am of Likud, Labor and Agudat Israel) used a much more centralized procedure. Goldberg and Hoffmann explain these variations in terms of interparty differences. Herut and Mapam both have all-powerful ideologies (in the case of Herut, 'one of fervent Israeli nationalism [which] implies an ideal of "One Israel" standing above ethnic considerations') which provide internal cohesion and militate against factions and against the notion of allowing small 'arranging committees' to draw up 'balanced' lists (1983: 72, 78). But in Agudat Israel and, especially, Labor, the existence of such factions made a centralized procedure necessary if party unity was to be preserved (1983: 76–7, 80–1). Goldberg and Hoffman conclude (1983: 78–9) that Labor

> is thus a classic illustration of how procedural centralization is inversely related to political decentralization. It was the pluralism of the Labor Party that required one committee, whether formal or informal, to assume responsibility for the list, while the ideological homogeneity of Mapam permitted its center to remain the final nominating authority.[10]

This hypothesis derives some support when tested against evidence from other countries. In Belgium the CVP's giving such a powerful role in its affairs to interest groups, and its use of 'model lists' to make it hard for ordinary members to upset the arrangements reached between them, derive from its character as less homogeneous than the other parties. In France the fragmented nature of the UDF may be part of the reason for its relatively centralized procedure (although the greater degree of centralization in the non-factionalized RPR than in the factionalized PS counts against the theory). In Italy and Japan the most factionalized parties (the DC and LDP) give ordinary members little if any say in the selection process.

Influences: a summary
None of these five factors can be disregarded, as each has a bearing on the precise nature and outcomes of the selection process in any party. A quantitative analysis, with the attendant difficulties of operationalizing variables which do not readily lend themselves to

quantification, would be needed to attempt to measure the impact of each, and the degree to which the nature of the selection process in any party can be predicted from a given set of independent variables. But it appears that they do not, even collectively, provide a complete explanation, and that even when the impact of each has been taken into account there remains a certain amount of 'residual variance'. To some extent, each party must be looked on as being sui generis. Parties do have some autonomy; their behaviour is not determined absolutely by their environment.

Consequences

In Chapter 1 it was suggested that the candidate selection process might have consequences in three main areas: the composition of parliaments, the behaviour of parliamentarians, and the cohesion of parties. We shall now examine our evidence on each of these points.

The composition of parliaments
Establishing cause and effect between candidate selection and the composition of parliaments is not easy. In a sense, the backgrounds of all deputies other than independents must reflect the selectors' values, especially under non-preferential electoral systems. Thus, even without examining any empirical evidence, one might argue that the composition of any parliament is, by definition, the product mainly of the selectors' values. A more interesting line of investigation is to ask whether there is any variation, between or within countries, which seems to reflect differences in selection procedures. If there is little such variation, or if the variation is closely linked to the nature of the party, this might suggest that the selection process is more of an intervening variable than an independent one in the recruitment process. The most important characteristics of parliamentarians to consider in this context are education, occupation, gender, age and local connections; other factors like religion or ethnicity may be relevant in some countries.

It seems to be a universal phenomenon that candidates and deputies are of higher socio-economic status, and have received more education, than the population at large (Putnam, 1976: 22–8). Equally common is that this applies more strongly to right-wing parties than to left-wing ones. All the evidence in this book supports these propositions.

Where this leaves the role of candidate selection is debatable. One line of argument would suggest that candidate selection is only an intervening variable. Candidates and deputies are wealthier and better educated than the general population not because the selectors specifically want such people but because of the familiar set of explanations as to why they find it easier to pursue a political career than the less well-off: their greater ability to speak articulately about political issues and to take time off work, their higher subjective political competence, and so on. Variations between parties can also be explained without recourse to candidate selections: if most candidates of farmers' parties are themselves farmers, if workers feature more strongly in the lists of parties supported by the working class than of those with predominantly bourgeois support, or if candidates of a party drawing support mainly from one religious or ethnic community themselves have the characteristic which distinguishes that community, this is hardly surprising, and we do not require an elaborate theory laying heavy stress on the selection process to make sense of it.

But, against this, it is surely mistaken to see candidate selection as a neutral factor in the recruitment process, a view which implies that the selected candidates are a cross-section of all aspirants or potential aspirants. This is inherently implausible. Some would-be candidates are likely to be discouraged from seeking a candidacy because they believe that the format of the selection process and/or the values of the selectors give them little chance of success. Others who do become aspirants may find that this is only too true. One example concerns being a long-standing party member or a member of a local elected council. Neither quality may contribute much to an aspirant's ability to win votes or to be a capable deputy, but in many countries the selectors are unlikely to favour people without at least one of these attributes, or preferably both.

The dearth of studies of selectors' values makes it hard to test their impact, but two pieces of research throw some light on the question. Timonen was able to compare the backgrounds (unfortunately with regard only to age, length of party membership, and age when joining the party) of unsuccessful aspirants, successful aspirants who were not elected to Parliament, and elected candidates, in the Finnish Social Democrats at the 1966 election. He found that the rejected aspirants tended to be younger and more recent converts than those selected. But since the elected candidates were generally older and longer-established party members than the unsuccessful candidates, it seems that the values of the selectors and the voters were fairly similar; the selectors were not introducing any distinctive set of values into the recruitment process (Pesonen, 1972: 217–18).

A study of the British parties' selection of candidates for the 1979 European Parliament elections showed that those eventually selected were not an exact cross-section of the original pool of aspirants. In the Conservative Party, interestingly, products of Britain's elite 'public' schools featured more prominently among rejected aspirants (72.9 percent) than selected ones (59.7 percent) (Holland, 1986: 193). But since practically three-fifths of those selected were public-school educated, it hardly seems justified to conclude that 'the possession of public-school credentials was not in itself a selection asset'. The very fact that two-thirds of all aspirants, compared with only a very small proportion of Conservative voters, had these credentials can hardly be unrelated to a widespread belief that Conservative selectors prefer to pick candidates with a public school background.

Bochel and Denver's British study again shows the value of directly studying the selectors' values rather than merely trying to draw inferences from the backgrounds of those selected. They found that Labour Party selectors had a preference in principle for working-class candidates, but in practice usually chose middle-class ones. This is attributed by the researchers (1983: 56–9) to the nature of the procedures used in the selection process, which emphasize the ability to address an audience articulately, and thus inevitably favour well-educated middle-class aspirants. The high proportion of teachers among Labour's candidates (32 percent compared with only 8 percent among Conservative candidates) may be seen as a consequence of this. Candidate selection, then, does matter. The format and procedures of the process, whose origins may be forgotten and which persist mainly through inertia, can even have the effect of thwarting the selectors' own declared wishes.

In trying to establish the impact of the selectors' values, one obvious basic distinction is between selectors in countries using PR and those where a single-member constituency system is used; the former aim above all to 'balance the ticket', a consideration which does not arise, at least within each constituency, when only one candidate is to be picked. Admittedly, it seems that the selectors rarely try to balance occupation per se, let alone education, and so Von Beyme (1985: 237) is probably correct in stating that 'there has been virtually no deliberate planning of the social composition of a parliamentary party in any Western democracy'. Sometimes, though, a rough occupational balance, in relative terms, is a by-product of balancing interest groups representing occupational sectors like farmers, employers and workers, as happens in parties like the Belgian CVP and the OeVP of Austria.

At the other extreme, ticket-balancing plays no part in Britain, since election is from single-member constituencies, and since no attempt is made by central party agencies to engineer any kind of national balance in the parliamentary group. The outcome is that

British MPs are of exceptionally high socio-economic status. Many have been to a public school; there are very few members of ethnic minority groups. Almost certainly, a better 'mix' of candidates would be selected if Britain had a multi-member constituency system. However, the absence of ticket-balancing does not necessarily produce such a socially elite body. When the political culture and the selectors' values are different, the resulting parliament is different, as is shown by the legislatures of Australia, New Zealand and Canada (see, for example, Williams, 1981: 88).

When it comes to gender, unlike education or occupation, parties are increasingly inclined to engage in the deliberate planning of which Von Beyme speaks. Some set precise quotas and thus ensure that their incoming parliamentary party will contain at least a certain proportion of women. Several attempts to explain the varying proportions of women in national parliaments have identified the electoral system as the most important independent variable, but the candidate selection process is all too often absent from these analyses, as if it were merely an artefact of the electoral system (for example, Castles, 1981; Rule, 1985). The chapters above show clearly that this is not the case. There is variation from party to party, and from election to election, within any one country. The dramatic increase in the percentage of women in the Storting, from 23 percent in 1981 to 34 percent in 1985, came about because the Norwegian selectors picked more women for safe list places in 1985, not because of any change in the electoral system. While a PR electoral system obviously makes the selection of women more likely, it is not the electoral system which does the selecting. The selectors are not the prisoners of the electoral system. The active role of the selection process in determining how many women enter Parliament should not be overlooked.

Our evidence on the age of parliamentarians is too fragmentary to allow a rigorous examination of any possible relationship between this factor and the selection process, but what evidence we have suggests strongly that there is no such relationship. Ticket-balancing appears to make no great difference here, because even where it exists it is doubtful whether parties pick many more young (under thirty) candidates than the 10 percent selected by the British parties in 1983. Indeed, it would be unrealistic to expect to find any general relationship, such as that proposed by Duverger, between the ages of parliamentarians and the degree of centralization of the selection process, given the many influences on the former. A party experiencing an upturn in its fortunes is likely to have many new and thus relatively young deputies. Other parties may have a set of long-serving parliamentarians who all retire at around the same time, leading to an apparent 'rejuvenation' which in fact has little to do with candidate selection practices.

But even if there is no general relationship between age and centralization of selection, it remains true that the values of the selectors will have an impact on the age of a party's candidates and thus its deputies. Two extreme examples can be given to illustrate this point. The Austrian parties, both the relatively centralized SPOe and the decentralized OeVP, operate a 'seniority principle' under which candidates start at the bottom of the list and work their way up it over a number of elections. Until fairly recently this was so rigid that when one person on the list died between elections everyone else simply moved up a place. The result, not surprisingly, was that Austrian deputies were exceptionally old, with an average age in the mid-fifties (Steiner, 1972: 235–6). In contrast, when Sanjay Gandhi favoured his Youth Congress followers in the nominations at India's 1980 elections, the resulting Indira Congress candidates were 'probably the youngest group to stand since the first elections in 1952' (Weiner, 1983: 43).

In much the same way, there does not seem to be any connection between centralization and the possession of local roots, but the selectors' values are still important, for, as we saw earlier, practically all selectorates, be they local or central, are reluctant to pick 'outsiders'.

When discussing the backgrounds of parliamentarians, special mention must be made of the Communist states of Eastern Europe. In all of these some care is taken to ensure that the resulting legislature is reasonably close to being a microcosm of the entire country, with regard to key variables like occupation, nationality and gender. This is easiest to manage where, as in the Soviet Union, there is only one candidate per constituency, so that the precise composition of the incoming parliament is known in advance. Writers on Soviet politics have been able to deduce that 'there was a system of "norms" in operation, which established the desired strengths of various sociological characteristics among the deputies' (Hill, 1976: 594; cf., for Romania, Nelson, 1982: 89). The Soviet case, incidentally, shows that ticket-balancing of a sort is not incompatible with an electoral system using single-member constituencies.

Behaviour of parliamentarians

In Chapter 1 it was suggested that the selection process might have an impact on two aspects of deputies' behaviour: the cohesiveness of voting in parliament, and the focus of their activity.

With regard to the first, it is clear that, for almost all Western parliaments, there are no significant variations to be explained. In practically every party, voting within parliament is highly disciplined, and such defections as do occur are more likely to be related to local constituency factors than to ideological disagreements with the party line. The outstanding exception when it comes to discipline is the US Congress, where party is only one among several factors influencing individual legislators' voting behaviour. Party unity in Congress, say Keefe and Ogul (1981: 286–300, 311–12), is 'fundamentally impaired by the inability of the national party to influence congressional nominations', but it might be more accurate to say that it is impaired by the inability of *any* party agency to control nominations. Roll-call analysis is generally regarded as a pointless exercise for almost all other national parliaments.

The evidence brought forward in this book, then, bears out Ozbudun's conclusion (1970: 339) that 'central control of candidate selection is not a crucial, nor even a necessary, condition of party cohesion'. Epstein (1980: 219, 225) has given the reasons for this. Because local party organizations 'want MPs loyal to the cause as defined nationally . . . the absence of central control and the sharp limits on central influence are not politically crucial. The vital effect of centralization is achieved without organizational centralization . . . The local party oligarchy has a built-in partisanship serving the national party without central dictation.' Where a party is not as cohesive as this quotation assumes, though, parliamentary indiscipline can occur. In Japan in 1979 two LDP faction leaders stood against each other in the Diet for the post of prime minister, and in 1980 abstentions on a vote of confidence led to the collapse of the LDP government. But in neither case were the dissidents punished by being denied renomination, for they had remained loyal to their own faction in the LDP, the essential prerequisite for reselection.

Such exceptional cases apart, even if the local set of selectors is dominated by a particular faction or tendency within the party, the deputies they pick do not, and are not expected to, vote against the mainstream party line in Parliament. However, this does not mean that the selectors' views have no impact on deputies' stands on policy matters. It was pointed out in Chapter 3 that the increased dominance of the left in constituency parties of the British Labour Party, and the introduction of mandatory reselection, has made Labour MPs increasingly cautious about voicing 'moderate' opinions in Parliament or in internal party forums. In addition, it has affected their voting behaviour in party leadership elections, a factor also mentioned for Ireland. In parties generally, it seems likely that deputies will have some regard, when speaking at party conferences or within the parliamentary party, for the views their selectors wish to hear, but we do not have enough evidence to explore this systematically.

There are some parliaments where the concentration of candidate selection in a few hands has been cited as giving the selector(s) control of the parliamentary group. Of the Greek PASOK it has been said that 'it is a relatively easy matter for Papandreou to control the party's MPs as long as they depend almost exclusively on him for their nomination' (Elephantis, 1981: 124). In Colombia the national executives demote candidates on the party list if they have deviated from the party line in Parliament, and, 'needless to say, such a system encourages party orthodoxy in the legislature' (Duff, 1971: 383). The Shah's control of Iranian candidate selection moulded 'the Majlis into a force possessing built-in malleability for executive control' (Bill, 1971: 364). In general, it is important to remember that the near-universal solidarity of party voting in Parliament is by no means unrelated to a well-founded fear that the selectors, national or local, are likely to deselect any deputy who continually violates party discipline. It may not matter much, in this sense, *which* party agency selects candidates, but it does matter that *some* party agency selects them.

On the second question, the impact of the selectors' values on the way deputies spend their working hours, there is not enough information to reach any precise conclusions.[11] The Belgian evidence on this point shows that deputies who believe that a certain type of behaviour is expected by their selectors spend an above-average amount of time on it. But even though deputies have to respond to the selectors' preference for candidates with strong local roots who will keep in close touch with constituency affairs, the average Belgian deputy reports spending 60 percent of his or her time on parliamentary work. In contrast, in Ireland, where the selectors have the same preferences, deputies say they spend 50 percent of their time on casework and less than 10 percent on parliamentary work. For most other parliaments (France is perhaps an exception) the clear impression is that constituency work, though usually significant, does not interfere unduly with national parliamentary business. In Israel selection by a national quasi-convention of members has led to some deputies, notably those without the backing of any internal party group or faction, turning to brokerage work on a national scale. In 1981 one prominent politician won a safe place on the Herut list after visiting most of the 900 selectors at their homes, while a veteran incumbent finished even higher on the list, as a result of 'four years of supplying personal assistance and support for Center members, from his position in the Knesset and the party', leaving his door 'open twenty-four hours a day for party members' (Goldberg and Hoffmann, 1983: 73).

When interest groups are among the selectors, their impact on deputies' behaviour is usually pronounced. The deputies are, naturally, expected to promote their backers' interests wherever possible; not, usually, by dissenting from the overall party line (though it is possible that this is among the factors explaining the low levels of party voting in Switzerland's Nationalrat – see Steiner, 1974: 69–70) or, as a rule, by promoting sectional legislation, but by using their influence, especially within parliamentary committees, to move policy incrementally in the desired direction. In parties like the Belgian CVP legislators are strongly oriented towards the interest group 'family' which nominated them. Some parliaments are highly penetrated by interest groups, such as the Austrian Nationalrat and, some argue, the West German Bundestag. In the former, deputies with expertise in a particular area are often members of the relevant interest group. They tend to 'take control of' issues in their area, and 'are able to advise the party leadership, both in Parliament and beyond, on the attitude to be taken' (Steiner, 1972: 307). Some might see this as a threat to the independence of the legislature, but it could also be seen as making it more relevant. The selection process of Zambia's UNIP has been identified as a factor in weakening that country's parliament. Since the selectors tend to pick a high proportion of party officials, important sectors of society are underrepresented, so 'interest groups continue to by-pass the Assembly in favour of direct relations with the executive' (Molteno and Scott, 1974: 178–9).

Parliaments might also be weakened when parties make a point of deselecting incumbents under a policy of 'rotation'. It has been argued that the Yugoslav rule that no deputy can serve more than two consecutive terms has this effect, by removing any incentive for deputies to try to become capable parliamentarians (Cohen, 1982: 41). In the Soviet Union the practice of deselecting most deputies after one term means that 'the Supreme Soviet remains dominated by an elite group of more permanent members' (Hill, 1972: 67). But in Italy a very different pattern was noted in Chapter 7: PCI deputies, who can expect to be deselected after two terms, devote more time to legislative work than other parties' deputies, mainly because of their greater commitment to the party as such and because they do not have to engage in a battle for preference votes.

Party cohesion

Turning finally to the question of the impact of candidate selection on party cohesion, it is clear that it plays a major role here.

Increasingly, in modern parties, the selection of candidates is the only area of party activity where ordinary members can expect to have a decisive voice. The making of formal party policy is usually the task of a large body, such as an annual conference, and, in any case, the relationship between formal policy and what the party's ministers do when in office may be hazy. The mundane but time-consuming tasks of keeping the party organization alive at local level, of campaigning at elections, and so on, would be almost entirely unrewarding if members were not given a genuine role in candidate selection. In some countries where selection is locally controlled, such as Britain, the power of nomination is seen as important in preserving activists' commitment to the party, and in Ireland, and perhaps elsewhere, it may dispose many of them to accept that decisions on other matters are the leadership's responsibility. In France the very minor role played by activists in selection in the right-wing parties has brought about a 'demobilization' of activists and has raised questions as to whether party activism is worthwhile. Of course, it has been argued that modern campaigning styles mean that parties no longer need a large number of members, who may be as much of a hindrance as a help to a vote-seeking parliamentary party (Epstein, 1980: 233–60; Sjöblom, 1983), so that the centre in most parties could be more assertive without suffering electorally even if activists did leave, but this would contravene the spirit in which most parties nominally operate, by openly converting the party into a vehicle for the leaders' political advancement.

In some cases, then, allowing members to participate in the selection process can help to preserve party cohesion, but there is also support for the opposite proposition, to the effect that excessively wide participation may be detrimental to cohesion in the case of parties with major internal divisions. In the Belgian CVP local party leaders put together 'model lists' which, under the rules governing their party primaries, are rarely altered by members. This procedure is adopted largely out of a fear that if members were able to vote in an unstructured fashion the result could be a list underrepresenting one of the interest groups which back the party, perhaps because of uneven participation in the primary by members of the various groups or because of capriciousness produced by the voting system used. In all the West German parties, conventions for list nominations are preceded by discussions among the Land party leaders, which produce a list reflecting the desired balance of interests. In the Italian DC, too, the exclusion of ordinary members can be seen in terms of the need to preserve a balance between the various factions and interests, although a slight imbalance would not be as disastrous as in Belgium or West Germany since the voters can correct it through their use of preference votes. In some of the Finnish parties members' selection of a set of candidates which does not respect a balance agreed among groups has created the need for 'awkward arbitration' (Nousiainen, 1971: 171).

In some parties the need to preserve unity seems to call for a degree of centralization. This applied to the factionalized PS and the 'cluster' UDF at France's 1986 election. Agreements on how many safe candidacies were to be received by each component were made at national level. This ensured that the largest groups retained their dominant position, and also prevented the various factions/ parties fighting it out, constituency by constituency, around the country, with detrimental consequences for party unity, which might have happened if wider membership participation was allowed.

We have already described the centralized procedure used in the Israeli Labor party, which has been attributed to the need to maintain a balance between factions, and from the same country comes a salutary warning of what can ensue if members are given complete control over candidate selection. The Democratic Movement for Change, which had given each of its 35,000 members a direct vote in picking its candidates in 1977, no longer existed by 1981. Its collapse became known as 'the DMC trauma', and 'was due largely to the imbalances among factions and other groups in the party created by its super-democratic procedures' (Goldberg and Hoffman, 1983: 71). There were no women and only one 'Oriental' among its elected candidates, while the small but well-organized Druze group won two safe places (Hoffman, 1980: 293). The possibility of such a trauma is a strong argument against divided parties allowing control over nominations to slip out of the hands of an elite into those of the membership at large, let alone the entire body of party voters. In this may be seen a parallel between 'plural' parties and plural societies: cohesion can be maintained only if the faction (or segment) leaders, who understand the rules of the game, reach accommodation among themselves, for the sub-elite activists are less willing to accept the compromises and trade-offs which are necessary if cohesion is to be preserved (cf. Lijphart, 1977: 53–4, 99–103).

Direct primaries on the American model, then, appear to be incompatible with the preservation of an existing balance within parties divided along either group or factional lines. More broadly, they are surely incompatible with any sort of strong party organization. Ranney (1975: 129) believes that, in the USA, 'the direct primary in most instances has not only eliminated boss control of nominations but party control as well', and Schlesinger

(1965: 781) states that 'nomination is less a case of an organization's selecting candidates according to qualifications than it is of providing the framework within which they contest for the nomination'. A party which lacks control over its nominations will find it difficult either to be able to offer enough inducements to members to sustain a substantial permanent organization, or to control its own members in parliament. Primaries 'empower mass communication media and various non-party organizations . . . to perform tasks that elsewhere belong to parties'. They undermine much of the rationale of a permanent organization, since politically active individuals are likely to conclude that their time and money 'can be better spent in supporting an ad hoc candidate organization' than a party (Epstein, 1980: 386; 1981: 59–60). Even if direct primaries in America are more of a symptom than a cause of the weakness of the parties (as is argued by Epstein, 1980: 210, 331 and 386, who observes that party cohesion in Congress was low even when most candidates were selected by the convention method), once established they undoubtedly reinforce that weakness (Epstein, 1980: 386). Ranney (1975: 131) concludes that 'the direct primary is the best way to keep the parties weak without destroying them altogether'. The American experience is unlikely to induce parties elsewhere to forfeit control over candidate selection.

This may not apply to primaries where party agencies screen aspirants and allow only those approved by the activists to enter the primary. In such cases, like that of Colorado mentioned at the start of this chapter, Ware (1979: 82) argues that 'cohesive parties' can continue to exist. This is perfectly plausible since this procedure is closely comparable to what obtains under preferential electoral systems, where party voters choose their deputies from among a small set of candidates selected by party activists. It may be, indeed, that much discussion in the political science literature of the differences between American primaries and European candidate selection focuses on the wrong point. It concentrates too much on the power of voters to choose and too little on the absence of party control over the choice available. Arguably, what makes American primaries (in most states) different from European practice is not the direct role of ordinary voters, which exists in many countries by virtue of the electoral system (see p. 239 above), but the inability of the party to determine which names are to be put before the voters to choose between.

Conclusion

Finally, we return briefly to the question posed at the start of this book: Just how important is candidate selection?

Its importance in the political recruitment process is borne out by each of our country chapters. The selectors' values influence, and in many cases determine, the backgrounds of legislators and to some extent their behaviour. Although many factors can be seen as influences upon the selection process, none is entitled to be regarded as a deterministic cause of the type of candidates it produces. In any study of political recruitment, candidate selection has to be seen as a key variable, not a peripheral factor whose nature can be largely taken for granted once we know enough about other variables such as the electoral system.

The importance of the selection of candidates for elections to a parliament might be seen as directly related to the importance of the parliament itself. The 'decline of parliaments' thesis raises the question of whether parliaments count for much in the late twentieth century. If political decisions are made by governments, after consultation with the civil service and major interest groups, with parliaments reduced to the status of a minor actor in the policy-making process, then does it really matter what kind of people enter parliament and how they spend their time?

This line of argument cannot be disregarded, but neither need it be accepted entirely. First, even where parliaments are not initiators of policy they may still be able, often through a committee system, to make significant adjustments to the shape of legislation. Second, where parliaments are weak this may be partly due to the nature of the deputies produced by the candidate selection process. We have already seen that the absence of interest group representatives from the ruling party's candidates has been cited as a cause of the secondary nature of Zambia's parliament, and the point may have wider application. Third, not all parliaments are in decline; it has been argued that Communist legislatures, often seen in the West as mere rubber stamps, are in fact becoming increasingly significant (White, 1982: 195). The reform of the Westminster committee system since 1979 has increased the role of the House of Commons (Drewry, 1985).

Fourth, and perhaps most important, being in parliament is often an essential step on the road to entering government, in which case the pool of potential ministers is determined by the candidate selectors. Ministers are generally drawn from parliament, whether or not this is constitutionally essential, and even in some countries where being a minister is incompatible with being a member of parliament, as in France and the Netherlands, most ministers in recent governments have previously been deputies. Of the countries covered in this book, only in Norway, where about a half of ministers have never belonged to parliament, is there a significant extra-parliamentary route to government.

Candidate selection has also been regarded as a crucial battle-ground in internal party conflict, as was noted in Chapter 1. Perhaps surprisingly, this is not really borne out by the evidence in this book, once account has been taken of the fundamental distinction between parties which do not control their nomination process (the USA) and parties which do (everywhere else). Outside America, only in countries employing single-member constituencies does candidate selection seem to be important in this respect. The British Labour Party constitutes one of the clearest examples, with the left and centre-right using the selection process to try to boost their strengths in the parliamentary party.

But in countries using PR electoral systems the pervasive notion of ticket-balancing removes much of the factional, as opposed to personal, conflict, since the various groups generally come to an arrangement, either at constituency level or at national level, on how many candidacies each is to receive. The basis of the division is usually something like the strength of each faction at the most recent party congress or the number of members each group has in the local party. In these cases, the factions do not fight each other bitterly for as many places as possible on the ticket in each constituency; they operate within a framework devised precisely to minimize inter-group conflict at the nomination stage. They accept, contrary to the statements of Schattschneider and Ranney quoted at the start of Chapter 1, that no one group or faction 'owns' the party or will ever have complete control of it. The ethos of parties operating under PR electoral systems prevents candidate selection becoming the 'crucial process' in this sense. Only in parties operating under 'winner takes all' systems do notions like ownership and complete control seem to be applicable. Schattschneider is right to say that to study candidate selection is to discover where power lies within a party, but in most cases it *signifies* how power is distributed rather than *deciding* it. His dictum needs to be rewritten: the nature of the nominating procedure reflects the nature of the party more than it determines it.

Notes

I should like to thank Michael Marsh for extensive comments on previous drafts.

1. In this chapter the source for all statements about one of the countries covered in this book is the relevant chapter, unless otherwise stated.

2. Technically, under the Dutch electoral system the whole of the Netherlands

constitutes one large constituency, so CDA and PvdA candidates are picked by sub-constituency units of the parties. But the country is divided into nineteen smaller electoral units, known as 'voting districts' or 'electoral sub-districts', and the parties can and usually do present different lists in each district, though usually with the same candidate heading these lists. While the *overall* number of seats won by each party is determined by its national share of the votes, the question of *which* seats it is allocated is decided by its strength in the various sub-districts. A party might therefore be awarded five seats in one sub-district but only one in another. Consequently, it makes sense, for our purposes, to look on each 'sub-district' as if it were a multi-member constituency, even though it does not fill exactly this role under the Netherlands' unique electoral system.

3. Being an incumbent could be regarded as either a subjective personal characteristic or an objective one. Since it reflects an achieved status rather than an ascribed one, it seems preferable to treat it as the former, although the point is arguable since the label 'incumbent' is undoubtedly a boost to an aspirant whatever his or her personal abilities may be. One might even ignore the factor of incumbency at this stage, and try to see the selection of so many incumbents as a mere consequence of the selectors seeking electorally appealing candidates, but this would be an unrealistically fine distinction which almost certainly does not reflect the reality of what goes on in the selectors' minds.

4. Asking aspirants for money in exchange for a candidacy should not be confused with the widespread practice of parties of all persuasions requiring successful candidates to pay part of their parliamentary salaries into party coffers (Paltiel, 1981: 151, sees this as characteristic of parties of the left, while Von Beyme, 1985: 197–8, regards it as more common among bourgeois parties).

5. Northern Ireland's MPs at Westminster are elected under the British single-member plurality system but, at elections to provincial legislatures or assemblies, PR (the STV system, as used in the Republic of Ireland) has been employed since 1972, having also been used up to 1929.

6. Of course, this is not to say that the former causes the latter, as it may well be that both are the products of other features of the country, such as its size and/or the extent of diversity.

7. Interestingly, a similar conclusion has been reached as to the impact, long assumed to be considerable, of electoral systems upon the closeness of parliamentarians' contact with their constituents. Bogdanor (1985b: 299) says that 'the electoral system is not a fundamental cause of variations in the focus of representation'.

8. Belgium, the Netherlands, Norway and Austria are categorized as having non-preferential systems since in practice voters' preferences very rarely overturn the party-determined list order, even though technically they are preferential systems.

9. The only survey evidence on this question of which we are aware comes from Austria, where respondents rated more influence on candidate selection as the fifth most important of ten possible 'priorities for the development of new democratic patterns'. Just under 9 percent of respondents regarded it as the most important priority (see Pelinka, 1985: 195).

10. Lest the word cause confusion, it should perhaps be pointed out again that the 'center' is in fact a large body, containing several hundred members, and equivalent to a national party convention.

11. Most of the contributors to a volume on relationships between voters and representatives (Bogdanor, 1985) observe that the question has not been studied in any depth in their country. Curiously, the selectors' values are not examined systematically as a factor which might affect deputies' behaviour.

References

Agor, Weston H. (ed.) (1971) *Latin American Legislatures: Their Role and Influence*. New York: Praeger.

Aksin, Benjamin (1979) 'The Likud', pp. 91–114 in Penniman (1979).

Andren, Nils (1961) *Modern Swedish Government*. Stockholm: Almqvist & Wiksell.

Arian, Asher (1979) 'Conclusion', pp. 283–302 in Penniman (1979).

Arian, Asher (ed.) (1983) *The Elections in Israel 1981*. Tel Aviv: Ramot.

Aronoff, Myron J. (1979) 'The Decline of the Israeli Labor Party: Causes and Significance', pp. 115–45 in Penniman (1979).

Arter, David (1980) 'Social Democracy in a West European Outpost: The Case of the Finnish SDP', *Polity*, 12 (3): 363–87.

Baaklini, Abdo I. (1977) 'Legislatures and Political Integration in Lebanon: 1840–1972', pp. 233–66 in Eldridge (1977).

Baker, Christopher E. (1971) 'The Costa Rican Legislative Assembly: A Preliminary Evaluation of the Decisional Function', pp. 53–111 in Agor (1971).

Barkan, Joel D. and John J. Okumu (1978) ' "Semi-Competitive" Elections, Clientelism, and Political Recruitment in a No-Party State: The Kenyan Experience', pp. 88–107 in Hermet, Rose and Rouquié (1978).

Bill, James A. (1971) 'The Politics of Legislative Monarchy: The Iranian Majlis', pp. 360–9 in Herbert Hirsch and M. Donald Hancock (eds), *Comparative Legislative Systems*. New York: Free Press.

Bochel, J.M. (1985) 'The Selection of Candidates: An Analytical Framework', paper presented at the European Consortium for Political Research workshop on Candidate Selection in Comparative Perspective, Barcelona.

Bochel, John and David Denver (1983) 'Candidate Selection in the Labour Party: What the Selectors Seek', *British Journal of Political Science*, 13 (1): 45–69.

Bogdanor, Vernon (ed.) (1985a) *Representatives of the People?: Parliamentarians and Constituents in Western Democracies*. Aldershot: Gower.

Bogdanor, Vernon (1985b) 'Conclusion', pp. 293–301 in Bogdanor (1985a).

Butler, David, Howard R. Penniman and Austin Ranney (eds) (1981) *Democracy at the Polls*. Washington DC: American Enterprise Institute.

Carter, April (1982) *Democratic Reform in Yugoslavia*. London: Frances Pinter.

Castles, Francis G. (1981) 'Female Legislative Representation and the Electoral System', *Politics*, 1 (2): 21–7.

Cohen, Lenard J. (1982) 'Politics as an Avocation: Legislative Professionalization and Participation in Yugoslavia', pp. 14–46 in Nelson and White (1982).

Cribb, Margaret Bridson (1977) 'The Country Party', pp. 143–57 in Penniman (1977).

Dodd, C.H. (1969) *Politics and Government in Turkey*. Manchester: Manchester University Press.

Drewry, Gavin (ed.) (1985) *The New Select Committees: A Study of the 1979 Reforms*. Oxford: Clarendon Press.

Duff, Ernest A. (1971) 'The Role of Congress in the Colombian Political System', pp. 369–402 in Agor (1971).

Elder, Neil, Alistair H. Thomas and David Arter (1982) *The Consensual Democracies*. Oxford: Martin Robertson.

Eldridge, Albert F. (ed.) (1977) *Legislatures in Plural Societies: The Search for Cohesion in National Development*. Durham, NC: Duke University Press.

Elephantis, Angelos (1981) 'The Crisis in the Greek Left', pp. 130–59 in Penniman (1981).

Epstein, Leon D. (1977) 'The Australian Party System', pp. 1–48 in Penniman (1977).
Epstein, Leon D. (1980) *Political Parties in Western Democracies*. New Brunswick, NJ: Transaction Books.
Epstein, Leon D. (1981) 'Political Parties: Organization', pp. 52–74 in Butler, Penniman and Ranney (1981).
Farrell, Michael (1980) *Northern Ireland: The Orange State*. London: Pluto.
Fitzmaurice, John (1981) *Politics in Denmark*. London: C. Hurst.
Goldberg, Giora and Steven A. Hoffmann (1983) 'Nominations in Israel: The Politics of Institutionalization', pp. 61–87 in Arian (1983).
Goodman, Jay S., Wayne R. Swanson and Elmer E. Cornwell (1970) 'Political Recruitment in Four Selection Systems', *Western Political Quarterly*, 23 (1): 92–103.
Hermet, Guy, Richard Rose and Alain Rouquié (eds) (1978) *Elections Without Choice*. London: Macmillan.
Hill, Ronald J. (1972) 'Continuity and Change in USSR Supreme Soviet Elections', *British Journal of Political Science*, 2 (1): 47–67.
Hill, Ronald J. (1973) 'Patterns of Deputy Selection to Local Soviets', *Soviet Studies*, 25 (2): 196–212.
Hill, Ronald J. (1976) 'The CPSU in a Soviet Election Campaign', *Soviet Studies*, 28 (4): 590–8.
Hoffman, Steven A. (1980) 'Candidate Selection in Israel's Parliament: The Realities of Change', *Middle East Journal*, 34: 285–301.
Holland, Martin (1986) *Candidates for Europe: The British Experience*. Aldershot: Gower.
Hughes, Colin (1983) 'A Close-Run Thing', pp. 216–47 in Penniman (1983).
Jackson, Keith (1980) 'Candidate Selection and the 1978 General Election', pp. 99–118 in Howard R. Penniman (ed.), *New Zealand at the Polls: The General Election of 1978*. Washington, DC: American Enterprise Institute.
Jewell, Malcolm E. (1977) 'Legislative Representation and National Integration', pp. 13–53 in Eldridge (1977).
Kavanagh, Dennis (1970) *Constituency Electioneering in Britain*. London: Longmans.
Keefe, William J. and Morris S. Ogul (1981) *The American Legislative Process*, 5th edition. Englewood Cliffs, NJ: Prentice-Hall.
Khalaf, Samir G. (1980) 'Lebanon', pp. 243–71 in Jacob M. Landau, Ergun Ozbudun and Frank Tachau (eds), *Electoral Politics in the Middle East*. London: Croom Helm.
Kohler, Beate (1982) *Political Forces in Spain, Greece and Portugal*. London: Butterworth Scientific.
Kohn, Walter S.G. (1980) *Women in National Legislatures*. New York: Praeger.
Lawson, Kay (1976) *The Comparative Study of Political Parties*. New York: St Martin's Press.
Lijphart, Arend (1977) *Democracy in Plural Societies*. New Haven and London: Yale University Press.
Loulis, J.C. (1981) 'New Democracy: The New Face of Conservatism', pp. 49–83 in Penniman (1981).
Luke, David Fashole (1985) 'Electoral Politics in Sierra Leone: An Appraisal of the 1982 Elections', *Journal of Commonwealth and Comparative Politics*, 23 (1): 30–42.
McDonald, Ronald H. (1971) 'Legislative Politics in Uruguay: A Preliminary Statement', pp. 113–35 in Agor (1971).

Marsh, Michael (1985) 'The Voters Decide? Preferential Voting in European List Systems', *European Journal of Political Research*, 13 (4): 365–78.

Martin, Denis (1978) 'The 1975 Tanzanian Elections: The Disturbing 6 per cent', pp. 108–28 in Hermet, Rose and Rouquié (1978).

Mendilow, Jonathan (1982) 'Party-Cluster Formations in Multi-Party Systems', *Political Studies*, 30 (4): 485–503.

Mendilow, Jonathan (1983) 'The Transformation of the Israeli Multi-Party System, 1965–1981', pp. 15–38 in Arian (1983).

Mezey, Michael L. (1979) *Comparative Legislatures*. Durham, NC: Duke University Press.

Mishler, William (1978) 'Nominating Attractive Candidates for Parliament: Recruitment to the Canadian House of Commons', *Legislative Studies Quarterly*, 3 (4): 581–99.

Molteno, Robert and Ian Scott (1974) 'The 1968 General Election and the Political System', pp. 155–96 in William Tordoff (ed.), *Politics in Zambia*. Manchester: Manchester University Press.

Mommsen-Reindl, Margareta (1980) 'Austria', pp. 278–97 in Peter H. Merkl (ed.), *Western European Party Systems*. New York: Free Press.

Nelson, Daniel (1982) 'People's Council Deputies in Romania', pp. 85–110 in Nelson and White (1982).

Nelson, Daniel and Stephen White (eds) (1982) *Communist Legislatures in Comparative Perspective*. London: Macmillan.

Nousiainen, Jaakko (1971) *The Finnish Political System*. Cambridge, MA: Harvard University Press.

Olson, David M. and Maurice D. Simon (1982) 'The Institutional Development of a Minimal Parliament: The Case of the Polish Sejm', pp. 47–84 in Nelson and White (1982).

Ozbudun, Ergun (1970) *Party Cohesion in Western Democracies: A Causal Analysis (Sage Professional Papers, Comparative Politics Series, 01–006)*. Beverly Hills, CA and London: Sage.

Palmer, Norman D. (1975) *Elections and Political Development: The South Asian Experience*. London: C. Hurst.

Paltiel, Khayyam Zev (1981) 'Campaign Finance: Contrasting Practices and Reforms', pp. 138–72 in Butler, Penniman and Ranney (1981).

Pasic, Najdan (1966) 'How the Manner of Nominating Candidates Affects the Character and Role of the Assembly', *Review of International Affairs* (Yugoslavia), September: 29–31 and October: 26–8.

Pelczynski, Zbigniew (1959) 'Poland 1957', pp. 119–79 in David E. Butler (ed.), *Elections Abroad*. London: Macmillan.

Pelinka, Anton (1985) 'The Case of Austria: Neo-Corporatism and Social Partnership', pp. 184–98 in Bogdanor (1985a).

Penniman, Howard R. (ed.) (1977) *Australia at the Polls: The National Elections of 1975*. Washington, DC: American Enterprise Institute.

Penniman, Howard R. (ed.) (1979) *Israel at the Polls: The Knesset Elections of 1977*. Washington, DC: American Enterprise Institute.

Penniman, Howard R. (ed.) (1981) *Greece at the Polls: The National Elections of 1974 and 1977*. Washington, DC: American Enterprise Institute.

Penniman, Howard R. (ed.) (1983) *Australia at the Polls: The National Elections of 1980 and 1983*. Washington, DC: American Enterprise Institute.

Pesonen, Pertti (1968) *An Election in Finland*. New Haven and London: Yale University Press.

Pesonen, Pertti (1972) 'Political Parties in the Finnish Eduskunta', pp. 199–233 in Samuel C. Patterson and John C. Wahlke (eds), *Comparative Legislative Behavior: Frontiers of Research*. New York: Wiley-Interscience.

Pravda, Alex (1978) 'Elections in Communist Party States', pp. 169–95 in Hermet, Rose and Rouquié (1978).

Putnam, Robert D. (1976) *The Comparative Study of Political Elites*. Englewood Cliffs, NJ: Prentice-Hall.

Ranney, Austin (1975) *Curing the Mischiefs of Faction: Party Reform in America*. Berkeley and London: University of California Press.

Ranney, Austin (1977) *Participation in American Presidential Nominations, 1976*. Washington, DC: American Enterprise Institute.

Ranney, Austin (1981) 'Candidate Selection', pp. 75–106 in Butler, Penniman and Ranney (1981).

Rawlinson, Martin (1983) 'The Liberal Party', pp. 35–54 in Penniman (1983).

Rule, Wilma (1985) 'Twenty-Three Democracies and Women's Parliamentary Representation', paper presented at the International Political Science Association meeting on Representation and Electoral Systems, Paris.

Sayari, Sabri (1980) 'Aspects of Party Organization in Turkey', *Middle East Journal*, 30: 187–99.

Schlesinger, Joseph A. (1965) 'Political Party Organization', pp. 764–801 in James G. March (ed.), *Handbook of Organizations*. Chicago, IL: Rand McNally.

Scott, Ruth K. and Ronald J. Hrebenar (1979) *Parties in Crisis*. New York: John Wiley.

Seliktar, Ofira (1980) 'Israel: Electoral Cleavages in a Nation in the Making', pp. 191–239 in Richard Rose (ed.), *Electoral Participation: A Comparative Analysis*. London and Beverly Hills, CA: Sage.

Sjöblom, Gunnar (1983) 'Political Change and Political Accountability: A Propositional Inventory of Causes and Effects', pp. 369–403 in Hans Daalder and Peter Mair (eds), *Western European Party Systems*. London and Beverly Hills, CA: Sage.

Steiner, Jurg (1974) *Amicable Agreement versus Majority Rule*. Chapel Hill, NC: University of North Carolina Press.

Steiner, Kurt (1972) *Politics in Austria*. Boston, MA: Little, Brown.

Sully, Melanie A. (1981) *Political Parties and Elections in Austria*. London: C. Hurst.

Summers, Anne (1983) 'Holding the Balance of Power? Women in Australian Electoral Politics', pp. 124–39 in Penniman (1983).

Thomas, Alistair H. (1985) 'Members of Parliament and Access to Politics in Scandinavia', pp. 199–223 in Bogdanor (1985a).

Torgovnik, Efraim (1979) 'A Movement for Change in a Stable System', pp. 147–71 in Penniman (1979).

Verner, Joel G. (1971) 'The Guatemalan National Congress: An Elite Analysis', pp. 293–324 in Agor (1971).

Von Beyme, Klaus (1985) *Political Parties in Western Democracies*. Aldershot: Gower.

Ware, Alan (1979) *The Logic of Party Democracy*. London: Macmillan.

Weiner, Myron (1983) *India at the Polls, 1980*. Washington, DC: American Enterprise Institute.

Weller, Patrick (1983) 'Labor in 1980', pp. 55–78 in Penniman (1983).

Wells, Henry (1980) 'The Conduct of Venezuelan Elections: Rules and Practice', pp. 30–55 in Howard R. Penniman (ed.), *Venezuela at the Polls, 1978*. Washington, DC: American Enterprise Institute.

White, Stephen (1982) 'Some Conclusions', pp. 191–95 in Nelson and White (1982).
Williams, Robert J. (1981) 'Candidate Selection', pp. 86–120 in Howard R. Penniman (ed.), *Canada at the Polls, 1979 and 1980*. Washington, DC: American Enterprise Institute.

About the contributors

David Denver is lecturer in Politics, University of Lancaster. He has recently co-edited *Electoral Change in Western Democracies*, and is currently engaged in a survey study of the political perceptions of young voters.

Lieven De Winter is researcher at the European University Institute, Florence, working on a doctoral thesis on 'Roles and Behaviour of Belgian Representatives'. He is also involved in Jean Blondel's project on cabinet decision-making in Western Europe. He has published several articles on party government, political clientelism and legislative behaviour in Belgium.

Michael Gallagher is lecturer in the Department of Politics, Trinity College, University of Dublin. He has written *The Irish Labour Party in Transition, 1957–1982* (1982) and *Political Parties in the Republic of Ireland* (1985). His current research interests include political parties, electoral systems and Irish politics.

Ruud Koole is the Head of the Documentatiecentrum Nederlandse Politieke Partijen at the University of Groningen, and a part-time lecturer in the Department of Political Science at the University of Leiden. He does research and publishes on Dutch political parties and edits the Yearbook of the Documentatiecentrum. He has also edited two symposia volumes: *Het Belang van Politieke Partijen* (1984) and *Binnenhof Binnenste Buiten: Slagen en Falen van de Nederlandse Parlementaire Democratie* (1986).

Monique Leijenaar is lecturer in the Department of Political Science at the University of Leiden. Her current research interests concern the electoral and parliamentary behaviour of women and research methods of political science. She has published articles on women in the political process and on methods of data collection. She is the author of *Vrouwen en politieke macht* (1983).

Michael Marsh is lecturer in Political Science at Trinity College, Dublin. He has published articles on Irish and comparative politics covering the fields of recruitment, electoral behaviour and political protest. He is currently completing a study of candidate appeal in Irish elections.

Geoffrey Roberts is Reader in European Studies and acting Head of the Department of European Studies, University of Manchester Institute of Science and Technology (UMIST). He is author of several books and articles, including *An Introduction to Comparative Politics* (Edward Arnold, 1986); *West European Politics Today* (with Jill Lovecy) (Manchester University Press, 1984); *West German Politics* (Macmillan, 1972). He is a member of the editorial board of the *European Journal of Political Research*. His current research is concerned with the organization and development of the West German Free Democratic Party.

Rei Shiratori is a professor of Political Science and Director of the Institute of Social Sciences at Tokai University in Tokyo. He is also the Chairman of the Institute for Political Studies in Japan (IPSJ). In the UK he is Professor of Government and Director of the Centre for the Study of Contemporary Japan in the University of Essex. He is the author of more than twenty books in Japanese, and the editor of *Japan in the 1980s* (1982) and *The Welfare State East and West* (1986, with R. Rose). He is now regarded as the most reliable scholar in the analysis of political parties, elections and voters' attitudes in Japan.

Jean-Louis Thiébault is *maître de conférences* of Political Science at the University of Lille 2. His recent works include studies of public policy and Western European cabinets and governments.

Henry Valen is Professor of Political Science at the University of Oslo. His research interests include problems of representation, political leadership and electoral behaviour. Among his major publications are: (with Daniel Katz) *Political Parties in Norway* (1964); (with Stein Rokkan) *The Mobilization of the Periphery* (1962) and *Norway: Conflict Structure and Mass Politics in a European Periphery* (1974); *Valg og Politikk* (*Elections and Politics in a Changing Society*) (1981); (with B.O. Aardal) *Et Valg i Perspektiv* (*An Election in Perspective*) (1983).

Douglas A. Wertman is an analyst in the West Europe/Canada Branch of the United States Information Agency's Office of Research. From early 1985 until summer 1987 he was Deputy Director of USIS Milan, Italy. Before joining USIA in 1980, he taught political science for six years, three of them at the Hopkins School of Advanced International Studies Bologna Center. He has contributed to all three *Italy at the Polls* volumes and is working on a book about the Italian Christian Democratic Party.

Index